EQUALITY IN EDUCATION LAW AND POLICY, 1954–2010

Educational equality has long been a vital concept in U.S. law and policy. Since *Brown v. Board of Education*, the concept of educational equality has remained markedly durable and animated major school reform efforts, including desegregation, school finance reform, the education of students with disabilities and English language learners, charter schools, voucher policies, the various iterations of the Elementary and Secondary Education Act (including No Child Left Behind), and the "Stimulus." Despite such attention, students' educational opportunities have remained persistently unequal as understandings of the goals underlying schooling, fundamental changes in educational governance, and the definition of an equal education have continually shifted. Drawing from law, education policy, history, and political science, this book examines how the concept of equality in education law and policy has transformed from *Brown* through the Stimulus, the major factors influencing this transformation, and the significant problems that school reforms accordingly continue to face.

Benjamin Michael Superfine is an associate professor in the College of Education at the University of Illinois at Chicago (UIC). Superfine received his J.D. and Ph.D. in Education Foundations and Policy from the University of Michigan. Before joining UIC, Superfine practiced law at Dow Lohnes PLLC in Washington, D.C. His work has been published in leading educational and legal journals, including the *American Educational Research Journal*, *American Journal of Education*, *Cardozo Law Review*, *Educational Policy*, *Kentucky Law Journal*, *Missouri Law Review*, *Review of Educational Research*, and *Teachers College Record*. Superfine was awarded the Steven S. Goldberg Award for Distinguished Scholarship in Education Law from the Education Law Association for his first book, *The Courts and Standards-Based Education Reform*. He was a States' Involvement in Federal Education Policy Fellow and is currently the Director of the UIC Research on Urban Education Policy Initiative.

Equality in Education Law and Policy, 1954–2010

Benjamin Michael Superfine

University of Illinois Chicago

CAMBRIDGE
UNIVERSITY PRESS

CAMBRIDGE
UNIVERSITY PRESS

32 Avenue of the Americas, New York NY 10013-2473, USA

Cambridge University Press is part of the University of Cambridge.

It furthers the University's mission by disseminating knowledge in the pursuit of education, learning and research at the highest international levels of excellence.

www.cambridge.org
Information on this title: www.cambridge.org/9781107460058

First published 2013
First paperback edition 2014

A catalogue record for this publication is available from the British Library

Library of Congress Cataloguing in Publication data
Superfine, Benjamin Michael.
   Equality in education law and policy, 1954–2010 / Benjamin Michael Superfine, University of Illinois Chicago.
     pages   cm
   Includes bibliographical references and index.
   ISBN 978-1-107-01692-7 (hbk.)
   1. Educational equalization – Law and legislation – United States – History.
   2. Educational equalization – United States – History.   3. Discrimination in education – Law and legislation – United States – History.   I. Title.
   KF4155.S87   2013
   344.73′0709045–dc23   2012042702

ISBN 978-1-107-01692-7 Hardback
ISBN 978-1-107-46005-8 Paperback

To Alison, Chloe, Estelle, and George

Contents

Acknowledgments

This book could not have been written without the help of many people.

Several people provided excellent feedback on particular chapters or drafts of this book: Alison Castro-Superfine, Suzanne Eckes, David Mayrowetz, Mark Smylie, Kevin Welner, and two anonymous reviewers provided especially extensive feedback. Their comments and advice were invaluable, and this book is significantly better for their gracious efforts. Of course, all mistakes and omissions are my own.

I am also grateful to the faculty and administration at the College of Education at the University of Illinois at Chicago for their continuing support. I am particularly grateful to Mark Smylie for his intellectual mentorship. He provided a sounding board for many of my ideas and more broadly helped me navigate the strange environment that is academia. I am also grateful to John Benjamin for his research support.

Most of the ideas in this book were developed and sharpened in several courses that I taught at the University of Illinois at Chicago. I am indebted to the undergraduate, master's, and doctoral students who have taken my classes more than they will ever know for the opportunity to discuss these ideas over and over again. My students' enthusiasm and passion for education reform are driving forces behind this book.

Last, I would like to thank my family. My wife, Alison Castro-Superfine, has been my go-to source for helping me hash through issues of teaching and learning, which are far too often ignored in works focusing on law and policy. More importantly, she has been a never-ending source of encouragement as she strategically pushed the right buttons at just the right times. Chloe, Estelle, and George kept me firmly grounded every day. I can never fully express how much all their love and support mean to me.

Frequently Used Abbreviations

ARRA	American Recovery and Reinvestment Act
AYP	Adequate Yearly Progress
CSTP	Cleveland Scholarship and Tutoring Program
ED	U.S. Department of Education
ELL	English Language Learner
ESEA	Elementary and Secondary Education Act
ESRA	Education Sciences Reform Act
Goals 2000	Goals 2000: Educate America Act
HEW	U.S. Department of Health, Education, and Welfare
HQT	Highly Qualified Teacher
IASA	Improving America's Schools Act
IDEA	Individuals with Disabilities Education Act
IEP	Individualized Education Program
IES	Institute of Education Sciences
KERA	Kentucky Education Reform Act
MCT	Minimum Competency Test
MPCP	Milwaukee Parental Choice Program
NAEP	National Assessment of Educational Progress
NDEA	National Defense Education Act
NEA	National Education Association
OSP	Opportunity Scholarship Program
OTL	Opportunity to Learn Standards
RtI	Response to Intervention
RTT	Race to the Top Fund
SFSF	State Fiscal Stabilization Fund

Introduction

Educational equality has long been a vital concept in U.S. law and policy. While its roots stretch back to the founding of the United States, educational equality took center stage in law and policy with the Supreme Court's decision in *Brown v. Board of Education* in 1954 and subsequent civil rights decisions and legislation.[1] Since the civil rights era, the concept of educational equality has remained markedly durable and has animated major school reform efforts, including desegregation, school finance reform, the education of students with disabilities and limited English proficiency, the various iterations of the Elementary and Secondary Education Act (ESEA) since 1965, and school choice (including charter schools and voucher policies).[2] This concept continues to find expression in major education policies currently being implemented that have commanded significant attention from the White House and the American public more generally, such as the No Child Left Behind Act (NCLB) and the American Recovery and Reinvestment Act (ARRA) (which is popularly referred to as the federal "Stimulus").[3] As such, the concept of educational equality has dramatically transformed since *Brown* as legal and policy movements appear, evolve, disappear, and recombine.

While the transformation of such a durable and pervasive concept in law and policy is inevitable over time, an examination of it sheds light on a handful of fundamental problems that have persistently plagued large-scale school reform efforts. Although equalizing educational opportunities for students has been a central aim of education law and policy since *Brown*, such opportunities have not been realized as our understandings of the primary goals underlying schooling and, in turn, the very definition of an equal education have continually shifted. Similarly, although fundamental changes in the nature of educational governance have tracked transformations in the concept of educational equality and the underlying goals of education, these governance changes have generally failed to achieve many of their desired effects as well. Grounded in muddled educational goals and responding only obliquely to significant problems they have faced in the past, reforms of educational governance have yielded mixed results at best and have often created a slew of unintended problems. As a result, we have devoted huge amounts of resources to law and policy efforts aimed at educational equality without achieving the significant and lasting results at scale that many of the reformers driving such changes have sought. Given such problems, we now risk taking an overly narrow, if not myopic, view of why we educate children in the United States without enough to show for our efforts.

This book accordingly examines the transformation of equality in education law and policy from *Brown* through the ARRA, the major factors influencing this transformation, and the significant problems raised by this transformation that modern school reform efforts continue to face. This examination particularly focuses on the relationship between the transformation of the concept of educational equality in legal and policy decisions, key shifts in understandings of the purposes of education underlying these decisions, and the evolution of educational governance structures. In examining such interrelated developments, this book asks several fundamental questions about the current state of education law and policy and how it got here since *Brown*: How have education law and policy reform efforts focused on equality reflected shifts in understandings of major political and social goals of education, such as supporting U.S. international competitiveness, a robustly functioning democracy, and broad-based social mobility? To what extent can these reforms serve as vehicles for supporting several different goals concurrently? How have the changing structures of educational governance, and federalism in particular, influenced (and been influenced by) the accomplishment of educational equality and these underlying goals? How has the notion of equality itself been translated in the context of such shifts? How have students' educational opportunities, which have long been dramatically unequal, ultimately been influenced by these changes? In short, this book investigates the development of equality in education law and policy in relation to major educational goals and governance structures and highlights a handful of major problems raised by these changes. This examination is particularly aimed at shedding light on how historical purposes and problems underlie more immediately visible ones that characterize current school reform efforts.

Although law and policy reform efforts have long centered on the concept of equality in a range of major domestic policy areas, such as employment, health, housing, and voting, the concept of equality has arguably assumed its most prominent role in education. Despite its centrality and the continual waves of reform efforts associated with it, the concept of an equal education has transformed dramatically over time. When this concept took center stage in *Brown*, it was largely structured around protecting the rights of underrepresented groups.[4] But as courts and legislatures continued to craft decisions about educational equality throughout the second half of the twentieth century and beginning of the twenty-first, the concept generally evolved into one that is situated in broad social structures and institutions. The legal and policy strategies used to address educational equality accordingly began to deal with increasingly complicated issues, grounded deeply within the workings of school systems, schools, and classroom practices, that stretch the traditional boundaries of governmental power and capability[5] – instead of dealing largely with concerns about equal access to schools, these strategies now focus on broader issues of school and student performance, and instituting accountability mechanisms tied to such performance.[6] As a result, many modern reforms in education law and policy have become concerned with increasing and equalizing students' demonstrated academic performance on measures such as standardized tests through the systemic restructuring of school systems.

Such transformations in equality have in turn been anchored in significant changes in educational governance. While federal courts were the primary governmental institution involved with reform efforts centered on educational equality during *Brown* and the heyday of the desegregation movement, these courts have faded into the background in this area over time.[7] However, state courts have taken on increasingly important roles by becoming involved in school finance reform litigation in almost every state, and state legislatures and agencies have become involved in setting educational standards and holding students and schools accountable for their performance.[8] At the same time, educational federalism underwent dramatic shifts as the role of the federal government in matters of educational equality began to grow and change with the passage of laws like the ESEA in the 1960s and its reauthorization as NCLB in 2002.[9] Still, educational decision making has become decentralized in other respects since the 1990s. The proliferation of school choice reforms, such as charter school and voucher policies, has positioned schools and school districts as primary sites of reform and accountability, and they have empowered more parents to make decisions about which schools their children attend.[10] Given such shifts in the loci of decision-making authority, "policy instruments" that structure the relationships among educational actors have evolved as well. For example, while the federal government heavily relied on basic grant mechanisms in the 1960s to improve states' educational systems for poor students, complex accountability systems focused on school, teacher, and student performance now structure major relationships between federal and state governments as well.

Educational equality in law and policy and the underlying governance structures have similarly transformed in the context of a shifting web of broad political and social goals.[11] Educational and political theorists have long underscored the importance of an equal education for the operation of a robust democracy.[12] Especially during the civil rights era, reformers also framed educational equality as a key element for increasing social mobility.[13] As highlighted by the education legislation enacted in the wake of *Sputnik*'s launch, reformers have positioned education as a needed support for international competitiveness as well.[14] With the attention of policy makers and the public currently focused on globalization, conceptual links between education and international economic competitiveness have recently cast an even longer shadow over education reform efforts in debates over modern policies such as NCLB.[15] Indeed, schools have consistently served as a battleground for struggles over wide-spanning social and political issues, and the legislative and judicial spheres have played key roles in these battles. This book analyzes how educational equality has transformed in light of such major changes in educational governance and goals, and the major problems still associated with these changes.

Although educational governance and goals are useful touchstones for an analysis of the transformation of equality, there are countless angles that one could potentially take in such an examination. Instead of focusing on educational goals and governance, one could highlight the significant political, economic, technological, and demographic shifts that swept through the United States since *Brown*. Alternatively, one could focus on how powerful interest groups and advocates have influenced education law and policy. Because an examination of the transformation of educational equality in law and policy since *Brown* would not be complete without discussing such changes, this book references these changes throughout. However, focusing on equality in relation to the touchstones of educational goals and governance is useful precisely because they mediate the influence of such broader shifts; as politics, economics, technology, and demographics change, so too do our notions of why schools operate and how they should be run. Examining the transformation of equality in relation to a couple of fundamental touchstones allows for an analysis that is broad and holistic yet not overly unwieldy or unintelligible.

The focus on educational goals, governance, and their relationship with educational equality is further based on a fundamental insight about the nature of education law and policy that appeared in *Brown*. In this case, the Supreme Court famously stated:

> Today, education is perhaps the most important function of state and local governments. Compulsory school attendance laws and the great expenditures for education both demonstrate our recognition of the importance of education to our democratic society. It is required even in the performance of our most basic public responsibilities, even service in the armed forces. It is the very foundation of good citizenship. Today it is a principal instrument in awakening the child to cultural values, in preparing him for later professional training, and in helping him to adjust normally to his environment. In these days, it is doubtful that any child may reasonably be expected to succeed in life if he is denied the opportunity of an education. Such an opportunity, where the state has taken to provide it, is a right which must be made available to all on equal terms.[16]

With this statement, the Supreme Court framed educational equality, a primary target of school reform efforts for at least the following half-century, directly in relation to the public institutions responsible for governing education and its underlying purposes. As the constitutional scholar Bruce Ackerman argued, *Brown* represents a synthesis of two major strands of constitutional thought – one focused on the concept of equality that emerged in response to Reconstruction and the Fourteenth Amendment in particular, and the other on the modern functions of governmental institutions that emerged in response to the New Deal.[17] Furthermore, as the educational scholars David Tyack and Larry Cuban argued, "Americans have translated their cultural anxieties and hopes into dramatic demands for educational reform."[18] While legal analyses of educational equality often ignore the range of purposes and politics underlying school reform, educational analyses often ignore the institutional complexities associated with it. This book aims at reinvigorating the fundamental insight of *Brown* that equality in education law and policy is effectively understood in relation to both governmental institutions and broad social and political purposes.

In addition to focusing on educational goals and governance as a way to make sense out of the transformation of equality, the examination in this book also emphasizes certain large-scale education reform strategies over others. This examination particularly focuses on desegregation, school finance reform, standards-based reform and accountability policies, and school choice, which researchers have historically identified as the primary types of equal opportunity reforms in education law and policy.[19] The examination also includes reform efforts in both judicial and legislative spheres involving the education of students with disabilities and English language learners (ELLs) because these types of reforms have at times dramatically altered the education law and policy landscape. However, analyses of these reforms are often folded into broader discussions about the other major types of reforms noted previously. This book also discusses several other types of education law and policy reform strategies throughout, such as the recent focus in federal education policy on conducting "scientifically based research" in education and funding reforms based on this kind of research. In this way, several laws and policies that are not directly aimed at leveraging educational equality or involve goals beyond educational equality are also included. Without an analysis of such areas and the major aspects of these reforms that do not immediately involve educational equality, this book could not present a complete picture of how educational equality has transformed. Still, the focus remains on the laws and policies involving equality that have played major roles in education since *Brown*.

The approach needed to conduct an examination that centers on educational equality, and particularly on educational governance and goals, over such a broad range of reforms is not easy. It involves an analysis of what various laws and policies say and the principles underlying their text; an understanding of courts, legislatures, agencies, and other governmental and nongovernmental entities as institutions with different characteristics that sometimes compete and sometimes cooperate; an examination of how educational laws and policies are implemented, move through various administrative levels, and ultimately influence what happens in schools and classrooms; knowledge of the political and historical contexts surrounding legal and policy reform efforts in education; and a sensitivity to how these contexts can influence understandings of educational goals that underlie these reform efforts.

This book accordingly synthesizes insights from various disciplines, including law, history, political science, and education policy. Legal opinions, statutes, and other legal texts (such as regulations and agency decisions) constitute the primary sources of evidence for this examination. As such, this book employs traditional methods of legal analysis to understand the rules and principles underlying these different texts, and to analyze how the concept of educational equality is treated in these texts in specific relation to educational goals and governance.[20] When examining law and policy events that are particularly central to the major issues in this book, other sources that provide more direct insight into the reasons underlying legal and policy change are also examined. For example, the *Congressional Record* is examined to illuminate the reasons and arguments underlying legislative change, and legal briefs and court transcripts are analyzed to understand how such issues are reflected in litigation.

A range of theoretically and empirically oriented secondary sources provide additional insight into the transformation of equality. This book draws on theoretical perspectives from the study of law and political science focusing on legal and policy change, how governmental institutions influence and are influenced by such change, and the implementation of public policy across administrative levels. This literature can help explain how and why legal and policy changes in the area of educational equality occurred over time and across governmental institutions. Historical and political science research are also used to situate legal and policy changes in their particular historical and political contexts. This literature is used to create a robust picture of the environment in which these changes occurred and the major actors involved with such changes and to illustrate why changes in educational goals and governance structures have been such powerful factors influencing changes in equality.

Finally, this book draws on education policy literature to understand the concrete effects of legal and policy decisions on schools and school systems. This literature helps illustrate what these reforms have looked like in practice and how they have changed (or failed to change) conditions outside courts and legislatures. Moreover, this literature provides an evidence-based view of the concrete problems education reform efforts have faced and the problems to which changes in educational governance could have potentially responded. Together, these disciplinary perspectives facilitate a broad analysis of how the concept of equality has transformed over time in education law and policy, the major factors that have influenced its transformation across institutional environments, and the major problems that law and policy reform efforts focused on educational equality continue to face.

Such an examination of the transformation of equality in education law and policy is particularly important and timely. We are currently at a historical moment that requires a strong and holistic understanding of how the concept of educational equality has fared since *Brown*. Although education was largely a local concern for much of U.S. history, law and policy became among the most significant tools for reforming schools in the wake of *Brown*.[21] Beginning with the desegregation movement, the federal and state roles in education have expanded dramatically, especially in issues related to equality. And with the Supreme Court's emphasis of the importance of education in *Brown*, governmental recognition of education's importance began to grow.[22] Building on this foundation, a range of legislative and judicial decisions at federal and state levels have aimed at increasing and equalizing students' educational opportunities and performance. With the acceleration of changes in educational federalism and the policy instruments used to structure the relationships among federal, state, and local governments, as exemplified by NCLB and the recent passage of the ARRA, it appears that such involvement will only intensify in the foreseeable future. Yet, despite the significant resources accompanying intensive judicial and legislative efforts to equalize educational opportunities, these efforts have often failed to achieve their goals.[23] In order to structure such ongoing efforts more effectively, it is imperative to understand how and why education law and policy have arrived at the state they are in today.

Moreover, the changing political and social contexts of school reform make such an examination more pressing than ever. The concept of an equal education has long played a central role in democratic theory and is key for facilitating social mobility in a country characterized by vast gaps in wealth and class.[24] While the notion of an equal education has also played a role in ideas about how to strengthen the U.S. economy, the ideas of educational efficiency and excellence have, at times, provided powerful competition to the idea of educational equality. As governmental and public attention to the place of the United States in a globalizing world only intensifies over the coming years, we risk taking an overly narrow view of the purposes and potential of school reform efforts. A nuanced understanding of how equality has transformed in education law and policy can provide an important guidepost for navigating difficult legal and policy decisions aimed at school reform in this quickly changing time.

On an even deeper level, an investigation of the transformation of equality in education law and policy has the potential to shed light on fundamental issues that lie at the heart of the modern American state. The transformation of educational equality takes place in the context of a highly fragmented legal and policy environment, laden with technical and administrative nuances, in the even larger context of a constitutional democracy composed of powerful institutions. Education itself is a legal and policy field that is highly politicized and shaped by organizations and individuals with significant economic and political stakes. Moreover, education has a limited research base and is heavily influenced by external forces from other fields, such as health and housing. As at least a partial result, U.S. schools have long needed improvement in several respects, have commanded attention as one of the most important domestic priority areas for the future of individuals in the United States and the country as a whole, and have proven stubbornly resistant to change.[25] The involvement of the concept of equality heightens these stakes and pressures that already inhere in education law and policy – equality is one of the core values underlying the U.S. polity, and it has long animated fundamental issues inherent in American law and policy. When examined together, such elements of educational equality – those that are based in policy, law, governance, politics, and science – can inform us not only about how to craft education law and policy more effectively, but also about how a value core to the U.S. political order can fare as we move forward.

Although researchers have devoted significant attention to judicial and legislative involvement with particular reform efforts aimed at equalizing educational opportunities, such analyses have been limited in scope and surprisingly have not included a systematic examination of how these efforts have transformed across institutions and over time. For example, several legal, educational, and policy researchers have examined courts' and legislatures' roles in the major areas of reform aimed at educational equality, such as desegregation, school finance reform, school choice, and standards, testing, and accountability systems.[26] Throughout these works, researchers have identified the major goals of reform, factors influencing the formation and implementation of goals, and the outcomes of these reforms. Moreover, some recent work has focused on the importance of educational governance structures for understanding such reforms, especially in light of the recent expansion of the federal role in education.[27] However, these works generally do not take a bird's-eye view of education law and policy reform efforts since *Brown*. And while many of the works in this field integrate insights from legal research, they often lack significant attention to shifting educational goals and the effects of such changes on schools and classrooms. On the flip side, while educational and political theorists have devoted significant attention to developments in the purposes of education throughout U.S. history, such examinations generally have not been deeply anchored in nuanced discussions of law and policy.[28] Finally, few works focused on education law and policy adequately account for the influence of institutional context in their analyses.

Conducting a broad and interdisciplinary analysis is therefore necessary in order to fill gaps in existing research and shed light on major longstanding problems in this area. For example, deeply understanding recent attempts to equalize students' educational opportunities through school finance litigation requires knowledge of how courts in these cases have begun to restructure traditional educational governance structures, which in turn requires knowledge of standards, testing, and accountability policies, which in turn requires an understanding of the shifting federal role in education, which in turn requires attention to key shifts in educational goals and their political operationalization over time. Without an analysis that traverses various reform efforts from different disciplinary perspectives, the major problems persistently associated with the transformation of equality cannot be fully appreciated. Indeed, there have been several calls for more research firmly grounded in knowledge of both education policy and the law, and this book represents an attempt to respond to this call.[29] In this way, this book not only is aimed at developing a nuanced and holistic map of how equality has transformed, but also responds to historical problems that persist not insignificantly because of their location at overlapping disciplinary boundaries.

OVERVIEW OF THE ARGUMENT

This book generally argues that the concept of equality in education law and policy has dramatically transformed since *Brown* was decided in 1954. This transformation has largely been driven by fundamental and interlocking shifts in educational governance and understandings of educational goals. As a result of these changes, modern education law and policy reform efforts focused on equality face a series of problems, ranging from muddled and conflicting goals to the concrete and sometimes undesirable effects of governance structures built on these goals. Despite the pervasiveness of such problems, a new approach to educational equality that is grounded in an understanding of the strengths and weaknesses of previous education law and policy reform efforts has the potential to address at least some of the major challenges.

On a more specific level, this book argues that although equality has been the focus of several different large-scale law and policy reform efforts, three major trajectories of the transformation of equality have appeared across these reforms. First, while educational equality originally was structured primarily to protect the rights of harmed groups, the concept shifted to focus on the reform of entire school systems that were built in ways that systemically produced inequalities. Second, while educational equality originally focused on educational inputs, such as access to predominantly white schools and funding, the concept shifted to focus on educational outputs, such as school and student performance. Third, while educational equality originally was structured around "sameness" between different groups of students, the concept shifted to an emphasis on ensuring that all students receive at least an adequate, or standard, level of educational opportunities and exhibit at least adequate academic achievement.

This transformation of equality has been driven largely by interrelated shifts in educational governance and understandings of educational goals. Throughout education law and policy decisions focused on equality since *Brown*, educational governance and goals have acted together as two of the most basic touchstones for framing changes in the definition of equality. In *Brown*, the concept of equality was largely framed in relation to the fundamental educational goals of facilitating social mobility and supporting an inclusive democracy. However, reflecting political, economic, and technological developments and the influence of educational interest groups and individuals, education law and policy reforms have strongly focused on supporting international economic competitiveness since the early 1980s and have reflected an increasingly free-market and efficiency-oriented ideology. Indeed, given such changes in the ideology underlying education law and policy, reforms such as school choice policies have been at least partly based on the notion that education is a private good for individuals to attain rather than a public good related to broader social purposes.[30]

Accompanying and often reflecting such changes in educational goals, educational governance arrangements have also undergone fundamental shifts. Immediately following *Brown*, federal courts loomed large and assumed a "command-and-control" approach to issues of educational equality by issuing top-down mandates in this area.[31] However, in response to shifts in understandings of educational goals, increasing experience with the actual implementation of equality-based reforms, and significant political developments, these governance arrangements shifted. Under the stated logic of "local control," federal courts largely withdrew from matters of educational equality and faded into the background over time, while many other governmental institutions, such as state and federal legislatures, assumed decision-making authority in this area.

In doing so, these institutions employed a wide range of strategies and policy tools to govern matters of educational equality. School choice policies focusing on charter schools and school vouchers proliferated with these changes in the loci of institutional authority. Perhaps most notably, the historical focus of the federal government shifted from employing basic grant mechanisms for improving students' educational opportunities to the heavy use of accountability systems focused on demonstrated academic performance of schools and students. Indeed, although public understandings of educational purposes and educational governance have changed for a variety of reasons, such changes have been strongly inter-related – when making decisions involving educational equality, governmental institutions like the U.S. Congress have explicitly considered the proper institutional arrangements for effecting particular educational purposes, such as social mobility and international competitiveness. So, where educational goals have provided the general direction for equality-based reforms, educational governance structures have constituted the basic framework for achieving these goals and have concretely structured the ways in which these reforms have come in contact with schools, classrooms, and ultimately teachers' instructional practices.

Such transformations in the concept of equality, as framed by changes in educational goals and educational governance, have animated the rise, fall, and recombination of specific legal and policy movements in education. The movement away from traditional civil rights efforts, such as desegregation, and to more modern forms of school reform, such as school choice and accountability structures (as embodied in policies such as NCLB and the ARRA), reflects these transformations. Significant changes within the shape of lasting types of reform efforts, such as school finance litigation (which has persisted since at least the 1960s), similarly reflect these transformations. The convergence of education reform movements, such as the growing relationship between school finance reform litigation and standards-based reforms, reflects these transformations as well.

Despite the durability and flexibility of education law and policy efforts aimed at effecting educational equality, these reforms have resulted in a handful of significant and persistent problems that education law and policy reform efforts continue to face. Although there have been some critical successes, such as the elimination of legal segregation in public schools, efforts at equalizing students' educational opportunities have ultimately yielded mixed results at best. All the while, traditional versions of the concept of equality are increasingly at risk of getting lost in the endless waves of reform as they compete with modern educational goals. At the same time, modern law and policy efforts focused on educational equality suffer from muddled educational goals and governance structures that often respond only obliquely to significant problems they have faced in the past and that create unintended problems.

In order to conduct an examination of the transformation of equality and the major problems that have emerged with it, this book is divided into seven primary parts in addition to the Introduction. In Chapter 2, this book situates the transformation of equality in its historical and theoretical contexts. This chapter begins with a discussion of the major theories and disciplinary perspectives that guide the subsequent analysis. This section particularly highlights a policy regimes framework that places political and policy developments in their historical contexts to understand policy change by focusing on the relationships among political ideas, institutions, and interests.[32] Given the focus on educational goals and governance, the relationship between ideas and institutions is particularly emphasized. This section also highlights the ways in which comparative institutional choice theory is helpful for understanding legal and policy decision making across different institutional environments.[33] This theory generally focuses on the comparative characteristics of governmental and nongovernmental institutions and accordingly provides a useful lens for analyzing legal and policy decisions that span various institutional contexts. Finally, this chapter focuses on the major factors that have historically influenced the implementation of law and policy across various institutional and organizational environments. Together, these theoretical frames facilitate a broad analysis of not only how the concept of equality has transformed but also the range of factors that have influenced its transformation.

With this backdrop in place, Chapters 3 through 7 turn to the analysis of substantive education law and policy decisions focused on school reform and equality beginning with *Brown*. Chapter 3 focuses on the early stages of civil rights litigation and legislation, which were primarily aimed at desegregating public schools. In addition to examining how particular purposes of the civil rights movement found expression in legal decisions, this chapter focuses on the beginning of the expansion of courts' and legislatures' role in education reform efforts. First, *Brown* and the way in which the Supreme Court framed the purposes of education and the role of governmental institutions are examined in detail. Although many have argued that *Brown* was ultimately ineffective or should have been decided differently, the way in which the Supreme Court addressed equality in *Brown* prefigured governmental treatment of educational equality for years after the case was decided. A deep analysis of *Brown* therefore provides a useful guidepost for the rest of the book.

After examining *Brown*, this chapter turns to the major desegregation cases decided by the Supreme Court through the early 1970s. This examination emphasizes the ways in which the Supreme Court located power within the judiciary (and federal district courts in particular) to oversee desegregation. Given this allocation of power, the analysis also focuses on the discretion accorded to other governmental institutions with commands such as the mandate to desegregate with "all deliberate speed," the criteria used by courts to determine when districts have satisfactorily desegregated, and strategies like busing that were approved to implement desegregation mandates. This chapter particularly examines the early development of the judiciary's conception of educational equality, as reflected by the shifting strategies approved by the Supreme Court to implement desegregation mandates and the list of ever-growing social issues underlying these decisions. Laced throughout this discussion is specific attention to the resistance to the Supreme Court's various mandates to desegregate and the entrance of the U.S. Congress into matters of educational equality with legislation like the Civil Rights Act of 1964 and the ESEA.[34]

Chapter 4 focuses on how educational equality was defined and addressed in law and policy during the maturing stages of the civil rights movement. On one hand, this chapter analyzes the broadening and deepening of legislative and judicial involvement in education. In the 1970s, states and localities gained experience working with the ESEA, and ESEA requirements began to change in light of its previous implementation. Still working under a civil rights paradigm, Congress also expanded its reach into areas like the education of students with disabilities with the Education for All Handicapped Children Act of 1975, and federal courts and Congress became deeply involved with reform focused on the education of ELL students.[35] At the same time, state courts and legislatures were beginning to become involved in school finance reform litigation and legislation. So, in some respects, this analysis covers the ways in which the treatment of equality in education law and policy represented a seemingly natural extension of the principles established in *Brown*.

But, on the other hand, this chapter also examines a fundamental shift in education law and policy away from reforms directly focused on educational equality. During the 1970s, cracks in the governance structures underlying equality-based reforms were becoming clearly visible. Throughout this decade, federal and state legislatures and courts were gaining experience working with the often difficult and politically problematic implementation of a range of equality-based reforms in education law and policy, including desegregation, school finance reform, and the ESEA. In this context, an increasingly conservative Supreme Court underscored the importance of local control over schools and backed away from addressing emerging complexities in desegregation. On the basis of similar logic, the Supreme Court ruled that states' methods of unequally financing local school districts were not unconstitutional and that such problems would need to be addressed, if at all, by state courts. The involvement of state courts and legislatures in school funding issues in the 1970s was driven precisely by this Supreme Court decision. So, in addition to addressing the expansion of civil rights legislation and litigation, this chapter charts the backlash to this movement, the redistribution of institutional authority in matters of educational equality, and the ways in which educational equality and the problems associated with it were accordingly conceptualized through the 1970s and early 1980s.

In Chapter 5, this book examines a fundamental shift in the politics and perceived purposes of educational law and policy in the 1980s, and the ways in which law and policy defined and addressed educational equality in the following years. The publication of *A Nation at Risk*, a report drafted by a federally appointed panel in 1983, reinvigorated the public focus on education as a lever for international competitiveness in a time characterized by economic downturn and the growth of telecommunications technology.[36] Given the widening cracks in educational governance and quickly shifting educational goals, equality-based reforms began to assume a very different structure. In part pushed by appeals to principles of business management and a growing governmental experience with a range of education reform efforts primarily focusing on educational inputs, the idea that governmental institutions should focus on educational outcomes became increasingly prevalent. Moreover, the notion of adequacy – a minimally sufficient level of educational resources that all students need to be provided or level of educational outcomes that all students need to attain – increasingly became mixed with reform efforts focusing on equality. Similarly, reform efforts focused less on protecting the rights of individual students and more on reforming the systemwide legal and policy regimes that structured students' educational opportunities.

This chapter accordingly analyzes how these developments emerged in major education law and policy movements from the early 1980s through the 1990s. *A Nation at Risk*, the emergence of the educational "excellence" movement, and the development of standards-based reforms and related accountability systems at the state level are particularly examined. Building on this examination, the dramatic expansion of the federal role in this area in the 1990s with the passage of laws such as the Goals 2000: Educate America Act and the Improving America's Schools Act are discussed.[37] While much of the investigation of these laws focuses on the federal emphasis on standards, accountability, and the systemic change of schools and school systems, this investigation also focuses on the synthesis of notions of adequacy and equality with the concept of the "opportunity-to-learn" knowledge and skills in standards. This chapter similarly focuses on fundamental changes in school finance reform litigation and legislation at the state level to emphasize the notion of adequacy of funding, the importance of assessing educational outcomes in school finance reform, and the need for broad, structural reforms of school systems to accompany funding reforms.

In Chapter 6, this book turns to critical developments in education law and policy efforts in the 1990s involving equality and the principle of local control. In particular, this chapter highlights how the principle of local control fueled both the expansion and the contraction of law and policy efforts focused on equality across major education reforms. This chapter specifically examines the ways in which the principle of local control powered the proliferation of education law and policy reforms in states involving school choice – a movement that focuses authority in schools and parents with policies authorizing reforms such as charter schools and school vouchers. First, the emergence of the voucher movement, the theories and politics underlying vouchers, and their effects on schools are discussed. Then, the charter school movement is discussed, with an emphasis on the theories and politics underlying it and its effects on schools. Finally, the major cases decided by the Supreme Court in the 1990s and 2000s involving desegregation are examined. Heavily emphasizing the principle of local control, Supreme Court decisions governing desegregation generally continued down the trajectory that they had assumed in the 1970s and increasingly facilitated the dismantling of desegregation decrees. The logic of these cases is particularly analyzed, in addition to the resulting actions of district courts overseeing desegregation mandates and the effects of these actions on schools.

In Chapter 7, this book turns to the modern era of school reform efforts involving educational equality. This chapter particularly examines NCLB, the way in which its underlying logic synthesizes historical concepts of equality and adequacy, the heavy focus NCLB places on educational outcomes through its accountability mechanisms, and the ways in which the law expanded federal power while still carving out specific roles for states and school districts. This section also analyzes the range of implementation problems NCLB has faced and the major effects of NCLB on schools, including the often inequitable effects of its strong accountability mechanisms. The discussion of NCLB notably includes attention to the alignment of NCLB with other major education law and policy reforms, such as the reauthorization of the Individuals with Disabilities Education Act and the Education Sciences Reform Act, which promotes the development of education reforms grounded in "scientifically based research." The recent focus on "scientifically based research" in federal law is especially important to consider because it is aimed at increasing the effectiveness of large-scale education reform efforts through its focus on a centralized, scientific brand of decision making that heavily relies on educational outcomes.

In addition, this chapter analyzes the ARRA. Although this law was primarily enacted to stabilize and stimulate the U.S. economy during the worst financial crisis since the Great Depression, the law devoted approximately $100 billion to education. In doing so, it aimed at not only keeping school systems afloat in difficult financial times, but also fixing existing education policy problems, sparking future education reform efforts, and laying the foundation for the Obama administration's subsequent education reforms. While some of the education provisions of the ARRA have continued to focus on enacting systemwide change at the state level, including the expansion of policies to hold teachers accountable for their performance, other parts of the ARRA have focused more on turning around low-performing schools through particular reform strategies. As such, the ARRA has reflected new dimensions of federal action in education. This section accordingly analyzes the purposes underlying the ARRA, the ways in which the ARRA frames and addresses educational inequalities, and the known effects of the ARRA thus far.

In Chapter 8, this book synthesizes the developments in education law and policy examined in the previous chapters and offers concluding thoughts. An overview and analytical summary of the major crosscutting issues appear first. Then, this chapter articulates four major principles for structuring education reform in the future. Finally, it presents concrete reform recommendations to illustrate how these principles can be fruitfully applied. These recommendations are largely based on more effectively understanding and capitalizing on institutional strengths in relation to educational goals through a model that draws on recent developments in the federal role and school finance litigation.

Given the broad scope of this analysis, there are of course several limitations. The book cannot cover every event within specific reform efforts, such as every single legal case aimed at desegregation or school finance reform. Because mapping the transformation of equality across governmental institutions over a period longer than fifty years is very complex, the discussions of reforms sometimes spill beyond the general period covered by individual chapters. Indeed, while the story of educational equality in law and policy is at its most coherent when viewed historically, marking off particular years as easy cutoff points for the discussion of several different reforms would be artificial and result in overly narrow discussions at best. Finally, given the complexity of the issues covered in this book, it is worth noting explicitly that there are no easy conclusions to be drawn or simple recommendations to be made that could act as "magic bullets" for the problems of inequality in education.

However, this book does aim at expanding our knowledge in important ways. The analysis covers major shifts in a primary area of education law and policy and includes detailed analyses of legislative and judicial decisions marking our understanding of long-term developments that have fundamentally shaped how schools and school systems are run. It investigates the goals underlying major legal and policy reforms, and how major governmental institutions have engaged with a core American value more generally. Finally, it attempts to provide a strong foundation for crafting future education law and policy reforms not simply in response to problems that have emerged with the most recent reform effort but with knowledge of some of the broader issues that persistently underlie such problems.

2

Government, Equality, and School Reform

Attempting to understand the transformation of education in law and policy across a span of more than fifty years is a complex and difficult task. One could pay attention to an almost limitless range of phenomena and evidence. Such an examination requires attention to how legislatures enact policies and the large range of factors influencing this process. While many of these factors could be labeled as "political," such as public opinion and bare partisan politics, it is also important to consider broad economic, technological, and demographic changes that could push politics in certain directions and influence the formation of educational policies. An examination of law and policy change in education also requires attention to how laws and constitutional requirements are interpreted (and arguably made) by courts and the large range of factors that influence this process. Given that legislative and judicial decisions are not self-executing, such an examination requires further attention to the institutions and individuals responsible for implementing educational law and policy, such as states, districts, schools, and teachers. On a more abstract level, it is just as important to consider the very content of the ideas about educational equality that emerge throughout these interrelated processes and the ways in which all these ideas, institutions, and political interests interact.

Although there are no definitive models for conducting such an examination, insights generated by previous research can inform the analysis. This chapter synthesizes literature from a handful of different disciplines, including law, political science, education policy, and history, to gain theoretical leverage on the transformation of educational equality in law and policy. To this end, "policy regimes theory" is first discussed as an overarching theoretical umbrella for the rest of the examination. This theory primarily stems from a historically oriented branch of political science that focuses on understanding the relationships among political ideas, interests, and institutions. These three areas are arguably the elemental building blocks of modern political science (and increasingly education policy) analysis.[1] While political interests and interest groups are discussed throughout, this chapter (and book more broadly) primarily focuses on the relationship between political ideas and institutions. Indeed, this relationship has traditionally been an important subject of education policy research and reflects the book's focus on the transformation of equality in light of shifts in educational purposes and governance.[2]

Despite the utility of policy regimes theory for understanding the transformation of equality, integrating additional theoretical insights can make this book's approach to the transformation of equality more robust. Literature on education policy and history has long highlighted prominent educational purposes that have emerged throughout U.S. history. This chapter discusses such literature to frame major political ideas underlying changes in the concept of educational equality over time. Moreover, while policy regimes theory has been used to understand sweeping education policy changes, such as the development of the federal role in education, this theory has been used in education largely to analyze legislative action and change.[3] Understanding the transformation of equality in education law and policy involves extensive attention to the courts and their relationship with legislatures as well. The institutional branch of policy regimes theory is thus fleshed out by drawing on comparative institutional choice theory, which focuses on understanding the strengths, weaknesses, and characteristics of governmental and nongovernmental institutions in relation to each other.

Finally, building on the discussion of how education laws and policies are formed, this chapter discusses the major factors that can influence the implementation of education law and policy decisions. Although this discussion cannot capture every factor influencing education policy implementation, it particularly focuses on the way education law and policy cascade through multiple institutional and organizational levels, including the federal government, states, districts, schools, and classrooms. In doing so, this discussion not only reveals how individual law and policy decisions have fared in concrete settings but also provides key insight into the transformation of equality over time as information from (and interpretations of) the implementation process feeds back into subsequent education law and policy decisions.

It is worth noting that none of the literature and theories included in this chapter is completely uncontested. Moreover, not even a broad examination focusing on ideas, interests, and institutions can account for every important aspect of how and why educational equality has transformed in law and policy. However, the theoretical insights presented in this chapter represent a useful way of thinking about governmental decision making and implementation, and the inclusion of these insights is ultimately the product of a search to explain how and why governmental bodies have acted in particular ways. Including this literature is ultimately aimed at pushing forward our understanding of education law and policy, and more broadly providing more theoretical leverage for understanding how law and policy operate and interact over time.

POLICY REGIMES THEORY

Given the focus of this book on the transformation of educational equality in relation to educational purposes and governance, policy regimes theory provides a useful lens for understanding educational decisions. Policy regimes theory broadly focuses on what are arguably the fundamental building blocks of change in law and policy – ideas, interests, and institutions.[4] While this theory generally grew out of international relations literature, researchers have employed it to focus on several areas of domestic policy, including environmental protection, immigration, and education.[5] The theory takes a broad approach to law and policy change by helping us place contemporary political and policy developments in the context of relevant historical developments.[6]

In contrast to some other theories of policy change, policy regimes theory stresses that policy change happens gradually.[7] Policy regimes are the sets of ideas, interests, and institutions that structure governmental activities in particular issue areas, and they tend to be stable over time.[8] Change in policy regimes occurs as regimes become stressed, alternative policy ideas emerge, crises of political legitimacy occur, and political power shifts.[9] A range of factors can stress policy regimes, including sudden disasters, visible political events, or cumulative processes like demographic shifts.[10] These sorts of factors can put pressure on organizational arrangements, undermine dominant policy ideas, and raise the visibility of new problems. As a result of disconnects between the elements of an older regime and new problems and issues that emerge, new policy paradigms can gain traction and become dominant. As the following sections reflect, the elements constituting a policy regime can be very complex and varied.

Interests

The study of political interests has long played a large role in political science. Researchers have particularly focused on the political interests of individuals and formal and informal groups, and how these entities have interacted. In this way, some researchers have argued that interests (and the power of the individuals and groups with certain interests) are the fundamental drivers of politics and political change.[11] Studies of interest groups have accordingly focused on who wields political power and influence, and whose views are represented in the U.S. democracy.

Interest groups have become increasingly important in national politics and policy in the United States since World War II. In the postwar era, large national interest groups developed and gained significant influence in the political process.[12] While collective action is generally difficult to effect, even groups with limited resources and political power managed to organize during this time.[13] As such groups emerged, several policy areas came to be ruled under "iron triangles" composed of small and rigid groups of legislators, bureaucrats, and interest group representatives.[14] Still, it appears that interest group influence on the political process has become much more complex since at least the 1990s as the openness of the political process around particular issues began to vary widely.[15]

Interest groups can be categorized in several different ways; for example, they can be for-profit, nonprofit, citizen-based, or mixed.[16] Some researchers have further distinguished among interest groups by the strategies they employ to influence policy.[17] For example, groups may use lobbying, litigation, administrative interventions, whistle-blowing, public relations, release of research reports, presentations to governmental agencies, letter writing, and campaign contributions. Such strategies may also be categorized by an insider versus outsider approach. Groups employing insider strategies may use legislative lobbying, litigation, and electioneering, while outsider groups may use protests and grassroots lobbying.[18] Still, there is little evidence that these broad categories into which interest groups can be divided reflect strong differences in how these groups actually operate and their ultimate influence.[19]

Given the centrality of interests to political analysis, researchers have identified several interest groups in education that have exercised significant power in shaping the political discourse and law and policy formation. For example, textbook and testing companies have long played an important role in driving curricular decisions.[20] Teacher unions have played large roles in shaping teacher workforce policy. A host of other groups have played important roles across education policy issues as well, including business organizations, advocacy groups for underrepresented populations, foundations, for-profit services providers (such as student tutoring companies), and nonprofit organizations.[21] Despite the general recognition that such interest groups have played important roles in education policy, our knowledge about their influence is generally limited.[22] As noted, this book largely focuses on the relationship between educational ideas and institutions. Still, given the important role of interest groups in education law and policy, references to political interests and interest groups appear throughout.

Ideas

The concept of ideas has become prominent among political thinkers who believe that policy change can be driven by something more than self- and group interests and the bare exercise of power to achieve goals motivated by these interests.[23] Ideas generally refer to views about how laws and policies do and should operate with regard to the public interest. It is difficult to divide interests from ideas clearly – interests can be seen simply as ideas that are selfishly motivated to privilege certain people or groups. Under this formulation, ideas are at best justifications for the selfish application of power. However, considering ideas as separate from interests reflects the notion that at least some ideas are framed around an honest pursuit of the public good and that these ideas can be very different from each other. Thus, it is important to examine not only the interests that ideas serve but also the substantive content of the ideas themselves.

Education law and policy have historically reflected several different ideas about both the public good and the private good for individuals and groups. As the education historian David Labaree argued, schools "occupy an awkward position at the intersection between what we hope society will become and what we think it really is, between political ideals and economic realities."[24] As a result, debates over schools and school reform have ultimately focused on whether schools should be aimed at adapting students to the needs of society as currently constructed or at transforming students into a mechanism for remaking society.[25] Under this logic, the ultimate problem facing the U.S. education system is the lack of agreement on the purpose of schooling.

According to Labaree, three major goals have historically motivated efforts to reform schools. When Whig leaders established common schools in the mid-nineteenth century, schools were largely aimed at fostering a democratic education, a public good that would benefit the nation as a whole.[26] This kind of education involves some sort of training for democratic citizenship. As other scholars and reformers have also argued, a truly democratic education requires citizens to receive some form of equal educational opportunity because equality of citizens' capacities to vote in an informed way is a core element of a democracy.[27] Since at least the late nineteenth century, social efficiency has constituted another important goal for education reformers.[28] This goal positions schools as vehicles for preparing students to be effective workers in the economically stratified society they will inhabit after school. Because this goal is aimed at increasing the efficiency of U.S. society as a whole, it constitutes another sort of public good. In line with this goal, schools became internally stratified over the course of much of the twentieth century, particularly by offering vocational and academic curricula.[29]

Social mobility also became a popular educational goal in the late nineteenth century. Under this goal, education is a private good that students should be provided so they can individually advance through the stratified society they will inhabit after they leave school.[30] This goal generally positions school systems as markets in which parents and students act as consumers of the goods they want. As discussed later, this goal has been strongly reflected in education reforms like school choice structures that allow parents to choose the type of education their children will receive. While each of these three goals has been dominant at different times throughout U.S. history, they have also changed and intermingled in various ways. For example, reformers during the civil rights era focused on schools as vehicles for both a more robust democracy and social mobility for minority students. To be sure, there are other potentially important educational goals.[31] However, the goals discussed previously have been some of the most pervasive ones driving large-scale education reforms focused on equality.

Considering educational goals is especially useful for an analysis of large-scale change in law and policy because these goals are anchored in even broader political concepts that stretch across a range of policy areas. The political theorist Deborah Stone articulated four major concepts that structure political debates in the United States: equity, security, efficiency, and liberty.[32] Generally, equity relates to sameness, security relates to a level of minimum sufficiency, efficiency relates to getting the most out of what one puts into an endeavor, and liberty relates to freedom. None of these concepts is objectively "right." Instead, each represents a different way to frame law and policy positions that may be more or less persuasive to different individuals and groups. Moreover, each of these concepts can be reasonably defined in a number of ways.

Stone illustrated the flexibility of these concepts with a discussion of eight major ways in which equity can be defined. Under one formulation, equity means that all persons receive exactly the same amount of a good (e.g., all persons have the same amount of resources allocated for their education). Under another formulation, equity means that every person can perform at the same level even if such performance requires a differential distribution of goods (e.g., people are provided additional resources to perform at the same level as other people on an achievement test). Under yet another formulation, equity means distributing goods in line with every person's desires (e.g., people who want certain curricular offerings are provided with these offerings, and people who want other curricular offerings are provided with other curricular offerings). The list goes on for the concept of equity and Stone's other concepts as well, emphasizing the malleability of these concepts and their power for structuring discourse around law and policy. Indeed, as mentioned previously, policy reformers stressing the need for a more democratic education generally posit that education should be the same for everyone to help instill a democratic identity and skills that can be equally exercised in activities such as voting. In contrast, advocates for using education as a tool for social mobility often stress that students should receive a differentiated education so they can be compared to each other and therefore compete with each other.

In addition to referring to broad social or individual goals and fundamental principles for structuring law and policy, ideas can also refer to more specific policy strategies that can be adopted.[33] For example, the political scientist John Kingdon examined how policy makers consider several different policy "alternatives" created by experts when deciding how to address a problem.[34] Each alternative strategy that can be translated into formal law is an idea. Moreover, policy makers adopt particular alternatives in part because they maintain certain assumptions about the way the social world works, often regardless of the empirical evidence (or because of lack of such evidence).[35] For example, while some policy makers may believe free market school reform strategies yield greater educational opportunities for children, other policy makers may believe that significant governmental regulation is necessary for increasing educational opportunities. Similarly, governmental decision makers may maintain certain assumptions about the utility of different institutions (such as the courts) and governance arrangements for promoting educational reform. As this book highlights, the ideas of equal educational opportunity and decentralized democratic control as an appropriate and effective means of governance have proven particularly difficult to reconcile at times.[36]

In short, the contents of ideas about law and policy are important factors shaping law and policy change in education and are fundamental elements of policy regimes. While some of these ideas deal specifically with educational issues and goals, others reflect broad political and philosophical principles that cut across a range of law and policy fields. These ideas can also reflect assumptions about particular law and policy approaches and how they operate. So, although "educational equality" is an idea that has resided at the heart of large-scale school reform since *Brown v. Board of Education*, what it means both in the abstract and in concrete practice has proven malleable at best.

Institutions

The concept of institutions has also played a central role in attempts to understand law and policy change. Broadly speaking, institutions are the organizations that structure the governance system of a law and policy domain and otherwise constitute the particular domain.[37] In contrast to those in many other industrialized nations, the U.S. education system is very fragmented and composed of a large range of institutions.[38] For example, federal and state legislatures, courts, and agencies have become significantly involved in education, and their roles have generally expanded over time. For-profit organizations like textbook suppliers and test developers have also played large roles, and think tanks, business groups, and foundations have increasingly shaped education law and policy analysis and reform since the 1990s. Teacher unions have dramatically influenced decisions about the teacher workforce. Perhaps most notably, the U.S. education system includes almost fifteen thousand school districts and ninety thousand schools, ultimately requiring education law and policy to be implemented across a large range of sometimes very different organizations with varying contexts.[39]

Although institutions are composed of individuals, institutions have different strengths, weaknesses, and characteristics that mark them as differently functioning organizations. For example, institutions have different goals, internal procedures, and structures, norms, and capacities. As some researchers have underscored, historical context can strongly influence the characteristics of particular institutions.[40] As discussed throughout this book, decades of experience with early large-scale education reforms, such as desegregation, have strongly influenced how institutions engaged with later reforms, such as testing and accountability policies.

Given the focus of this book on education law and policy, comparative institutional choice theory provides a useful lens to understand the different ways in which different governmental institutions operate in the context of large-scale decisions about educational equality. The guiding principle of a comparative institutional choice approach is that, in making any law or policy prescription, one must always "decide who decides."[41] Because different institutions are more or less suited for the achievement of substantive policy goals, such as creating an education system with more equal learning opportunities for students, debates focusing only on the substantive aspects of law and policy decisions are incomplete. As the legal scholar Neil Komesar highlighted, no single institution is perfect for governing any specific issue because "the choice is always a choice among highly imperfect alternatives."[42]

The political branches constitute one of the major institutions in U.S. law and policy under comparative institutional choice theory.[43] Under Komesar's formulation, the political branches include legislative and executive entities. Federal and state legislatures have proven particularly important in education law and policy. State constitutions vest educational authority at the state level, and education has traditionally been considered a state and local concern. State legislatures accordingly have driven a significant amount of education reform, especially since the second half of the twentieth century, in areas such as school finance, standards, and testing policies. The U.S. Congress has taken on an increasingly important role over this time as well by providing funding for schools, protecting student rights, and later pushing states to implement standards, testing, and accountability policies.

Legislatures have certain strengths that other governmental institutions do not. They have access to a wide range of information and possess much flexibility in their decision-making processes. In addition to conducting formal hearings and having much looser rules than courts for the presentation of information, legislators interact with various interest groups and interested parties on more informal bases. Because of the character of such organizational structures and processes, legislatures are often comparatively well positioned for making decisions that depend on an array of complex information. Legislatures also possess the ability to balance a range of competing political interests in their decision-making processes, but they are strongly influenced by the vagaries of the political process as well. As a result, powerful political minorities (such as wealthy interest groups) or powerful majorities (such as an unusually large and motivated group of voters) may "bias" this process and make it difficult to make decisions that are well suited for accomplishing certain social goals. Moreover, although legislatures are comparatively well positioned to gather and analyze a variety of information, technical and otherwise, it is far from clear that legislatures can expertly engage in this process on a consistent basis, especially where the relevant information is extremely complex or technical.[44]

Although agencies share some of the same characteristics as legislatures, they are different in key respects. Because agencies specialize in one type of issue, administrative bureaucrats possess expertise in a field in a way that is very difficult for legislators or judges to possess.[45] Agencies also possess a higher capacity and flexibility to deal with the day-to-day decisions needed to administer policies.[46] However, agency decisions also have the potential to be strongly biased – though likely more technically savvy than legislators, administrative bureaucrats ultimately must follow the orders of the appropriate chief executive entity (such as the president).[47] So, although agencies may possess a greater capacity to analyze a large amount of technical information, their decision-making processes are also more likely to be skewed by political concerns. As federal and state agencies are generally the first organizations responsible for administering and managing policies enacted by legislatures, agencies have historically played important roles in the implementation of reforms centered on educational equality.

Since the Supreme Court decided *Brown* in 1954, the courts have become one of the most significant drivers of large-scale education reform in the United States, especially in issues of educational equality. The courts have been the primary institution overseeing school desegregation and have heavily influenced school finance reform, the education of students with disabilities, and the education of English language learners. The courts have continued to play important roles in cases governing testing and the legality of reforms decentralizing school governance, such as voucher and charter school policies. Judicial decision making can be based on several important elements, including relevant legal text, the evidence in particular cases, personal preferences of judges, and judges' readings of the political climate.[48]

Given the extent to which reformers have looked to the courts in education, the courts have certain institutional strengths that make them particularly important in the area of educational equality. As their decisions focused on protecting the rights of minority groups reflect, the courts offer reformers a potential means to overcome political inertia and to affect governmental decision making when other governmental branches fail to act to address perceived policy problems.[49] Because some courts are comparatively insulated from the political process (because of factors such as life appointments of federal court judges) and the nature of the adversarial process is formalized, the courts tend to engage in a more "evenhanded" brand of decision making than other institutions.[50] In other words, compared to the decision-making processes of the political branches, the adjudicative process equalizes the representation of positions and how information is conveyed to the decision maker. As such, the courts are a venue where minority groups can argue for the value of different policy choices before a governmental institution that is generally more impartial than the political branches.[51]

Some observers have accordingly described the courts as a countermajoritarian institution. As the countermajoritarian argument goes, unelected judges are antidemocratic when they act contrary to the will of the majority by overturning the actions of elected representatives (such as laws passed by Congress) by deeming them unconstitutional.[52] However, legal researchers have also highlighted robust historical connections between constitutional decision making and majority will. When viewed historically, the Supreme Court has rarely opposed strong majorities and has almost never done so for long periods.[53] This is not to say that the Supreme Court (and lower level courts as well) never assumes a countermajoritarian role or decides against majority preference where that preference is clear and significant. A broad political consensus simply seems to create some sort of boundary that courts are reluctant to cross for extended periods.

Still, judicial concern about politics and popular will outside the court-house seems to influence what happens within this boundary in several important ways as well. On a very basic level, courts cannot decide cases without reference to broad understandings about U.S. culture and society that are shared by a large number of people or such decisions simply would be unintelligible.[54] Moreover, popular sentiment can strongly influence the courts during times of significant constitutional change. As the constitutional scholar Bruce Ackerman argued, the "People" were activated and unusually involved in significant shifts in constitutional law during the founding, Reconstruction, and New Deal.[55] Some degree of popular consensus, which seems larger than bare majority preference, can also be an important ingredient in constitutional decision making on a more everyday and direct basis.[56] When courts make decisions in high-profile constitutional cases, they enter into "conversations" with the public that evolve over time about the ways in which we do and should live in light of social, technological, and economic changes and in light of how such decisions are actually implemented.[57] While the courts may not independently undertake or sustain unpopular policies, they can still push the debate in a certain direction in the face of divided public opinion and ultimately respond to that opinion as it develops.

Despite the potential advantages of such processes, the courts' sphere of decision making and capacities to engage in effective decision making about education policy are limited in several important respects. Because the costs of litigation are high, many issues involving public policy never enter the courts in the first place.[58] Even when the courts consider education policy issues, many court decisions prescribing unpopular changes in education policy may not be fully implemented as a result of countervailing political forces.[59] Once courts rule in cases involving social policy, they have little ability to direct and oversee the implementation of their rulings.[60] Given both the value of learning from other branches and an understanding that effective implementation of legal commitments requires continuing support, the courts have often looked to positions taken by the political branches as a guide for decision making.[61]

Although the courts have some tools available to them that can help them sort through technical matters of education policy (such as the ability to appoint a "special master"),[62] they have also faced many difficulties understanding scientific arguments undergirding factual claims.[63] The legal structures governing issues heard by courts can also have a large impact on the way in which courts decide educational issues.[64] Because plaintiffs often bring education cases involving large-scale social policies under legal theories based on vague statutory or constitutional provisions (such as the requirement for "equal protection" that has driven desegregation litigation), the relevant rules and doctrines in these cases can be ambiguous.[65] Accordingly, courts deciding in cases involving large-scale education reform often attempt to understand complex technical information, find violations of the law, and craft remedies without concrete guidance.

The market is also a particularly important institution to consider given its centrality in recent laws and policies governing school choice.[66] The market can be especially useful when changes in the goals of schools involve too much controversy to be implemented in pluralistic and interest-driven political systems.[67] Given that particular arrangements of governmental institutions can be fairly stable and favor some priorities over others, the market can provide an opportunity for other goals to be realized.[68] Moreover, many have argued that markets can facilitate increased variation, competition, innovation, and excellence and can help tailor products to individual preferences.[69] Yet, the power of markets can suffer when there is widespread imperfection of information, and small, individualized harms are unlikely to be considered in market decisions when there are interests with large stakes.[70] While education laws and policies involving the market are particularly considered in this book in the context of school choice policies, the focus remains largely on governmental institutions because of their central role in the history of large-scale school reform.

There are, of course, countless other factors that could potentially influence the ways in which institutions involve law and policy decisions. However, it is impossible to consider all of these factors in the course of conducting a focused analysis. The factors highlighted previously are the primary ones discussed by the researchers employing an institutional approach toward governmental organizations, and research on education law and policy consistently reflects them. As Komesar broadly stated, "The tradeoff is between a political process that integrates far more information but with a more significant risk of bias and an adjudicative process that suppresses information but decreases distortions in its presentation. The adjudicative process hears and considers less, but is more evenhanded in what it considers."[71] Given the important but shifting roles of governmental institutions in making decisions about educational equality, considering such differences can shed much light on the transformation of educational equality in law and policy.

THE IMPLEMENTATION OF EDUCATION LAW AND POLICY

Although law and policy change in education is very complex, focusing on such change only tells part of the story. Once law and policy decisions are made in education, they must be implemented by a range of actors across a variety of administrative levels in often many different contexts. Problems therefore may emerge in several places in the implementation process that prevent education law and policy decisions from being played out in line with their underlying intentions. While some of the divergences from original intentions may reflect a natural and even necessary adaptation of law and policy decisions to local contexts, other divergences may reflect fundamental problems with these decisions, such as a weak theory of action for leveraging educational change. As such, implementation often reveals issues in law and policy ideas that have long been present but not fully clear until these ideas have contact with concrete reality.

Factors influencing the implementation of education law and policy can be found in an almost countless number of places, including law and policy decisions themselves. Because law and policy actors have particular goals when they make these decisions (given the host of complex issues surrounding policy regimes), these actors identify and target particular problems to be addressed by their reforms in certain ways. As such, the tractability of the targeted problems can significantly influence the effectiveness of educational reform. When the targeted population (such as teachers or principals) exhibits a large diversity of behavior, significant behavioral change is required, or there is little solid scientific basis for reform, implementation problems are particularly likely.[72]

In addition, the various organizations and institutions through which law and policy are transmitted can significantly influence the implementation of education law and policy. For example, the implementation of many federal education policies (like No Child Left Behind) is often described as "from the capitol to the classroom" because the process includes several layers through which the policy must travel, including federal agencies, state agencies, districts, schools, and classrooms. Organizations at each layer have the potential to influence the course of implementation. The administrative structures and norms of these institutions and organizations and the division of authority and duties across personnel can block or facilitate reforms aimed at changing schools.[73] In light of such factors, individuals within organizations must interpret legal and policy mandates in order to decide whether and/or how to ignore, adapt, or adopt reforms in practice.[74] Indeed, administrative personnel may focus on piecemeal changes mandated by reforms that originate at higher levels and accordingly may lack a holistic approach to the implementation of such changes.[75] In communicating with other organizations and gathering information from them about education reform, even the precise content of the objects that cross administrative levels, such as memoranda, assessments, and curricular documents, can be crucial for fostering effective implementation.[76]

School-level factors play one of the most important roles in the implementation of laws and policies that are aimed at changing what happens in schools and classrooms. As researchers have long noted, variation in the implementation of reform at the school level is the norm rather than the exception.[77] Because of factors such as how reforms fit with existing practices, policies, and norms of schools, and the will and skill of school leaders, individual schools fashion different interpretations of how reforms should be enacted. In turn, schools often emphasize different components of reforms.[78] Similarly, individual teachers interpret reforms in light of their individual experiences, beliefs, skills, and knowledge and accordingly can interpret the same policy ideas in various ways.[79] As such, "street level bureaucrats" like teachers and local administrators have been found to be arguably the most important actors in the entire education law and policy implementation process.[80]

Other factors structuring organizations' environments and the relationships among organizations can also influence the implementation of education law and policy reform. Organizational relationships in education law and policy are forged in a complex and dynamic federalist governance system that has traditionally placed most decision-making power in the hands of local and state officials. However, as discussed throughout this book, this system has undergone a rapid expansion of the federal and state roles. In addition to the "vertical" relationships that span from the capitol to the classroom, "horizontal" relationships, such as those between different agencies in a state, can also influence implementation as organizations assume responsibility for different administrative functions.

"Policy instruments" that formally structure the relationships of organizations for specific policies can significantly influence implementation as well. For example, federal laws aimed at educational reform have traditionally involved a range of tools to shape the behavior of educators and administrators, including mandates, inducements, capacity-building efforts, and system-changing efforts.[81] Given that there are very different types of educational organizations with varying contexts, the use of each policy instrument can yield a range of effects.[82] Moreover, the environment in which an organization resides can significantly influence implementation.[83] For example, the political and economic climate can impact how schools respond to strong mandates to increase student performance in a time of tightening budgets. Similarly, other connected policy domains can significantly influence how organizations implement education law and policy, including domains like housing, health care, and taxation.[84]

Because the implementation of education law and policy is very complex, assessing the effectiveness of reform efforts is not easy. The education historians David Tyack and Larry Cuban proposed that education law and policy can be assessed along at least three dimensions: outcomes, longevity, and fidelity.[85] Under this formulation, outcomes are the bottom-line measures of effectiveness given the goals of a policy, such as student test score growth for policies aimed at boosting student achievement. Longevity relates to the length of time a law or policy stays in place; fidelity relates to the extent to which implementers carry out their tasks in line with the types of practices envisioned under the policy. While these categories are very useful for assessing implementation, many other categories are arguably useful as well, such as the extent to which a law or policy results in unintended consequences. Stressing that no policy is successful and is implemented everywhere all the time, the education policy researcher Meredith Honig argued that implementation and success are the products of complex interactions among policies, people, and places.[86] Therefore, laws and policies that are successful are generally adapted to their local contexts and should accordingly be judged by their success in particular places at particular moments in time.

In short, the implementation of education law and policy entails extensive variation by nature. Implementation is driven by the complex and sometimes idiosyncratic interaction of law and policy, people, and places. Although it would be easy to conceive of implementation as a linear process that begins when a decision is made and ends when implementers receive their orders and possibly do what they are told, the reality of implementation is not so simple. Instead of such formal and easily identifiable pathways, implementation is composed of a web of relationships that may be constantly changing even as the initial law and policy requirements stay the same (or change too over time). Under this logic, formal law and policy decisions should be seen as building blocks rather than road maps for action.[87] Such a conception of implementation highlights a fundamental tension inherent in large-scale education reform – while education law and policy are aimed at broadly changing educational practices, implementation must occur across highly variable contexts that may require different sorts of treatment in order for change to occur. Given this tension, implementation often reveals new problems to solve in the process of addressing old ones. As a result, new law and policy decisions are often made at least partly in light of emerging problems and help drive forward the evolution of law and policy over time.[88]

CONCLUSION

Examining the transformation of educational equality in law and policy is a complex endeavor that requires attention to a large range of factors and ultimately different types of evidence. Because this book focuses on the concept of educational equality in law and policy, legislation and judicial decisions are the primary touchstones for this examination. Still, such an examination requires attention to much more. As policy regimes theory emphasizes, analyzing law and policy change in relation to ideas, interests, and institutions can yield valuable insights into not only how law and policy have changed but also why. Such a focus is especially useful for considering law and policy change when integrated with comparative institutional choice theory. Where there are multiple institutions at play, such as legislatures, courts, and agencies at federal and state levels, it is vitally important to consider the shifting institutional contexts in which change occurs. Indeed, because overlapping reforms have emerged in various places, it is arguably impossible to understand how educational equality has transformed in law and policy over time and to make recommendations for future action without taking such a holistic approach.

At the same time, it is also important to focus on how law and policy decisions involving educational equality generally have been implemented. While there are a variety of factors influencing how education law and policy decisions are made, the actual experience of the implementation process is one of the most significant. Implementation is perhaps more complex than making these decisions in the first place and ultimately determines the fate of most reform efforts. While large-scale education reform efforts may be well conceived and carefully designed, execution almost always falls short of original goals, and actions taken under reform efforts are varied by nature. This disjuncture between the centralized nature of many reform efforts and the variation entailed by implementation is a tension to which this book repeatedly returns.

Moreover, looking at where the rubber hits the road in the implementation process can be very revealing about a host of issues that are often hidden but inherent in decisions when they are made. Although researchers have often considered separately the formation of law and policy and implementation, the line between these stages is blurry at best. Many researchers have considered law and policy as things that are first enacted and then implemented once enactment is completed. Following this logic, there are important points where law and policy clearly change, like the successful passage of a law or a decision by the Supreme Court. As noted, this book focuses on such events throughout. However, the relationship between enacting law and policy decisions and implementing them is not so simple when carefully scrutinized. Throughout both stages, multiple institutions and individuals with certain interests and often long and shared histories work in connection with each other in dynamic environments. While one policy is enacted by a legislature, a related court decision may be in the process of implementation. The implementation of this court decision could affect how the policy is implemented across administrative levels and how courts and legislatures make decisions the next time around. Similarly, ideas originally driving a policy will be interpreted and accepted, rejected, or most likely modified by implementers after its formal passage. This process may reveal aspects of the ideas underlying a policy that were always present but could not be fully understood until the ideas had contact with the real world.

Seen from this perspective, education law and policy reforms and their implementation occur in overlapping loops through a sort of evolutionary, historical process. The transformation of the idea of equality in law and policy happens over time, in light of political interests, across institutions that are vertically and horizontally related to each other, and in an ever-changing environment. Only by considering such relationships together can the transformation of equality in education law and policy be fully appreciated. Given such complexities, this book now turns to an examination of the first phases of governmentally required desegregation. In doing so, it lays the groundwork for understanding how a range of law and policy reforms centering on educational equality sprang out of (or occurred in response to) this initial salvo.

3

Brown and the Foundations of
Educational Equality

When the Supreme Court decided *Brown v. Board of Education* in 1954, it set off a wave of education reform that has continued to ripple in law and policy through the beginning of the twenty-first century. Although the justices of the Supreme Court did not expect desegregation litigation to continue indefinitely, the Court decided a major desegregation case as late as 2007. The desegregation movement has also continued to resonate by providing the conceptual and political foundations for most major, large-scale education law and policy reform efforts that have swept through the United States since *Brown*. Reforms ranging from school finance litigation to legislation focusing on testing and charter schools share roots in the principles of educational equality articulated in *Brown* and the Supreme Court opinions that followed it.

The principles of equality contained in *Brown* have also resonated through areas of U.S. law and policy besides education. In the years following *Brown*, reformers pioneered the area of public law litigation. Instead of simply adjudicating private disputes through a structured, adversarial process, courts became involved in a new kind of case that involves multiple parties and aims at reforming the diffuse institutional structures of government.[1] This sort of litigation surfaced in a range of cases, including those focused on voting rights, prisoners' rights, and employees' rights. Given the civil rights approach taken by the Supreme Court in *Brown*, the case has also assumed a hallowed place in our collective ideas about U.S. government and even society and is widely considered one of the most important cases decided by the Supreme Court in U.S. history. *Brown* has often been used as a "litmus test" for theories of constitutional interpretation and the suitability of lawyers to be appointed federal judges – if one's theory of interpretation cannot justify and explain *Brown*, that theory is arguably invalid.[2] As such, *Brown* has provided an enduring anchor for debates about the role of law and policy in shaping fundamental issues of equality in American society in a range of social areas, including employment, health, and marriage.[3]

Despite the iconic status that *Brown* has assumed, the early years of desegregation were marked by both major successes and glaring problems. When the Supreme Court ruled in *Brown* that racial segregation in public schools is unconstitutional, the Court essentially framed governmental institutions (and courts in particular) as a legitimate driving force for educational equality. As interpreted by the Supreme Court, equality was to be understood not simply in relation to the rights of particular groups of students, but also in relation to the purposes of education and the governmental structures needed to achieve these purposes. Still, the Court left the concept of equality and how to achieve it largely undefined, and it continued to do so with its decision in *Brown II* a year later, which required desegregation to proceed with the ambiguous and arguably paradoxical tempo of "all deliberate speed." After a decade in which very little desegregation actually occurred and courts rarely exercised their authority, the courts took a much firmer and more precise hand in overseeing desegregation efforts, just as the federal executive and legislative branches also began to focus on desegregation. As a result, school systems desegregated much more quickly, and what equality meant became clearer as desegregation was defined in legal opinions, legislation, and practice.

As desegregation efforts continued to broaden into politically contentious issues areas, such as busing and the reform of school districts in the North and West that never had operated under formal requirements to segregate students, the concept of equality was continually redefined under the microscope of American politics. The opinion in *Brown* articulated the concept of educational equality in simple and largely aspirational terms with few dimensions. In the decade that followed, educational equality appeared to be nothing more than an empty promise. Yet, in the 1960s, the concept of educational equality grew teeth and precision. Still, as the concept was tested in new contexts, significant debates arose about exactly what equality meant: Did equality simply refer to the protection of rights, or did it require the restructuring of school systems? Did equality only require the end of formal desegregation under law or actual integration? Did equality extend to racially homogeneous schools that were not clearly the products of a governmental intent to segregate students? What sorts of goals would these different constructions of equality serve, and what strategies would be both effective and appropriate to achieve these goals? These sorts of questions riddled the early years of desegregation in law and policy and have continued to drive many debates over education law and policy reforms.

In order to examine the early years of desegregation law and policy, this chapter first provides a brief overview of the education law and policy landscape involving desegregation in the years before *Brown*. Then, an analysis of *Brown* is conducted, with a particular emphasis on how the Supreme Court framed the purposes of education and the role of governmental institutions in relation to education equality. After examining *Brown*, the analysis turns to *Brown II* and the opposition to desegregation during the era of "massive resistance." Then, this chapter examines how courts and other governmental branches became increasingly involved in desegregation with a series of Supreme Court and lower federal court decisions, the Civil Rights Act of 1964, the Elementary and Secondary and Education Act of 1965, and the implementation of these decisions and laws in school systems. The increasing willingness of governmental entities to force desegregation in the South, the use of busing strategies, and the movement of desegregation cases to the North and West are particularly examined. Throughout, this chapter highlights not only the legal and policy principles and requirements used to govern desegregation, but also the changing political context, combinations of institutional action, and evidence of the effects of the reform efforts.

DESEGREGATION BEFORE *BROWN*

Although this book focuses on education law and policy beginning with *Brown*, the events leading up to *Brown* provide an important starting point for discussing the significance of the decision and the reforms that followed. As with *Brown*, many of the reform efforts focused on educational equality in the pre-*Brown* years were rooted in the equal protection clause of the Fourteenth Amendment of the U.S. Constitution, which states, "No State shall ... deny to any person within its jurisdiction the equal protection of the laws."[4] The Fourteenth Amendment was adopted in 1868 as one of the Reconstruction amendments shortly after the Civil War. As one of the Reconstruction amendments, the it was broadly aimed at protecting African American citizens from discrimination after slavery had been abolished. As such, the amendment became the primary legal grounds for constitutional litigation centered on protecting the rights of African American citizens in the post–Civil War era.

Given the ambiguity of the phrase "equal protection of the laws," the courts worked out the meaning of the equal protection clause over time through a continual process of interpretation and reinterpretation. In the 1896 case *Plessy v. Ferguson*, the Supreme Court famously articulated the requirements of the equal protection clause when it considered the constitutionality of a Louisiana law mandating separate railcars for African American and white passengers.[5] Finding that all the railcars were of the same quality, the Court ruled that "separate but equal" treatment was sufficient to satisfy the Fourteenth Amendment and that the Louisiana law was therefore constitutional. As the sole dissenter in the case, Justice Harlan argued for a different construction of equal protection – that the Constitution is color-blind and that African American and white citizens must therefore be treated in exactly the same way, which the doctrine of separate but equal did not accomplish. As a result of its decision in *Plessy*, the Court essentially allowed southern states' "Jim Crow" laws, which required racial segregation and usually led to inferior accommodations for African American citizens in practice, to stand.

Despite the apparent relevance of the Fourteenth Amendment to education, equal protection litigation did not focus on education until well into the twentieth century. Public education was not widespread when the Supreme Court decided *Plessy*, and compulsory education laws were not enacted in every state until 1920.[6] Although there were some cases focused on education around this time, the Supreme Court jurisprudence of the 1920s and 1930s centered on race largely focused on the creation of procedural rights for accused criminals and protection of African American citizens from the most glaring exploitations of Jim Crow laws.[7] The National Association for the Advancement of Colored People (NAACP), founded in 1909, spearheaded most of these efforts to protect the rights of African American citizens.

In the years leading up to World War II and during the war itself, the groundwork was laid for changes in reform strategies. During this time, attitudes and practices regarding race generally became more progressive.[8] Although World War II was grounded in a prodemocratic ideology, many African American soldiers became cynical about the war's purposes because they were fighting in a segregated army. In addition to demographic shifts and industrialization, the war created economic opportunities for African American citizens and ultimately an urban African American middle class with increased political power. Along with a burgeoning national dedication to civil rights that accompanied the war, such changes increased the political pressure to address racial practices in the southern region of the United States.

Two Supreme Cases in the postwar years particularly reflected this pressure and forecasted the change of constitutional doctrine that would soon follow. In 1950, the Supreme Court ruled in *Sweatt v. Painter* and *McLaurin v. Oklahoma State Regents*, cases that both involved graduate school education for African American students.[9] In *McLaurin*, the Court held that it was unconstitutional to separate an African American graduate student from white graduate students because it impaired the ability of the African American student to engage in the types of discussions and classroom activities needed to learn his profession. In *Sweatt*, the Court similarly found that interacting with peers was essential to receiving an equal education in law school and that denying law school admission to an African American student on the basis of race was therefore unconstitutional. While the "separate but equal" doctrine was still in full force and both cases involved a consideration of physical facilities, the intangible aspects of an education had begun to emerge as an important element of equal protection in the school setting. It was this shift in the understanding of equality that would fully emerge in *Brown*.

BROWN V. BOARD OF EDUCATION

On May 17, 1954, the Supreme Court announced its decision in *Brown v. Board of Education* and launched a new era in education law and policy. The unanimous decision in *Brown* declared racial segregation in public schools unconstitutional under the equal protection clause of the Fourteenth Amendment. In doing so, the Supreme Court not only invalidated a series of Jim Crow laws in the South focused on education but addressed the very purposes of education and the role of government in shaping wide-spanning issues that resided at the heart of the U.S. political and social order.

When *Brown* was decided, racial segregation in public schools was required under law in seventeen states and Washington, D.C., and by local ordinance in four states.[10] Spearheaded by the NAACP, *Brown* was filed by thirteen parents on behalf of their twenty children as a class action suit against the Board of Education of Topeka, Kansas. The case directly attacked the policy of racial segregation in elementary schools in Topeka, which was permitted under Kansas law. When *Brown* was ultimately heard by the Supreme Court in 1953, it was combined with four other cases sponsored by the NAACP that had also been filed around the country: *Briggs v. Elliott, Davis v. County School Board of Prince Edward County, Gebhart v. Belton,* and *Bolling v. Sharpe.*[11] Several months after the initial oral arguments in 1953, the Court was unwilling to issue an opinion and took the rare step of asking the parties to reargue the case during the following term. The Court specifically ordered the parties to submit briefs on a range of questions, including the original purposes of the Fourteenth Amendment and whether it permits segregation.

While there are several possible reasons why the Court wanted to hear an additional set of oral arguments, a few reasons stand out as the most important.[12] Although it appeared after the first set of oral arguments that the Court would find segregation in public schools unconstitutional, it was likely that four justices would dissent – given the doctrine of *stare decisis* (that legal precedents should be followed) and the idea that legislatures are better positioned to make policy decisions than courts, some justices believed that declaring segregation unconstitutional in public schools would be inappropriate. Because there would likely have been a strong political response to *Brown*, the members of the Court seemed to agree that a unanimous decision was highly desirable. Delaying the opinion would also give the Eisenhower administration a chance to weigh in, which was critical for assessing how well *Brown* would be enforced once the issue was out of the hands of the Court. Indeed, during the time before reargument, the U.S. Department of Justice under Eisenhower filed an *amicus curiae* brief supporting the NAACP position.[13] However, instead of focusing on the moral dimension of the rights of African American citizens, the brief emphasized that U.S. segregationist laws had a negative impact on the relations of the United States with other countries because the practice raised doubts about the U.S. commitment to democracy. During the three days of the second set of oral arguments in 1953, the Department of Justice verbally articulated this position as well, along with the parties who responded to the set of issues raised by the Court for reargument.

After several more months of deliberations, the Supreme Court made its decision, and Chief Justice Earl Warren read the unanimous opinion in *Brown* to a packed courtroom. The opinion itself was relatively short and focused on the major issues raised by the case. After covering the history of the Fourteenth Amendment and finding that the historical record regarding its intent was inconclusive, the Supreme Court briefly noted the cases leading up to *Brown* (such as *Plessy*) and the cases that were combined with *Brown*. Veering away from the applicable law, the Court then famously proceeded to discuss the importance of education in U.S. society:

> Today, education is perhaps the most important function of state and local governments. Compulsory school attendance laws and the great expenditures for education both demonstrate our recognition of the importance of education to our democratic society. It is required in the performance of our most basic responsibilities, even service in the armed forces. It is the very

foundation of good citizenship. Today it is a principal instrument in awakening the child to cultural values, in preparing him for later professional training, and in helping him to adjust normally to his environment. In these days, it is doubtful that any child may reasonably be expected to succeed in life if he is denied the opportunity of an education. Such an opportunity, where the state has undertaken to provide it, is a right which must be made available to all on equal terms.[14]

While the language of this statement is lofty and ambiguous, its line of reasoning is notable. First, the Court framed education not simply as something that could help a student succeed economically and socially but also as a key element of maintaining a democratic society. The Court thus framed education not just as a private good to be distributed for individual benefit but also as a public good impacting the United States as a whole. Second, the Court indicated that education is a central activity of governmental institutions. In doing so, the Court positioned education (and especially an equal education) as a good that requires concerted attention from the government in order for its goals to be accomplished.

Grounded in this philosophical discussion of education, the Supreme Court began its discussion of how a segregated education impacts African American students. The Court wrote, "To separate [African American students] from others of a similar age and qualifications solely because of their race generates a feeling of inferiority as to their status in the community that may affect their hearts and minds in a way unlikely ever to be undone."[15] Particularly noting its decision in *Sweatt*, the Court emphasized that intangible considerations are applicable when considering types of harms that are unconstitutional under the Fourteenth Amendment.[16] In addition to attempting to reconcile the finding of psychological harm with precedent, the Court also looked to social science. The Court particularly indicated that the finding of psychological harm was "amply supported by modern authority" and inserted a footnote that included a list of social science studies stressing this point.[17] This list of studies began with the "Clark doll study," which focused on whether children had positive or negative associations with African American and white dolls.

Although the Supreme Court did not clearly indicate the extent to which social science was necessary to support the finding of psychological harm, its use in *Brown* has garnered much scholarly attention. It has been praised for allowing reformers to use scientific evidence in litigation as proof of the harms of discrimination.[18] It has particularly freed reformers from the need to prove individualized harm for each plaintiff involved in litigation.[19] However, the Court's use of social science has also been strongly criticized. The legal scholar Herbert Wechsler argued that the Court's reliance on social science "narrowed the [equal education] doctrine, diluted the influence of broader notions of justice, and risked privileging social science evidence over background constitutional values."[20] Moreover, several critics have highlighted the Court's lack of institutional expertise with social science and have specifically noted methodological and interpretive problems with the studies cited by the Court in *Brown*, such as the Clark doll study.[21] Despite this debate, some scholars have stressed that the Court actually did not rely heavily on social science, especially given that the studies were only cited in a footnote.[22]

Grounded in such legal and social science reasoning, the Court clearly stated that segregation in public education is unconstitutional: "We conclude that in the field of public education the doctrine of 'separate but equal' has no place. Separate educational facilities are inherently unequal."[23] On the same day, the Court also decided *Bolling v. Sharpe*, a companion case to *Brown* addressing school desegregation in Washington, D.C. Although the Court found that the Fourteenth Amendment only applies to the states (as clearly stated in the language of the amendment), the Court found segregation in the District of Columbia unconstitutional under the Fifth Amendment of the U.S. Constitution.[24] Continuing its attack on segregation, the Court released a series of *per curiam* opinions after *Brown* that declared segregated state parks, beaches, golf courses, and public transportation to be unconstitutional. *Per curiam* opinions are of particular note in these cases because they are delivered in the name of the court rather than particular judges and generally signify the uncontroversial nature of a decision.

Still, clearly concerned about the political response to *Brown*, the Court did not specify in *Brown* how schools should actually be desegregated. The justices were particularly undecided about whether fast or gradual desegregation would engender more social turmoil and resistance.[25] *Brown II*, handed down by the Court in 1955 a year after *Brown*, addressed this question.[26] Erring on the side of gradualism, the Court famously stated that public schools needed to be desegregated "with all deliberate speed" and that African American students must be admitted to public schools "as soon as practicable on a nondiscriminatory basis."[27] The Court also placed responsibility for overseeing desegregation with local federal district courts. The Court specified that remedies could address transportation, personnel, and the district attendance zones. The Court further emphasized that district courts were best positioned to determine how much time is necessary for school districts to desegregate in light of their particular local contexts. District courts were thus given "practical flexibility" to shape remedies for school districts in light of the "equitable principles" articulated in *Brown I*.[28] Because of its vague language and gradualism, *Brown II* has been strongly attacked by a range of critics, perhaps most notably for seeming to invite evasion instead of even minimal attempts at compliance.[29]

The Response to Brown

Despite the boldness of the principles laid out in *Brown I*, the response in the decade that followed was marked by utter lack of cooperation and sometimes shocking displays of violence. In contrast to states in the Deep South, the southern border states responded to *Brown* quickly. As early as 1955, nine of the seventeen states with laws mandating segregated schools and the District of Columbia had changed their laws and assigned some students to schools on a nonracial basis.[30] However, the remaining eight states did very little and acted largely to avoid the requirements of *Brown*. The decade following *Brown* has thus been dubbed the era of "massive resistance" as southern politics moved to the far right in response to the decision. White opinion in the South became significantly more radical, and elections involved militant segregationists who enthusiastically touted their unwillingness to comply with *Brown*.[31] In 1956, 101 members of the Senate and House of Representatives signed the Southern Manifesto, a document opposing racial integration in public places.[32] Sitting politicians also made public statements directly opposing desegregation. For example, Governor Herman Talmadge (D-GA) indicated his willingness to avoid desegregation even if Georgia was the only state in the nation to do so, and the Louisiana legislature criticized the Supreme Court's "usurpation of power" of the states.[33]

In this context, Southern states implemented a handful of strategies to avoid desegregation. Between 1955 and 1957, these states enacted at least 120 laws to counter the requirements of *Brown*.[34] These laws were aimed at avoiding the Supreme Court's mandate in several different ways, including authorizing school closures, preventing integrated schools from being funded, and funneling public funds to private schools. School districts also engaged in strategies designed to comply nominally with *Brown* but result in little desegregation in practice.[35] "Freedom-of-choice" plans were among the most common strategies. Under these plans, parents were free to send their child to any school, given certain eligibility and capacity requirements. While a very small number of African American students attended previously white schools under such plans, almost no white students attended previously African American schools. Geographic zoning strategies were also common. Under this strategy, districts instituted "color-blind" attendance zones for schools. However, these zoning strategies consistently resulted in segregated school attendance patterns in practice.

In addition to such responses to *Brown* by southern politicians and governmental institutions, reactions were heated and volatile on the ground.[36] Ku Klux Klan membership experienced a significant resurgence, while southern membership in the NAACP radically decreased. In 1957, Governor Orval Faubus (D-AR) famously ordered the Arkansas National Guard to stop African American students from entering Central High School in Little Rock. After President Eisenhower federalized the Arkansas National Guard and ordered the soldiers to return to their armories, he sent other federal troops to protect the African American students from the angry white mob surrounding Central High School. As the 1950s wore on, the frequency and intensity of protests to the South's failure to desegregate increased in the form of activities such as public demonstrations, sit-ins, and boycotts. In response, southern law enforcement became increasingly violent, and police forces responded to public protests with beatings, fire hoses, and police dogs. High-profile civil rights leaders and activists were murdered, and a church used as a meeting place for civil rights leaders was bombed in Birmingham, Alabama, in 1963. In an era in which television had become commonplace, images of violence in the South were broadcast around the country.

Given the pushback to the mandate to desegregate in the South, the courts did very little to enforce *Brown*. District court judges, charged with overseeing desegregation at the local level, faced substantial political pressure to allow the strategies to avoid desegregation proposed by districts to proceed.[37] Some judges experienced more extreme forms of pressure, including hate mail, harassing telephone calls, and even cross burning. As at least a partial result, southern district courts generally permitted the token compliance of school districts and were satisfied with the most minimal of responses to *Brown*. For example, a South Carolina district court upheld the constitutionality of a freedom-of-choice plan in *Briggs v. Elliott* in 1955.[38] In doing so, the district court interpreted *Brown* as meaning that the "Constitution ... does not require integration. It merely forbids discrimination."[39] Other district courts in the South cited this opinion as a guiding interpretation of *Brown*.[40]

In the time between *Brown II* and the mid-1960s, the Supreme Court also did very little to enforce its decision by issuing few opinions and denying applications for review regarding desegregation. The Court issued its first desegregation opinion since *Brown II* in 1958 with *Cooper v. Aaron*.[41] In this case, the Court unanimously found that the resistance to desegregation in Little Rock violated *Brown* and that actions traceable to the state government were not grounds for delay. In another decision in this early era of desegregation in *Goss v. Board of Education*, the Court unanimously rejected a district court's approval of geographic zoning plans in Tennessee in 1963.[42] These plans explicitly allowed students to request a school transfer if they would be assigned to a school where they would be in the racial minority. In 1964, a unanimous Supreme Court issued *Griffin v. County School Board of Prince Edward County* and rejected a scheme that closed local public schools and provided state and county tuition grants and tax credits to private schools, which remained segregated.[43] Still, these decisions did very little on the whole to speed up the pace of desegregation.

Given the pushback to *Brown* and utter lack of enforcement, almost no segregation occurred in the South in the years immediately following *Brown*. Through 1960, 1.4 million African American students in the South attended completely segregated schools, and by 1964, only one out of eighty-five African American students attended integrated schools in the eleven southern states that had been part of the Confederacy.[44] Yet, by the mid-1960s, public pressure to address segregation in the South had begun to mount.[45] Reports and footage of violence in the South shocked northerners and even international audiences. Demographic and economic changes spurred by World War II also continued to provide African Americans with more political power. These forces set the stage for a radical new direction in how the federal government would approach desegregation.

LEGISLATIVE AND EXECUTIVE INVOLVEMENT IN DESEGREGATION

For much of U.S. history, the federal legislative and executive branches played only a small role in education. In the late eighteenth century, Congress reserved millions of acres for public education in a series of land ordinances under which new states were required to reserve land for public schools.[46] While the U.S. Department of Education was created in 1867, it was soon reorganized as the Bureau of Education (and later renamed the Office of Education) and primarily focused on the collection and dissemination of educational statistics.[47] During the first half of the twentieth century, a series of federal laws provided funding to states for fairly narrow purposes, such as giving financial assistance to veterans to attend college under the 1944 "GI Bill" and providing lunch for students under the National School Lunch Act of 1946.[48]

The role of the federal government in education began to change significantly in the 1950s. In the wake of *Sputnik*'s launch, Congress enacted the National Defense Education Act (NDEA) in 1958, which directed funds to localities in order to promote innovation in education, especially in the areas of science and foreign languages.[49] This law was passed in the midst of the cold war and reflected a growing sense of the need for the United States to compete militarily and technologically with the Soviet Union.[50] Especially given that the U.S. Constitution did not mention education or explicitly place any educational power with the federal government, the federal legislative and executive branches largely maintained a "hands-off" approach to education during this time.[51] While the NDEA provided funds to schools to support particular subject areas, the law gave schools much authority over their spending. Yet, the law reflected a notable shift in a political climate that historically had been hostile to centralized, federal power in education.

With the emergence of the civil rights movement and judicial involvement in desegregation, changes in the federal role in education accelerated. In the mid-1960s, public pressure to desegregate schools was beginning to peak. After the assassination of President John F. Kennedy in 1963, Vice President Lyndon B. Johnson succeeded to the presidency and was elected to the office in 1964 by a substantial margin. With the strong backing of the Democratic Party and a liberal majority in each chamber of Congress, President Johnson designed and pushed through Congress the "Great Society" legislation. This package of domestic programs was aimed at addressing civil rights as part of President Johnson's "War on Poverty," which reflected the core of President Johnson's political agenda. The package of legislation included the Civil Rights Act of 1964, the Economic Opportunity Act of 1964, the Voting Rights Act of 1965, the Social Security Act of 1965 (which authorized Medicare and Medicaid), and the Elementary and Secondary Education Act of 1965 (ESEA).[52] In 1965, the Johnson administration also launched Project Head Start, a program aimed at providing education, health, and social services to young children in low-income families.[53] The laws aimed at reforming education occupied a critical position in President Johnson's plan. As a former schoolteacher, President Johnson believed that education was vital for breaking the "cycle of poverty" and providing students with social mobility. As such, he saw federal leadership in education as a natural and important extension of the

New Deal.[54] The Civil Rights Act and the ESEA were two of the primary laws aimed at doing so.

The Civil Rights Act of 1964

As one of the first of the sweeping federal laws aimed at addressing civil rights, the Civil Rights Act of 1964 protected the rights of racial minorities in a range of areas, including employment, public facilities, and the administration of federal programs. Given the ongoing focus on school desegregation, the Civil Rights Act was especially important for structuring the protections of racial minorities in education. Title IV of the Civil Rights Act enabled the U.S. attorney general to bring an action to enforce this law on behalf of individuals when it would further the "orderly achievement of desegregation in public education."[55] Title IV notably defined desegregation as "the assignment of students to public schools ... without regard to their race, color, religion, or national origin" but explicitly clarified that such desegregation does not mean "the assignment of students to public schools in order to overcome racial imbalance."[56] Congress inserted this clarification into the Civil Rights Act to alleviate opponents' concerns that the law would mandate busing or other strategies that require integration rather that just prohibiting explicit segregation.[57]

Title VI of the Civil Rights Act contained other major provisions affecting desegregation. It required that "no person in the United States shall, on the ground of race, color, or national origin, be excluded from participation in, be denied the benefits of, or be subjected to discrimination under any program or activity receiving Federal financial assistance."[58] Title VI further authorized the U.S. Department of Health, Education, and Welfare (HEW) to withhold federal funds from school districts that were found to be in violation of Title VI.[59] This power provided the federal government with a substantial amount of leverage over school districts: In 1964, the federal government provided $176 million to the school systems in the seventeen states that practiced segregation under law at the time of *Brown*.[60] As discussed later, this leverage became even stronger with the passage of the ESEA in 1965 and the funding that followed.

Regulations and guidelines issued under Title VI provided additional specificity to the law's requirements. The original Title VI guidelines, issued by the Office of Education (contained in HEW), only called for "good faith" compliance toward starting integration and indicated that school districts could comply with Title VI by submitting a desegregation plan to the agency or going under a court order. In response to such permissive requirements, southern states such as Mississippi generally did very little to comply and continued to operate ineffective freedom-of-choice plans through 1965.[61] However, HEW revised these guidelines in 1966 to put much more pressure on school systems.[62] The 1966 guidelines articulated three major requirements for desegregation: First, freedom-of-choice plans would need to result in a doubling or tripling of school transfers on a racial basis. Second, plans would need to result in "substantial progress" in the desegregation of schools and teachers by requiring 16 to 18 percent of all African American students to attend predominantly white schools. Third, plans would need to close schools for African American students when they were inferior. Although the new guidelines were clearly more stringent than the previous version and promised to accelerate the desegregation process in areas of the South that had shown strong resistance, the guidelines were also criticized by conservatives for failing to follow the distinction between desegregation and integration laid out in the language of the Civil Rights Act.[63]

In addition to broadening the scope of the powers of HEW, the guidelines provided the courts with needed help for evaluating school districts' desegregation plans. Given the lack of Supreme Court involvement in desegregation since *Brown* and the ambiguity in *Brown I* and *Brown II* about how desegregation should proceed, lower courts were largely left to themselves to decide whether state and district actions were sufficient to comply with the requirement to desegregate. The guidelines provided the courts with more concrete ideas about how desegregation should proceed. The Court of Appeals of the Fifth Circuit, which oversaw the Deep South, adopted these guidelines as a standard for deciding desegregation cases in its 1966 decision in *U.S. v. Jefferson County Board of Education.*[64]

While Judge John Minor Wisdom of the Fifth Circuit was careful to indicate that the guidelines, created by a federal agency, could not bind the courts' interpretation of the Constitution, he stated that HEW's standards were substantially the same as the Court's and that district courts should make few exceptions to the guidelines. Moreover, Judge Wisdom indicated that twelve years of desegregation litigation had revealed that there is little distinction between the notions of desegregation and integration, and that adherence to the guidelines would produce a needed uniformity among court decisions. Seemingly giving a stamp of approval to the Fifth Circuit's adoption of the guidelines as a working standard for constitutionally acceptable desegregation, the Supreme Court refused to review the case.[65] Together with a reactivation of the Supreme Court in desegregation, the attention of the Congress and a federal agency would soon produce the most effective period of desegregation in U.S. history.

The Elementary and Secondary Education Act of 1965

Given President Johnson's view that education is vital for social mobility, the ESEA was also a major part of the War on Poverty. Grounded in the successful passage of the NDEA in 1958 and the Civil Rights Act in 1964, the ESEA represented a breakthrough in the federal role in education and a politically feasible way for Congress to respond to pressure from the civil rights movement.[66] Title I, the centerpiece of the ESEA, was a categorical grant program that provided financial aid to states and districts through a strict formula structured around the number of low-income students attending particular schools. Under this formula, the federal government sent funds to states, which then distributed the funds to districts and ultimately to schools. The other titles of the ESEA addressed a wide range of educational issues. Title II provided supplementary support for instructional materials and school libraries. Title III provided funds for supplementary educational services and centers. Title IV provided funds for research and training. Title V provided funds to support state departments of education in their implementation of the ESEA. Title VI contained general provisions. When the ESEA was first passed, Title I was appropriated $1.06 billion out of a total $1.3 billion for the entire law.[67] In the two years following the passage of the law, the annual budget of the U.S. Office of Education in HEW also increased from $1.5 billion to $4 billion.[68] While these new funding streams were directly aimed at providing compensatory education to low-income students, they also aided desegregation efforts by significantly raising the stakes for districts found in violation of Title VI of the Civil Rights Act.

The requirements governing the distribution and use of Title I funds clearly reflected the politics underlying its passage. In order to appease those who opposed the ESEA because of concerns that students in religious schools would not be treated fairly, Title I provided federal funds to both public and private schools.[69] Because opponents were also very concerned about the expansion of the federal role in education, the content and character of the programs originally funded with Title I dollars were also largely left to local program recipients. States only approved and monitored local choices, and the federal government only provided approvals as well.[70] During the discussions leading up to the law's passage, Congress specifically debated how much power the federal government would be given to set even basic criteria for the use of Title I funds in districts, and, as a result, states and districts were only required to submit assurances that funds were being spent in the proper ways. Given the broad definition of poverty included in Title I, the program also sent funds to almost every House district and 90 percent of Senate districts.[71] As a program that distributed funds so widely and ultimately entailed no specific changes to educational practices, the program proved very popular.

In line with the idea that policy can create politics, the passage of the ESEA further spurred the emergence and involvement of several important interest groups in federal education policy. The ESEA particularly acted as a "beachhead" for groups that wanted to expand the federal role's assistance to children, including the National Advisory Council for the Education of Disadvantaged Children, National Welfare Rights Organization, Legal Standards and Education Project of the NAACP, Lawyers Committee for Civil Rights under Law, and National Association of Administrators of State and Federal Assisted Education Programs.[72] Moreover, with the passage of the ESEA, the National Education Association, the largest teachers' union in the country, started to become increasingly involved in national politics and the Democratic Party. The influence of such groups ultimately would help drive the expansion and modification of the ESEA through an ongoing reauthorization process. While modifications to the ESEA and various expansions would change the law significantly over the years, it has proven quite durable and remained in effect through 2010 as No Child Left Behind. And although the law has faced a range of significant implementation problems (as discussed in Chapters 4, 5, and 7), it has continued to provide large amounts of funding to schools around the country specifically for the education of low-income students.

GREEN V. COUNTY SCHOOL BOARD OF NEW KENT COUNTY

As both the federal executive and legislative branches were quickly becoming more involved in education and civil rights in the mid-1960s, the federal courts were also entering a new era for judicial involvement with desegregation. The Supreme Court's decision in *Green v. County School Board of New Kent County* strongly signaled that the time for increased judicial engagement had arrived.[73] *Green* centered on the school system of New Kent County, located in a rural area of eastern Virginia. Approximately half the population of New Kent County was white and half was African American, and there was very little residential segregation in the area. The school system served 740 African American students and 550 white students and had only two schools that were previously segregated under the Virginia Constitution and legal mandates – New Kent School (for white students) and Watkins School (for African American students).[74] After

Brown, the school board of New Kent County continued to operate segregated schools under the authority of several laws enacted by Virginia
during the era of massive resistance. Although courts found many of these
laws unconstitutional, a pupil placement law requiring students to petition
the state board to change schools was not repealed until 1966. Through
late 1964, students did not apply for admission to the school they were
not originally assigned, and New Kent continued to be attended only by
white students, while Watkins remained completely attended by African
American students. Reformers filed *Green v. County School Board of New
Kent County* to address these issues.

In 1965, five months after reformers initiated the *Green* litigation, the
school board adopted a freedom-of-choice plan to continue to remain eligible for federal funding. This plan allowed students to choose the school
they wanted to attend annually and required students entering first and
eighth grade to choose a school. If students did not choose a school, they
would be assigned to the school they had previously attended. By 1967,
115 African American students enrolled in New Kent, but no white students chose to attend Watkins. Both the federal district court overseeing
New Kent County and the Fourth Circuit Court of Appeals found the New
Kent County's freedom-of-choice plan to be constitutional with minor
modifications. The Fourth Circuit particularly indicated that the school
board was not required to assign students to schools to achieve greater
integration.[75]

When the Supreme Court considered this case on appeal, it focused
on the distinction between desegregation and integration but went in
completely the opposite direction from the Fourth Circuit. The Court's
unanimous 1968 decision in *Green* strongly emphasized that school boards
operating dual school systems under law were required to take "whatever
steps might be necessary to convert to a unitary system in which racial discrimination would be eliminated root and branch."[76] Moreover, focusing
on the failure of the New Kent school board to adopt its freedom-of-choice
plan until eleven years after *Brown* was decided, the Court stated that
the school board was required to "come forward with a plan that promises realistically to work, and promises to realistically work now."[77] And
while the Court did not state that freedom-of-choice plans could never be
considered a constitutional response to remedying segregation, any plan
aimed at remedying desegregation would need to have real prospects for
accomplishing the goal of creating a unitary, nonracial system. According
to the Court, the freedom-of-choice plan adopted by New Kent County
clearly was not a sufficient step for transitioning to a unitary system.

Focusing on what a constitutionally appropriate plan would look like, the Supreme Court articulated what were subsequently labeled as the *Green* factors. In order to comply with the Fourteenth Amendment, school boards would need to take "affirmative steps" to create a unitary system to desegregate not only the student bodies of schools, but also several elements of school operations: faculty, staff, transportation, extracurricular activities, and facilities.[78] In this way, the Supreme Court did not simply require student assignment to schools without regard to race; it also required student assignment tailored to achieve integrated study bodies, along with a wide range of administrative and operational changes designed to achieve integration across various school functions. In *Raney v. Board of Education*, a case decided on the same day as *Green*, the Supreme Court found unconstitutional a desegregation plan that resulted in schools attended only by African American students and populated by 85 percent of African American students in the school system.[79]

Despite the specificity the Supreme Court began to add to the requirements of the Fourteenth Amendment, its decision in *Green* immediately gave rise to a wave of cases aimed at fleshing out the requirements and limits of the case. The task of interpreting *Green* centered in part on the use of ratios to achieve integration. District courts began to focus on determining the racial composition of school systems and schools within these systems, whether racial imbalances were permissible, and the steps that could be taken to remedy such imbalances.[80] On the basis of such ratios, many courts approved plans requiring majority to minority transfer provisions and supervised decisions about the location and capacity of new schools. In 1969, the Supreme Court decided *United States v. Montgomery County Board of Education*, a case involving ratios of white to African American faculty members. In this case, the Supreme Court reinstated a district court decision that a school board must move toward a goal where the ratio of white to African American faculty members is substantially the same in each school as it is throughout the entire school system.[81] Although the Court emphasized that precise ratios were not required for every school in every circumstance, it did indicate that ratios could be an effective tool for achieving integration.

Following *Green*, the Supreme Court continued to emphasize the imperative to dismantle segregated school systems immediately. In *Alexander v. Holmes County Board of Education*, decided the year after *Green*, the Supreme Court released a one paragraph *per curiam* opinion chastising the Fifth Circuit Court of Appeals for allowing school districts additional time to create and submit new plans for integration.[82] The Court particularly noted that the "standard of allowing 'all deliberate speed' for desegregation is no longer constitutionally permissible."[83] In this case, NAACP lawyers notably presented a motion to allow the school districts to be granted this time because the school year was to begin only two months later.[84] However, the Supreme Court remained focused on immediately speeding the pace of desegregation.

Given the intense focus on desegregation toward the end of the 1960s of a range of governmental actors, the racial composition of schools quickly changed. When *Brown* was decided in 1954, 0.001 percent of African American students attended majority white schools in the South.[85] Only 1.18 percent of African American students attended desegregated schools in 1964, and only 6.1 percent of these students attended desegregated schools in 1966.[86] However, this figure shot up to 16.9 percent in 1967, 32 percent in 1969, and 90 percent in 1973.[87] Still, by the end of the 1960s and beginning of the 1970s, it was becoming clear that underlying problems grouped around methods to address racial imbalance in schools were beginning to emerge.

BUSING AND *SWANN V. CHARLOTTE-MECKLENBURG BOARD OF EDUCATION*

Although the pace of school desegregation significantly increased by the late 1960s, residential segregation remained an issue largely untouched by desegregation plans. Given that members of the same race often lived near each other, transportation and student busing quickly became key issues in the attempts to address racial imbalances in schools. For the most part, busing had not received national attention under the Kennedy administration in the early 1960s – while students in the South were being bused to various schools, this form of busing was largely aimed at maintaining school segregation rather than leveraging desegregation.[88] However, busing became a focal point for political controversy under the Johnson administration.

Proponents of busing particularly argued that it was a necessary strategy to combat residential desegregation and integrate schools. Opponents of busing highlighted the principle of equality for their own purposes. As discussed previously, the Civil Rights Act of 1964 contained hard won provisions stating that desegregation did not mean racial balancing and by extension did not require the busing of students to address racial imbalances in schools. During the 1964 presidential campaign against President Johnson, the presidential candidate Senator Barry Goldwater (R-AZ) stated that busing was an example of "misguided egalitarianism" and that racial quotas would become a "substitute for the principle of equal opportunity in every aspect of social life."[89] Although Goldwater was perceived as an extremist even by some members of his own party and lost the election to Johnson in a landslide, this sentiment forecasted the legal and political problems that would soon follow. Indeed, the 1966 HEW guidelines for the Civil Rights Act faced significant political pushback by requiring specific levels of integration in schools.

In 1968, the busing controversy became the direct subject of litigation when reformers sued in *Swann v. Charlotte-Mecklenburg Board of Education.*[90] This case centered on Charlotte-Mecklenburg County, North Carolina, which ran a large school district serving more than eighty-four thousand students in 107 schools. There was a significant amount of residential segregation in the area. While there was a large African American population in the city of Charlotte, there was a predominantly white population in the suburban areas of Mecklenburg County. Of the approximately twenty-four thousand African American students in the school system, approximately fourteen thousand students attended schools that were at least 99 percent African American. Although the district had adopted geographic zoning and freedom-of-choice plans in 1965 that were approved by the Fourth Circuit Court of Appeals, the racial composition of most schools persisted because of the residential segregation in the area. Spurred by the Supreme Court's decision in *Green,* the Charlotte-Mecklenburg school board was sued again in 1968 for failing to achieve a unitary school system.

After several hearings and an extensive presentation of evidence, the district court found that certain actions of the school board were discriminatory and that residential patterns in the county resulted partly from federal, state, and local governmental actions.[91] The district court particularly found that the school board had located schools in areas populated predominantly by African Americans and fixed the size of schools to accommodate only the needs of immediate neighborhoods, which in turn resulted in segregated schools. The district court then ordered the school board to present a desegregation plan. After finding the board's plan unacceptable, the district court required the board to adopt a plan submitted by a court-appointed expert, Dr. John Finger, that extensively relied on busing students. In addition to rezoning the school district, the "Finger Plan" required grouping outlying schools with inner city schools, transporting African American students to predominantly white schools, and transporting white students to predominantly African American schools. The district court also indicated that while achieving an exact racial balance in schools may be impossible, the school district should make efforts to reach a 71 percent–29 percent ratio of student races in schools so that no school is predominantly either white or African American. However, upon reviewing the district court's decision, the Fourth Circuit proclaimed that it failed the "test of reasonableness."[92]

Emphasizing the "dilatory tactics" of many school authorities and historical resistance to desegregation, the Supreme Court sided with the district court in its last unanimous decision on desegregation.[93] The Court particularly focused on the need to clarify guidelines for desegregation, especially given demographic shifts to metropolitan areas with dense and moving populations, the presence of several schools in large school districts, and complex traffic patterns around these districts. After highlighting the district court's use of mathematical ratios for racial balance as "no more than a starting point" in the process of shaping a remedy rather than an inflexible requirement, the Supreme Court approved the district court's use of a ratio as within its discretionary powers and tailored to the school districts' particular circumstances.[94] While the Supreme Court also indicated that schools of predominantly one race in a district of mixed population do not conclusively signify desegregation under law, the Court stated that such school assignments require close scrutiny.

The Supreme Court also approved the district court's alteration of attendance zones and busing requirements. While acknowledging that there are limits to a district court's authority to craft remedies for dismantling segregated school systems, the Court refused to establish even "substantially fixed guidelines" as to how far a court can go.[95] Emphasizing the objective of creating a unitary school system, previous attempts to avoid desegregating schools in Charlotte-Mecklenburg, and the "informed judgment" of the district court, the Supreme Court approved the district court's use of attendance zones. Similarly stressing that it could not construct rigid guidelines for transportation given the "infinite variety of problems presented in thousands of situations," the Court approved of the use of busing to desegregate schools.[96] While the Court did indicate that factors such as the time or distance of travel and age of students could make a busing plan unworkable, the Supreme Court found that courts were able to reconcile the competing values involved in the construction of busing plans.

After the Supreme Court released its decision in *Swann*, the use of ratios, redrawing of attendance zones, and busing of students became commonplace strategies used by school districts and approved by district courts to combat segregation. While these strategies were fairly effective at integrating schools, they also involved significant costs, as discussed at length in several congressional hearings. For example, in Nashville, Tennessee, the high school day was shortened from seven to six hours, the beginnings of the school day for 141 schools were staggered to begin at twenty-minute intervals from 7:00 to 10:00 AM, and transportation became unavailable for field trips. The costs of additional equipment, operation, and maintenance were $1,418,100 for eighty-seven buses, $177,000 for maintenance equipment, $70,000 for operation costs for one year, and $56,000 for the installation of safety loading zones.[97] When funds were not available for such expenses, school districts sometimes were required to reduce the quality or number of educational programs and services.[98] While more difficult to measure, busing directly impacted students by moving them out of familiar surroundings.[99]

In light of such problems, the political climate became increasingly hostile to the methods used by courts to desegregate schools. Many white, middle-class parents and students began to move away from cities and into the suburbs to avoid requirements that would result in more integrated schools. In 1972, President Nixon proposed legislation to limit courts' authority to bus students.[100] Although this legislation was defeated in the Senate by filibuster, Congress approved a provision in the Education Amendments of 1972 that federal funds could not be used for transportation to overcome racial balance except on express written voluntary request of school officials. There was also significant local resistance in liberal northern states that had begun to employ busing. For example, Governor Francis Sargent (R-MA) vetoed attempts to repeal Massachusetts' Racial Imbalance Act, which prohibited the use of state funds to facilitate racial balance in school districts. Indeed, Boston, Massachusetts, experienced several high-profile and violent protests in response to a court order that required significant busing to desegregate Boston schools.[101] Reflecting such resistance to busing, a Harris poll in 1970 showed that 77 percent of white respondents opposed busing to integrate schools, while 16 percent supported busing and 7 percent were undecided. The same poll showed that the African American community was almost split, with 46 percent of respondents supporting busing, 40 percent opposed to busing, and 14 percent undecided. Such opposition would soon surface not just in local areas and Congress but even the Supreme Court as well.

DESEGREGATION IN THE NORTH AND WEST AND *KEYES V. SCHOOL DISTRICT NO. 1*

Although desegregation litigation had largely focused on the South through the 1960s, school districts in the North and West became the center for some of the most important struggles in school desegregation beginning in the 1970s. While schools in the North and West generally had not been segregated by explicit legal mandates, many schools were nevertheless attended by students of predominantly one race. Given how widespread this phenomenon was, courts and other governmental institutions had begun to distinguish among different types of segregation. Although the exact contours of this distinction varied across courts and circuits, certain categories of segregation began to emerge. *De jure* segregation generally referred to segregation caused by the law or intent of government officials to create or maintain segregated schools and was clearly unconstitutional. De facto segregation generally referred to segregation caused by factors other than governmental intent to segregate schools (such as residential housing patterns) and was thought to be permissible under the Fourteenth Amendment by several courts. Classifying the type of segregation present in schools in the North and West was very difficult – in the absence of explicit legal mandates to segregate schools, courts were required to discern intent to segregate students from the actions of school officials, such as creating attendance zones and constructing schools in ways that reflected purposeful maintenance of racially segregated student bodies.

While the Supreme Court first noted the de facto/de jure distinction in *Swann*, it did not become a central issue in desegregation cases until litigation turned to the North and West. In *Keyes v. School District No. 1*, this distinction played a pivotal role.[102] *Keyes* involved the Denver, Colorado, school district, which was the first nonsouthern urban district to undergo extensive desegregation litigation.[103] Although some other districts in the North and West had already experienced some desegregation litigation, including Pasadena and San Francisco, California, and Pontiac, Michigan, these cases had not been appealed to the Supreme Court.[104] Courts in these cases generally took the stance that any form of segregation was unconstitutional and racial balancing was an appropriate remedy. Moreover, courts in these cases generally concluded that actions purposefully aimed at maintaining racial imbalance constituted de jure segregation. The Supreme Court's decision in *Keyes*, centering on the conceptually thorny question of what the de facto/de jure distinction means, was its first non-unanimous desegregation decision.

The Denver school district was a perfect location for fleshing out this distinction. In 1969, the district had 119 schools with 96,580 students. The Park Hill area, located in the northeast portion of Denver, had schools that were predominantly attended by African Americans. In early 1969, the Denver school board adopted three resolutions designed to desegregate schools in Park Hill.[105] However, the resolutions were rescinded and replaced with a voluntary student transfer program after an election that resulted in a new school board majority. The Denver school district was then sued to reinstate the resolutions, desegregate the schools, and provide an equal educational opportunity to students in the school district "as a whole."[106] The district court found that the school board had purposefully engaged in racial segregation of the Park Hill schools since 1960 through strategies such as placing a small elementary school in the middle of a predominantly African American community near Park Hill, gerrymandering school attendance zones, and excessively employing mobile classroom units.[107]

The plaintiffs, however, were not simply interested in desegregating Park Hill schools. They were interested in desegregating the district as a whole, including the heavily segregated schools in the core city area of the district that served thousands of students. Upon examining the history of the core city schools, the district court did not find that school officials had engaged in a purposeful and systematic program of racial segregation; according to the district court, the segregated conditions in the core city schools were caused by residential housing patterns. Moreover, the district court found that the finding of intentional de jure segregation in Park Hill should not affect its examination of other areas of the city. As a result, the district court concluded that the finding of intentional discrimination in Park Hill was not sufficient to "dictate the conclusion that this is de jure segregation [across the entire district] which calls for an all-out effort to desegregate. It is more like de facto segregation, with respect to which the rule is that the court cannot order desegregation to provide a better balance."[108]

Still, the district court did find that the predominantly African American core city schools were educationally inferior to the predominantly white schools. Although desegregation could not be decreed for these schools, the school board was required to improve the quality of the educationally inferior schools and provide compensatory education. On appeal, the Tenth Circuit Court of Appeals agreed with the district court's analysis and treatment of the Park City schools.[109] However, the Tenth Circuit found that it was improper to order the implementation of school improvement programs in the core city schools. Accepting that student assignment to these schools was constitutional, the Tenth Circuit indicated that it was powerless to resolve educational problems arising from factors other than governmental action.

In a majority opinion written by Justice Brennan, the Supreme Court rejected the decisions of the district court and the Tenth Circuit and found that both courts employed the wrong legal standard for finding de jure desegregation. The Court highlighted that school officials carried out a "systematic program of segregating a substantial portion of the students, schools, teachers, and facilities within the school system," and that "it is only common sense to conclude that there exists a predicate for a finding of the existence of a dual school system."[110] The Court particularly found that the practice of purposefully maintaining predominantly African American student bodies in some schools kept other schools predominantly white. In other words, the various strategies employed to segregate Park Hill schools by race appeared to have a reciprocal effect on the racial compositions of other schools and residential neighborhoods (which would in turn cause further racial isolation in schools).

Given the potential for such a relationship to exist between the Park Hill schools and the core city schools in Denver, the Supreme Court established that a finding of intentionally segregative school board actions in one part of a school system "creates a presumption that other segregated schooling within the system is not adventitious."[111] The Court particularly highlighted that where school officials have purposefully engaged in segregation in one part of a district, there is a high probability that they have engaged in similar activities in another part. Still, the Court emphasized that a district could rebut this presumption – although the burden would lie with a district to rebut the presumption that purposeful segregation in one part of the district caused segregation, contributed to segregation, or reflected intent to segregate in another part, overcoming this presumption would be possible with enough evidence. Grounded in such logic, the Court clarified the de jure/de facto distinction: While governmental intent or purpose to segregate is the differentiating factor between the two, a finding of de jure segregation in one area can spill into other related areas unless the finding is proven to be "isolated and individual."[112] Given the large Hispanic population in Denver, the Court indicated that Hispanics also experienced discrimination somewhat like that experienced by African Americans and that they should be considered an identifiable racial group for equal protection analyses as well.

Although four other justices voted with Justice Brennan, the Supreme Court was fracturing along key conceptual lines. Justices Douglas and Powell wrote concurring opinions arguing that there should be no difference between de jure and de facto segregation. Justice Douglas emphasized that where neighborhoods are created along racial lines that restrict certain areas to the "elite," the "undesirables" move elsewhere. According to these justices, there was no meaningful way to untangle de jure and de facto segregation conceptually because the composition of nearby neighborhoods and school attendance patterns were so entangled. Justice Rehnquist, appointed by President Nixon in the year before *Keyes* was decided, dissented. Rehnquist objected to the basic idea that *Brown* required some sort of integration and argued against the Court's earlier extension of *Brown* in *Green*. Rehnquist particularly argued that *Brown* required only a prohibition against discrimination.

After the Supreme Court handed down its opinion in *Keyes*, the district court was charged with applying the new legal standard to the situation in Denver. This court approved a desegregation plan covering the entire district with strategies including rezoning attendance areas and busing. *Keyes* soon spurred a wave of other lawsuits in the North and West involving busing in areas such as Los Angeles and Stockton, California; Wilmington, Delaware; Indianapolis, Indiana; Boston and Springfield, Massachusetts; Detroit, Michigan; Minneapolis, Minnesota; and Dayton, Columbus, and Cleveland, Ohio.[113] Indeed, grounded in *Keyes*, these lawsuits fell into a fairly uniform pattern by the late 1970s.[114] Plaintiffs in these cases first attempted to show evidence that a school board had engaged in a purposeful practice to segregate in some areas. Such evidence included faculty hiring and assignment patterns, drawing of attendance zones, patterns of school closing and construction, use of temporary rooms to address overcrowding where reassignment was possible, and withdrawing actions taken by an old school board to desegregate schools. Having established purposeful intent to segregate, there was a presumption that de jure segregation occurred across the district. School boards then attempted to contest this presumption by introducing evidence that they had historically attempted to create neighborhood school systems and that the racial composition of schools simply reflects the racial composition of surrounding neighborhoods.

Although *Keyes* ultimately made it easier for reformers to win desegregation cases and cause entire districts across the United States to implement desegregation plans, the trajectory of desegregation litigation was about to change again. *Keyes* was the last Supreme Court case that significantly expanded constitutional doctrine in a way that made desegregation efforts more likely, and the lack of a unanimous verdict signaled that cracks in the government's treatment of desegregation were beginning to emerge. As desegregation continued and new dimensions of the problem were continually being considered, core concepts at the heart of desegregation that had once begun to sharpen were now becoming muddy again. Just as importantly, the political climate was quickly turning.

CONCLUSION

With its decision in *Brown v. Board of Education*, the Supreme Court transformed the concept of an equal education into a force that would drive large-scale education reform efforts in education for decades. Although the idea of an equal education had played a central role in some major cases before 1954, *Brown* has become elevated almost to the status of a founding myth in U.S. history and is arguably one of the most important cases ever decided by the Supreme Court. The case situates education as a key function of government in a society that highly prizes the notion of equality. *Brown* contains the seeds for the growth and transformation of the notion of equality through U.S. law and policy more broadly. On a deeper level, the case touches on core values and the fundamental role of governmental institutions in American society.

Despite the power and importance of *Brown*, the opinion in *Brown* was only a starting point for what turned into an ongoing conversation about the meaning of educational equality. While *Brown* clearly indicated that educational equality could not be characterized as "separate but equal," the Supreme Court's short opinion was unclear about what educational equality actually means beyond the inherent inequality of separate facilities. The case itself was decided under the ambiguous language of the Fourteenth Amendment that provides "equal protection." In addition to (or perhaps growing out of) the requirements of the equal protection clause, the main anchor for the logic of the case was the deceptively complex notion that education must be equal in ways that can support a robust democracy and social mobility. In this way, the concept of an equal education already contained an inherent tension: While democracy is a public good – a social end – social mobility is generally a private good that relates to an individual's social and economic position and how one can improve it. This tension would become much clearer in the decades that followed. Moreover, the decision in *Brown* appears to have been anchored partly in the goal of improving the international standing of the United States, which constitutes a very different sort of public good. As later chapters discuss, crafting laws and policies to accomplish one of these goals can lead to a very different education system than one tailored to other goals.

Given the ambiguity of *Brown*, the Supreme Court decisions following it also reflect the malleability of educational equality in law and policy. Although *Brown II* did not substantively define what an equal education means, it addressed how quickly desegregation must proceed with the vague and almost paradoxical language of "with all deliberate speed."

After the decade-long delay in attending to the meaning and implementation of *Brown* during the era of massive resistance, the concept of educational equality became more specific. Evaluating the constitutionality of freedom-of-choice plans, *Green* sharpened the concept by articulating precisely what elements of schooling must be desegregated, and *Swann* and related cases went so far as approving the use of precise mathematical ratios of a school's demographics to characterize educational equality. The Civil Rights Act and especially its guidelines, which quickly went through major revisions, ultimately pushed toward defining educational equality as integration and substantive equality of facilities. In concert with the funds provided by the ESEA, the Civil Rights Act and its guidelines also provided a specific enforcement mechanism focused on withholding funds. *Swann* approved busing as a legitimate (and ultimately primary) tool to achieve educational equality. While the approval of busing was important as a way to formalize a concrete practice as a central part of educational equality, it was also critical because it legitimized a fundamental move in the definition of equality – building on the Civil Rights Act guidelines, the Supreme Court also began to blur the idea of dismantling laws requiring segregation with integration. *Keyes* further fleshed out the definition of educational equality by articulating the difference between de facto and de jure segregation, even to the extent of establishing legal presumptions where certain conditions are met. As such, the concept of equality in education law and policy was defined as much by the concrete practices used to effect desegregation as by abstract legal language.

This transformation of educational equality appears to have been driven by several interrelated factors. Political pressures, grounded in broad social, economic, and technological changes, significantly influenced how the concept of educational equality transformed. When *Brown* was decided, changes such as the rise of an urban African American middle class made the political climate sufficiently ripe for the Supreme Court to act without an overwhelming groundswell of political support. However, the era of massive resistance, marked by very little governmental action directed at defining or implementing commands for equal protection, was largely the product of political resistance to *Brown*. But especially given the shockingly violent resistance to *Brown*, the political climate around the country became more open to desegregation in the mid-1960s. This was precisely the time when Congress and the presidency became active in desegregation and when the Supreme Court reengaged. Still, as the "rubber hit the road" with the onset of busing, the political climate again began to turn against the desegregation movement. Indeed, the ideological composition of the

Supreme Court also began to shift as resistance from the Court to ongoing desegregation began to emerge.

The governance structure in which the concept of educational equality was implemented also appears to have had a significant influence on how the concept was defined. Desegregation proceeded largely through the top-down decision making of the courts. The Supreme Court refined and clarified most of the major requirements of educational equality in cases such as *Green, Swann,* and *Keyes.* Framed by the Supreme Court's statements that desegregation needed to be tailored to local conditions, district courts and circuit courts were left some room for discretion and responded differently to situations with which they were confronted. Such differences among responses were sometimes legitimate. For example, given lack of guidance, lower courts had different interpretations of what de jure segregation meant. However, other differences were clearly illegitimate, such as the failure of many lower courts to act during the era of massive resistance. Still, beginning in the mid-1960s, district courts largely approved or disapproved of desegregation plans in ways that were directly keyed to understandings of Supreme Court jurisprudence.

As noted previously, the governance structure of educational equality also shifted in the mid-1960s with the enactment and enforcement of the Civil Rights Act and ESEA. While these legislative and executive actions were clear sources of definitional power by themselves, these actions were particularly important vis-à-vis their interaction with the courts; in the context of vague constitutional provisions and Supreme Court rulings, lower courts looked to these laws (and especially guidelines) for more precise standards for educational equality. As later chapters discuss, such governance structures continued to shift significantly in the years to come. Courts ruling in cases involving educational equality would soon begin to take roles other than those of top-down deciders, and legislative action became much more important for defining educational equality.

The concept of educational equality was also strongly influenced by the nature of how ideas are fleshed out through the ongoing process of implementation. After law or policy decisions are made, they are generally revisited after a certain period of time has passed. While these decisions are sometimes revisited simply in terms of their effectiveness or political viability, they are often considered in light of problems that can only become clear through the process of implementation. As a result, decisions are modified and refined, if not ultimately reversed. For example, parts of the Civil Rights Act and *Green* were directly aimed at combating freedom-of-choice plans. In these instances, law and policy decisions were made and revisited in light of particular strategies that emerged as a common response to diminish the effectiveness of desegregation. Similarly, the extent to which residential segregation would impact desegregation efforts was not quite so clear to many at the time of *Brown*. But as desegregation efforts continued, residential segregation emerged as one of the most significant barriers to school desegregation. The concept of equality appears to have shifted partially in response to this issue – the removal of formal legal mandates to segregate schools was insufficient to desegregate schools. Some form of integration, along with the tools needed to implement integration (such as busing and geographic rezoning), was necessary if an equal education meant the elimination of predominantly one-race schools. Indeed, while equality is a core American value, it is simply a muddy concept that can only be refined in light of its continual application and reapplication to real world situations.

Given the shifting nature of such factors and their relationships with each other, the effectiveness of desegregation law and policy varied significantly from *Brown* through the early 1970s. When the Supreme Court ruled in *Brown I* and *II*, it acted as the sole governing body making a decision primarily affecting an area with extreme political resistance. In doing so, the Court was very successful at laying the foundation for canonical legal principles and a social touchstone for generations to come. But in this context, the Court was ineffective at leveraging immediate change on the ground, especially in the Deep South. However, desegregation law and policy became much more effective in the mid-1960s. During this time, the political climate had become much more favorable to desegregation, and the legislative and executive branches joined the courts and added their legal and political might to the desegregation effort. Just as importantly, the more precise standards for desegregation, crafted by executive and legislative action, helped the courts flesh out their own vague requirements. In part grounded in such action, the courts became much more effective agents of holding school districts accountable for desegregation. Indeed, the courts did so just as they proceeded to grapple with thorny conceptual questions about precisely what equality means in light of changing conditions brought to light by implementation. As a result of such actions, quantitative evaluations clearly indicate that schools in the South were being rapidly desegregated between the late 1960s and early 1970s in what is perhaps one of the most successful periods of education reform in U.S. history.

These early stages of the desegregation movement reflect both the strengths and the weaknesses of the governmental institutions at play. As the Supreme Court demonstrated in *Brown* and the other major desegrega-tion cases, the courts can be a very useful institution for working through philosophical principles that hold much weight in the collective social con-sciousness. Moreover, the courts can be trailblazers in areas where the political climate does not favor change. Yet, reflecting its unwillingness to remain out of step with the prevailing political climate for long periods, the Supreme Court became almost dormant in the decade after *Brown*. Indeed, the Court's relative lack of activity during this period reflects its institutional inabilities to push complex reforms in times of political isola-tion, given its lack of enforcement and managerial capacities.

However, the courts acted largely in line with their strengths when desegregation efforts were at their most effective from the mid-1960s through early 1970s. The courts continued to work through important philosophical and moral concepts and kept desegregation efforts mov-ing forward despite remaining political opposition. At the same time, the courts were able to draw on precise standards worked out by other bodies with more institutional expertise and could draw on the threat of enforcement from other governmental institutions with stronger capaci-ties to do so. Desegregation efforts during this period similarly reflect the strengths and weaknesses of the legislative and executive branches. Both of these institutions acted in ways that were more immediately in line with the political climate than the courts. Although these institutions did not act quickly after *Brown*, they activated as the political climate further shifted in the 1960s and contributed in precisely the ways in which the courts could not.

So, in the context of these interacting factors, the slippery concept of educational equality was hammered into law and policy in a way that never stopped moving and continually offered glimpses into complexi-ties that would soon come to light. The idea of educational equality itself was always lofty and iconic. At times it was toothless and vague, while at other times it was sharp and precise. Still, just as the desegregation move-ment was at its most effective in the early 1970s, cracks were starting to emerge, giving hints that the concept was being stretched to its political and legal edge.

4

The Maturation of Educational Equality

Through the late 1960s and 1970s, the concept of an equal education continued to expand and be tested in a crucible of law, politics, and the harsh realities of the implementation process. Building on the logic of desegregation, both courts and legislatures devoted substantial attention to fleshing out the educational rights of students with disabilities and English language learners (ELLs). The issue of school funding equity also appeared before federal and state courts and state legislatures, and it would continue to be a major focus of education reform through the beginning of the twenty-first century. At the same time, the Elementary and Secondary Education Act (ESEA) was maturing as a deeply entrenched program that channeled billions of dollars per year toward schools with high enrollments of poor and minority students. As such, the federal and state roles in education continued to grow in a way centered on the idea of equality.

Yet, traces of the cracks in equality-based reform that had begun to appear in the desegregation cases of the early 1970s quickly widened. Underscoring the value of local control of education, the Supreme Court reversed its course on desegregation with rulings that made it more difficult for schools to become integrated. The Court also refused to find that inequitable school funding in states was unconstitutional under the Fourteenth Amendment (although the Court did leave open the possibility that inequitable school funding structures could be found unconstitutional under state constitutions). Accompanying this shift in the courts was growing political doubt about the efficacy of centralized governance structures to accomplish lofty social goals associated with educational equality.

This chapter traces the transformation of educational equality in law and policy in the late 1960s and 1970s and follows certain tendrils of this transformation that stretch into the 1980s. First, cases in which the Supreme Court fundamentally altered its approach to desegregation and ultimately began to withdraw judicial oversight from segregation in schools are examined. Then, this chapter considers the concurrent movement in courts and legislatures to expand the concept of equality dramatically. This discussion starts with the beginnings of school finance reform litigation and particularly focuses on the move of this litigation from federal to state courts. The expansion of judicial and legislative reach over issues of educational equality into the protection of students with disabilities and ELL students is then examined, in addition to the implementation and reauthorization of the ESEA through the 1970s. In this way, this chapter focuses on how and why the concept of educational equality quickly expanded just as deep cracks in its legal and policy foundation were coming to light.

THE TURN IN DESEGREGATION LITIGATION

The beginning of the 1970s marked a clear turn in the trajectory of desegregation litigation. As *Keyes v. School District No. 1* reflected, the concept of equality was transforming and expanding as litigation moved to the North and West, and this shift did not sit well with all members of the Supreme Court.[1] Richard Nixon had assumed the presidency in 1969 and by early 1972 had appointed four members of the Supreme Court, including Justice William Rehnquist, who was the sole dissenter in *Keyes v. School District No. 1*. Rehnquist was a conservative lawyer who had been a Supreme Court clerk when *Brown v. Board of Education* was decided. As a clerk, Rehnquist had drafted a memorandum supporting the "separate but equal" doctrine while the Court was considering *Brown*.[2] While Rehnquist's decisions in later desegregation cases particularly reflected his conservative political philosophy, the rest of Nixon's appointees provided support for such a philosophy in key desegregation cases as well.

Milliken v. Bradley strongly reflected the influx of these new judicial perspectives in the Supreme Court and became one of the most pivotal cases in the history of desegregation.[3] Decided by the Court in 1974, one year after *Keyes*, *Milliken* also addressed the thorny issue of desegregation in the North and West. In *Milliken*, the Detroit branch of the National Association for the Advancement of Colored People (NAACP) spearheaded a lawsuit aimed at desegregating the Detroit public school system (DPS). At the time when the suit was filed in 1971, Detroit had a population of approximately 1,500,000 residents and 290,000 students.[4] As a result of years of white families moving from Detroit to the surrounding suburbs, the proportion of the African American population in Detroit had rapidly increased. In 1961, African Americans were 45.8 percent of the overall population in Detroit, while in 1973, African Americans were 69.8 percent of the overall population. These demographics made the prospects of a desegregation effort focused only on DPS limited at best. Still, the Detroit Board of Education adopted a voluntary desegregation plan in 1970 aimed at eliminating the racial identity of every school in DPS. Later that year, the Michigan legislature enacted Act 48, which essentially prevented the implementation of the voluntary desegregation plan. The NAACP sued in federal court under the Fourteenth Amendment to allow the desegregation plan to move forward.

The district court's treatment of the case was far-reaching. After a forty-one-day trial, the court found that the Detroit Board of Education was responsible for intentionally causing the segregated conditions in DPS. According to the court, the school board had created attendance zones that would likely segregate students, operated a busing program that created segregated conditions, and constructed schools in places that had a segregative effect on student attendance patterns. The district court also found that the state of Michigan was responsible for failing to authorize or fund the transportation of DPS students while it provided a full range of support to predominantly white suburban districts. The court made clear that residential segregation in the Detroit metropolitan area was due to governmental action and inaction at federal, state, and local levels, combined with actions of private organizations like loan institutions and real estate associations.

Focusing on the actions of the state, the court also found that Act 48 had the purpose and effect of maintaining segregation by impeding, delaying, and minimizing racial integration in DPS. The court notably held that the state of Michigan was also liable for the acts of the Detroit Board of Education because the school board was a subordinate entity of the state. On the basis of such findings and conclusions, the district court approved a metropolitan desegregation plan centered on extensive busing that included Detroit and fifty-three of the eighty-five surrounding school districts. Noting that "any less comprehensive a solution than a metropolitan area plan would result in an all-black school system immediately surrounded by practically all-white suburban school systems," the Sixth Circuit Court of Appeals upheld the adoption of the metropolitan desegregation plan.[5]

The Supreme Court did not look favorably on the decisions of the lower courts. In a 5–4 decision that included all of President Nixon' s appointees, the Court declared the metropolitan area desegregation plan to be too extensive a remedy. In an opinion penned by the recently appointed

Chief Justice Warren E. Burger, a majority of the court found no significant violation of the Fourteenth Amendment in districts other than DPS or evidence that the district lines were based on race. The majority opinion also stated that the Michigan "educational structure involved in this case, in common with most States, provides for a large measure of local control."[6] According to this opinion, the implementation of a metropolitan remedy would effectively require the consolidation of fifty-four independent school districts into a "vast new super school district."[7] Further emphasizing the legal principle that the scope of the remedy should follow the scope of the violation, the Court found that a metropolitan remedy extending into the suburban districts was unwarranted; such a remedy would only be warranted where the suburban districts had also engaged in unconstitutional segregation or the lines separating school districts were the result of a governmental intent to segregate students. As a result, DPS, which had a predominantly African American student body, was forced to pursue desegregation only within its district lines.

After the Supreme Court decided *Milliken*, the case was remanded to the district court, which required both parties to submit desegregation plans.[8] In addition to using busing to facilitate student reassignment within the school district, the school board's plan called for the implementation of thirteen compensatory programs, including in-service training for teachers and administrators, guidance and counseling programs, and revised testing procedures. While the school board admitted that it was possible that none of the programs was essential to correct the constitutional violation in DPS, the court ultimately required their implementation as part of the desegregation plan and required the state of Michigan to pay for the programs. The state challenged the court's order, but the Supreme Court approved the district court's decision by a unanimous vote in *Milliken II* in 1977.

Soon after *Milliken II*, compensatory education programs became widespread in desegregation plans across the country.[9] While desegregation plans involving these programs were structured differently across school districts, the programs included activities such as remedial reading, counseling and career guidance, more testing and monitoring of student achievement, planning to improve relations between schools and communities, institution of a new student code, vocational education, and multicultural studies. However, evaluations of these programs revealed their limited effectiveness in increasing or equalizing students' educational opportunities. These programs were often implemented without an overarching plan for addressing segregation and used for activities that district personnel wanted to undertake anyway. Moreover, districts rarely conducted robust evaluations of these programs, the programs often failed to involve meaningful outcomes at the end, and funding only lasted for a limited period. Indeed, some commentators concluded that the primary function of these programs seemed to be simply "to serve as a way for school districts and states to sustain a temporary and superficial punishment for discrimination" rather than actually enhancing educational opportunities.[10]

As *Milliken II* was making its way through the courts, the Supreme Court also decided *Washington v. Davis*, a case that made it much more difficult for plaintiffs to prevail in lawsuits focused on racial discrimination under the equal protection clause.[11] In this case, the Washington, D.C., police department decided not to hire two African Americans who had failed a verbal skills test. African Americans had generally failed this test at a disproportionately high rate compared to their white counterparts. However, the Court ruled that under the Fourteenth Amendment, governmental action may not be held unconstitutional "solely because it has a racially disproportionate impact."[12] Instead, the Court ruled that a discriminatory purpose is required to find a governmental decision unconstitutional under the equal protection clause. So, in order for courts to find that a governmental entity has unconstitutionally discriminated under the equal protection clause, courts need to find a discriminatory racial purpose expressly built into a law or policy decision, or evidence that such a purpose motivated a decision. The combination of *Milliken I* and *Washington v. Davis* in effect marked the beginning of the end for judicial oversight of desegregation.

After these decisions, the Supreme Court largely withdrew from desegregation for more than a decade. From the late 1970s through the late 1980s, desegregation efforts primarily proceeded through district court oversight of desegregation plans, although usually without the aid of an interdistrict remedy. Integration generally increased in the South until the late 1980s, and the proportion of African American students in intensely segregated schools generally decreased.[13] However, in the 1986 case *Riddick v. School Board of the City of Norfolk, Virginia*, a federal district court declared a school district to be "unitary" for the first time and allowed it to dissolve its desegregation plan, thus restoring control to school district authorities.[14] This decision was the first of several by district courts around the country declaring school districts unitary as further and complete desegregation appeared impossible. Largely as a result, the proportion of African American students in schools with more than half minority students was greater by 1991 than the proportion before *Swann* in 1971. Through the

1980s, the level of segregation for Latino students also remained high across the United States, but especially in the Northwest, in the Chicago area, and in California and Texas. It was not until the 1990s that the Supreme Court became reactivated in the area of desegregation, and as Chapter 6 discusses, this activity was largely to facilitate the further dismantling of desegregation plans.

This is not to say that attempts to desegregate schools were never effective during the mid-1970s and beyond. For example, after San Francisco residents had a mixed response to initial desegregation efforts, the NAACP launched a lawsuit in 1978.[15] The federal district court overseeing San Francisco eventually entered a consent decree, or legal plan detailing the steps required to desegregate the city's schools. This plan was very precise and included not only requirements for desegregation, but also several strategies aimed at boosting student learning, such as requirements for teacher professional development and the adoption of philosophical tenets designed to raise teacher expectations for all students. Moreover, the implementation of the decree was especially effective when the district court built political support for the decree by pushing members of the legal community to work with members of the local educational community. Indeed, the implementation of the consent decree appears to have proceeded the most smoothly when the court facilitated reform by pushing stakeholders to hold meetings to address the salient issues and calling stakeholders into court on a regular basis to report their progress.

Despite such periods of effective desegregation in particular places, it has proven very difficult to sustain this process over an extended period. The implementation of the San Francisco consent decree was very effective only over short chunks of time, such as from 1983 to 1985 and 1993 to 1995.[16] To ensure that desegregation proceeds smoothly with stakeholder input, a court generally needs to ensure that the subtle range of opinion that exists within a community is appropriately represented and the capacities of citizen groups to develop and implement reform are not taxed as well.[17] Courts also need to remain deeply enmeshed with reform over the course of years, even though there may be judicial turnover.[18] Despite the inevitable changes in educational and political leadership as well, both of these communities similarly must continue to engage with and support reform for extended periods. As some scholars have argued, courts have often dissolved citizen committees once the implementation process has gotten well under way, and it has proven extremely difficult to sustain involvement from all the different stakeholders over the course of years.[19] As at least a partial result of Supreme Court decisions in the 1970s and the difficulty of maintaining wide-reaching stakeholder involvement, effective school desegregation efforts proved very difficult to develop and implement over time. So, although desegregation litigation experienced some critical successes in its maturing years, the combination of Supreme Court decisions in the 1970s and difficulty of overseeing successful reform at the district court level made such successes isolated and ultimately fleeting.

THE EXPANSION OF EQUALITY

The Birth of School Finance Reform Litigation

Even as the limitations of desegregation litigation began to come into focus in the 1970s, reform efforts centered on educational equality spread into several other areas of law and policy. Launched in the wake of desegregation litigation, school finance litigation became one of the most widespread forms of education reform in the United States. While school finance litigation primarily began in the late 1960s and significantly transformed over time, this type of reform has been remarkably durable. Through 2010, reformers had continued to employ school finance lawsuits in attempts to enhance students' educational opportunities, and this type of litigation had appeared in forty-five states.

School finance litigation generally has targeted the ways in which schools and districts are funded. Local wealth or property value has traditionally constituted one of the major drivers of school and district funding because this funding has often been strongly determined by property taxes. As a result, school funding mechanisms have often resulted in dramatic per pupil spending difference across districts within states. Although many states have centralized education funding at the state level to a certain degree to mitigate the effects of such a funding system, significant disparities have persisted. Moreover, because race and wealth have been so intertwined, annual per pupil spending in education has often been highly unequal for students of different races.

While school finance litigation first appeared in the early nineteenth century, the modern era of school finance litigation began in the late 1960s. Since this time, school finance litigation has targeted educational funding structures by aiming at the equalization and augmentation of education financing. Although the NAACP and its allies chose to focus on the fundamental existence of segregated schools in the lead-up to *Brown*, several factors pushed reform efforts centered on educational equality toward school finance reform.[20] As desegregation litigation proceeded in the years after

Brown, barriers to integrated schools were becoming increasingly evident. As federal courts began to find limits to the reach of the equal protection clause, it was becoming likely that the Supreme Court would limit constitutionally required desegregation to cases of de jure segregation, thereby failing to address problems rooted solely in residential segregation. At the same time, remedies such as busing had raised problems of their own, and white families were increasingly moving from cities to the suburbs. Still, federal courts had been perceived as an effective and friendly venue for reformers to leverage changes in the law to address social problems. As the civil rights movement broadened its reach, reformers naturally returned to the courts. Reformers particularly saw an opportunity to build into the law recognition of equal rights based not only on race but also on wealth.

Serrano v. Priest, the first major school finance case, was initiated in 1968 in a California state court. In this case, the plaintiffs argued that California's method of funding public education was unconstitutional under the equal protection clause of the U.S. Constitution because it resulted in a disparity of funding across districts and schools. In 1971, the California Supreme Court ruled that the state's school funding scheme violated the Fourteenth Amendment.[21] In 1973, the New Jersey Supreme Court similarly found its state school funding system unconstitutional in *Robinson v. Cahill* because it violated the state constitution's requirement for a "thorough and efficient education."[22] Despite these early successes, this initial burst of school finance litigation quickly shifted direction. Indeed, this burst was only the first of at least three "waves" that school finance litigation would eventually go through as it faced a series of legal, political, and educational barriers.[23]

San Antonio Independent School District v. Rodriguez

As the first wave of school finance litigation was proceeding in California and New Jersey, a school finance case was also making its way through the federal court system in Texas. In 1968, the Edgewood Concerned Parent Association sued the San Antonio Independent School District (SISD), six other districts, the Bexar County School Trustees, and the State of Texas for enacting and implementing a school funding system that violated the equal protection clause of the U.S. Constitution. This funding system included a "foundation program" that used both state and local contributions to fund schools and was partly aimed at equalizing school spending levels among districts. Federal funds also contributed a small portion of money to schools. This funding system resulted in substantial differences in per pupil expenditures across districts because of differences in property values. While SISD (the least affluent district in the San Antonio area) spent $356 per pupil annually, Alamo Heights School District (the most affluent school district in the area) spent $594 per pupil annually. According to the plaintiffs, the differences in per pupil expenditures created by this funding system violated the equal protection clause just as segregation in public schools did.

The federal courts that heard the case analyzed the Texas school funding system under a framework for evaluating equal protection claims that began to develop as early as 1938 in *U.S. v. Carolene Products*, a case dealing with the constitutionality of New Deal legislation.[24] Under this framework, a court must first decide whether governmental action has acted to the disadvantage of a "suspect class" or impinged upon a "fundamental right." A suspect class is any classification of a group suggesting that members of the group are likely subjects of discrimination. The Supreme Court has explicitly recognized categories such as race, national origin, and alienage as suspect classes. A fundamental right is a right that is explicitly or implicitly protected by the Constitution, including the rights generally listed in the Bill of Rights and unenumerated rights such as the right to an abortion.

If the government does act to the disadvantage of a suspect class or impinges on a fundamental right, a court employs "strict scrutiny," or the most stringent standard of judicial review, to assess the constitutionality of the action. In order to be constitutional under strict scrutiny, the governmental action must be justified by a "compelling governmental interest," must be "narrowly tailored" to achieve that interest, and must use the least restrictive means for achieving that interest. If the government does not act to the disadvantage of a suspect class or does not impinge on a fundamental right, a court may use other standards, such as "intermediate scrutiny" or "rational basis review." Like strict scrutiny, intermediate scrutiny is triggered by governmental action involving certain classes or rights, including the class of gender. Rational basis is the default level of review and simply requires governmental action to be "rationally related" to a "legitimate" governmental interest. While most governmental action satisfies rational basis review fairly easily, it is very difficult for governmental actions to be deemed constitutional when being evaluated through the lens of strict scrutiny. The core of the plaintiffs' legal approach thus focused on convincing courts to view the school finance system with strict scrutiny.

In order to apply this legal framework in *Rodriguez*, the courts were first required to decide whether the Texas school funding system involved a suspect class or impinged upon a fundamental right. Relying on decisions dealing with the rights of the poor to equal treatment in the criminal trial and appellate processes and on cases disapproving of wealth restrictions on the right to vote, the district court found that wealth was a suspect class.[25] Building on this finding, the district court further found that the local property tax system discriminated on the basis of wealth. On the basis of Supreme Court decisions underscoring the importance of education (such as *Brown*), the district court also found that there is a fundamental right to education. The court thus employed strict scrutiny when evaluating the constitutionality of the state's funding system. Because the court found no compelling state justification for disadvantaging the poor or impinging upon students' fundamental right to an education, it deemed the Texas school funding system unconstitutional.

However, in a 5–4 decision in 1973, the Supreme Court disagreed with the district court and found the Texas school funding system constitutional under the equal protection clause.[26] Examining a series of earlier Supreme Court decisions in areas such as voting, the Court found that wealth in fact is not a suspect class – the Court found that there is no definable category of "poor" people in early case law and no indication that the funding system resulted in the "absolute deprivation of education."[27] Indeed, the Court explicitly indicated that the equal protection clause does not require "absolute equality or precisely equal advantages."[28] The Court also found that education is not a fundamental right. After indicating that the key to discovering whether a right is fundamental cannot be determined by the relative societal significance of education as compared to other established fundamental rights (such as the right to travel), the Court stated that such a right can only be found if it is explicitly or implicitly guaranteed by the Constitution. The U.S. Constitution clearly does not protect education explicitly.

However, Justice Brennan forcefully argued in his dissent that education is in fact implicitly protected under the Constitution. According to Justice Brennan, education should be considered a fundamental right because it is necessary to effect other rights that are explicitly guaranteed by the Constitution, including the right to participate in a democracy and freedom of speech. Indeed, the majority agreed that "(t)he electoral process, if reality is to conform to the democratic ideal, depends on an informed electorate: a voter cannot cast his ballot intelligently unless his reading skills and thought processes have been adequately developed."[29] Still, the majority found that the Constitution does not implicitly protect education as a fundamental right because the Court "never presumed to possess either the ability or the authority to guarantee to the citizenry the most effective speech or the most informed electoral choice."[30]

Given that the Supreme Court did not deem wealth to be a suspect class or education to be a fundamental right, the Court evaluated the Texas school funding system under rational basis review instead of strict scrutiny. Stressing the importance of local control of education, the Court found that although the funding system was not perfect, it was reasonably related to a legitimate state purpose – the system encouraged participation in and significant control of schools at the district level. The Court thus deemed the Texas school funding system to be constitutional despite the differences in per pupil expenditures across rich and poor districts. With its decision in *San Antonio Independent School District v. Rodriguez*, the Court effectively foreclosed the possibility of further school finance litigation under the equal protection clause and ended the first wave of school finance litigation. However, the Court left open the possibility that school finance litigation could continue under state constitutions and effectively launched the second wave of school finance litigation.

The Second Wave of School Finance Litigation

The second wave of school finance litigation began immediately after the Supreme Court decided *San Antonio Independent School District v. Rodriguez* and lasted through the end of the 1980s. In second wave cases, plaintiffs continued to rely on equal protection arguments but shifted both the venue and legal basis for their arguments. Following the possibilities left open by the Court in *Rodriguez*, plaintiffs now relied on equal protection clauses contained in state constitutions, which are broadly similar to the equal protection clause of the U.S. Constitution.[31] Some plaintiffs also relied on "education" clauses contained in state constitutions. Every state constitution contains an "education" clause, which generally requires states to provide students with a "thorough and efficient" education or some similar type of education.[32] The plaintiffs' arguments in *Robinson v. Cahill* were in part based on an education clause in the New Jersey Constitution. Grounding their arguments in a state equal protection clause, education clause, or both types of clauses taken together, plaintiffs generally argued that states must equalize school funding or educational opportunities across schools and districts.[33]

While second wave cases were more successful than first wave cases, their effectiveness was ultimately limited.[34] Because equality is by nature a vague concept, it can be defined in several different ways in the context of school finance reform litigation, including in terms of tax capacity, per pupil expenditures, the goods or services bought with funds, and student performance. There has never been any clear legal basis for determining which construction should be used. Moreover, each of these constructions suffers from particular problems. While a construction such as per pupil expenditures can be easily quantified, the causal links between spending and students' educational opportunities are unclear, and some courts have underscored the lack of such links.[35] And while a construction such as education services is more closely related to actual educational opportunities, this construction cannot be quantified easily and would require courts to delve more deeply into the inner workings of schools than they have generally felt competent to do.[36] Indeed, without clear constitutional standards for deciding what an equal education is, some state courts have labeled decisions about the equality of school funding laws as a "political question" that lacks "judicially manageable standards" and thus a question for state legislatures and not courts to resolve. Given that successful equality arguments have often required the shift of resources from wealthy districts to poor districts, equality arguments have also faced heated political opposition and have been attacked for decreasing local control of education.[37] As a result of such problems, states won about two-thirds of the second wave cases and were not required to adjust their school finance systems.[38]

In the second wave cases won by plaintiffs seeking school funding reform, courts generally ordered state legislatures to address the inequities of state funding systems. However, these cases faced their own share of problems. Court orders in these cases were often vague about how school funding systems should be restructured.[39] And even in successful second wave cases, judicial reasoning often reflected a tension between the concepts of equality and adequacy, which exacerbated the vagueness of court orders.[40] As a result, state legislatures employed a variety of approaches. Some states enacted power equalization schemes, which ensured that each district would receive a certain amount of funding if it taxed at certain rates. Other states focused more on limiting educational spending to reduce disparities. In California, such an approach combined with Proposition 13 – a constitutional cap on increases in local property taxes adopted by the state's voters – to reduce educational spending dramatically.[41]

Even in the cases won by plaintiffs, the rhetoric of equality proved politically problematic as state legislatures often failed to fulfill their obligations to the satisfaction of the plaintiffs and repeatedly returned to court. The school finance litigation in New Jersey presents a stark example of this problem, as school finance litigation proceeded from the late 1960s through

2010 in different forms.[42] Moreover, while there is evidence that educational funding has been somewhat equalized by successful second wave litigation, there is very little evidence that this litigation has been effective in equalizing students' educational opportunities even where funding was equalized.[43] As several researchers have emphasized over the years, there is no boilerplate approach for transforming increased funding into increased educational opportunities for students, and states' approaches to school finance have suffered from this lack of such an approach.[44]

In short, the concept of equality as it had grown out of *Brown* and the desegregation cases showed tremendous resiliency even after a significant defeat in the Supreme Court. Although the equal protection clause of the U.S. Constitution was ultimately not a viable foundation for school finance reform, the concept of equality in education law and policy dramatically expanded to apply to differences in wealth as school finance litigation spread around the country. But given familiar definitional problems of the concept of equality, vague legal requirements, the limited institutional expertise of courts in education, the continuing interplay between the courts and the political branch of state legislatures, and the sheer lack of knowledge about how to transform educational funding into educational opportunities consistently, this litigation was ripe for yet another change by the end of the 1980s.[45] Placed in the context of other major education reform efforts undertaken around the same time, this transition in school finance reform litigation is closely examined in Chapter 5.

The Education of Students with Disabilities

In addition to expanding into school finance, efforts to equalize students' educational opportunities expanded to consider students with disabilities. For much of U.S. history, students with disabilities were often excluded from schools and instead isolated in "prisonlike institutions" or "dead-end programs."[46] Reflecting the pervasive stigma of being disabled, the Supreme Court upheld the constitutionality of a Virginia law requiring sterilization of mentally retarded citizens for the protection of the state in *Buck v. Bell* in 1927.[47] Writing the decision for an eight justice majority, Justice Oliver Wendell Holmes famously wrote in this case, "Three generations of imbeciles are enough."[48] However, beginning primarily in the 1960s, the disability rights movement began to aim at replicating the civil rights victories of African Americans and the women's rights movement. In doing so, advocates for the rights of students with disabilities launched what is arguably the most successful type of school reform focused on equality.

The law and policy reform efforts to equalize the educational opportunities of disabled students have proceeded across several major governmental institutions. These efforts primarily began in the courts. In the 1971 case *Pennsylvania Association for Retarded Citizens v. Commonwealth of Pennsylvania* (*PARC*), an advocacy organization sued the state of Pennsylvania under both the Fourteenth Amendment of the Constitution and Pennsylvania law.[49] Citing the principles of equality established in *Brown*, the organization particularly argued that mentally retarded students in Pennsylvania were not receiving a public education even though they were capable of benefiting from one. A federal district court in Pennsylvania agreed that all students can benefit from an education and that education is essential for citizens to function in society. The court ruled that children in Pennsylvania between the ages of six and twenty-one who have mental retardation must be provided a "free and appropriate public education" and that parents who are dissatisfied with their child's placement have the right to due process, or a hearing.

In 1972, a Washington, D.C., federal district court decided *Mills v. Board of Education of District of Columbia* (*Mills*), a case involving similar issues to those in *PARC*.[50] In *Mills*, the Washington, D.C., school district cited financial problems for excluding seven students from schools because they were labeled as having behavioral problems, mental retardation, mental disturbances, or hyperactivity. The school district was sued under the equal protection clause and Washington, D.C., law. The court ruled that under both the Constitution and Washington, D.C., law the school district had a clear duty to include and retain the students, provide them with a public education, and grant them due process hearings before terminating any educational benefits. Together, *Mills* and *PARC* were instrumental in establishing the foundation for the procedural protections for placement decisions about students with disabilities in the public school system. While *Mills* and *PARC* were arguably the most important of such cases in the early 1970s, they were not the only cases. By 1973, at least twenty-seven such lawsuits were pending or had been decided in courts across the United States.[51]

Responding to advocates' efforts across the country and victories in courts, Congress quickly became involved in the movement to equalize educational opportunities for students with disabilities. In 1973, Congress enacted the Rehabilitation Act, the first major law aimed at protecting the rights of disabled citizens and funding programs focused on helping disabled citizens.[52] Section 504 of the Rehabilitation Act provided, "No otherwise qualified individual with a disability ... shall, solely by reason of his disability, be excluded from participation in, or be denied the benefits of, or be subjected to discrimination under any program or activity receiving Federal financial assistance."[53] The regulations promulgated under section 504 largely mirrored and formalized the requirements for a free appropriate education and due process articulated in *Mills* and *PARC*.[54]

In 1975, Congress further expanded its commitment to protecting the rights of students with disabilities with the passage of the Education for All Handicapped Children Act (EAHCA).[55] By the mid-1970s, disability rights advocates had become concerned about losing lawsuits and worried that the Supreme Court would ultimately reject a constitutional argument in favor of equal education for students with disabilities, especially after the Court's decision in *San Antonio Independent School District v. Rodriguez*. On the basis of decisions such as *Mills* and *PARC*, laws such as the Rehabilitation Act passed in the early 1970s, as had a series of state laws recently enacted around the country protecting disabled students' right to a public education, and advocates turned their attention to Congress.[56] The EACHA bill sailed through Congress with very little opposition and was ultimately signed by President Gerald Ford.[57]

The EAHCA incorporated in federal law several principles underlying existing state laws and judicial decisions such as *Mills* and *PARC*. The EAHCA provided that all students have the right to receive a "free appropriate public education" and that public schools may not turn away students with disabilities. The law also included provisions prioritizing the placement of disabled students in the "least restrictive environment" so that these students are educated with their nondisabled peers to the greatest possible extent. The law further contained procedures for developing an "individualized education program" (IEP) for disabled students. An IEP is a document written annually by a person associated with the school system who is "qualified to provide or supervise the provision of specially designed instruction to meet the unique needs of children with disabilities, the teacher, the parents, or the guardian of such child, and, whenever appropriate, such child."[58] The IEP lists unique goals for the student and the services that are needed to benefit from an education. The process of creating an IEP was required to be tailored to individual students and developed according to their unique needs. Moreover, the law formalized the due process procedures when parents did not agree with the disability classification or decisions about their children in the IEP. Parents were given the power to initiate a due process hearing before an impartial due process officer, which could ultimately be appealed in the federal court system. Through 2010, these basic IEP requirements continued to operate under federal law, and there are no indications that these requirements will be removed.

Despite such broad attention to ensuring that students receive a free appropriate public education in the least restrictive environment and the very specific procedural protections instituted under the EACHA, the law contained very little in the way of specific substantive protections. As a result, federal courts have attempted to clarify substantive aspects of the EACHA as plaintiffs brought various types of lawsuits. The courts can be an especially important institution in the area of disabled students' rights because federal compliance monitoring has revealed that 90 percent of states fail to ensure proper oversight of school districts.[59] Since the passage of the EACHA, the Supreme Court has issued twelve rulings clarifying the law.[60] These decisions have covered a range of issues, including what constitutes a free appropriate public education, what constitutes education related services versus medical services, attorney's fee awards, placements and tuition reimbursement at private schools, and student discipline.[61]

For example, the Supreme Court's 1982 decision in *Board of Education of Hendrick Hudson School District v. Rowley* helped clarify what constitutes a free appropriate education.[62] In this case, a deaf girl was integrated into a regular classroom, was doing fairly well in school, and was refused a sign interpreter by her school district. The lawsuit aimed at forcing the district to provide the girl with an interpreter. The Supreme Court ruled that an interpreter was not required under the EACHA because the law did not promise the maximum feasible education – only that the child gain some educational benefit. Still, federal circuit courts have interpreted *Rowley* in different ways. While some courts have interpreted *Rowley* as requiring that disabled students receive services that enable them to do more than pass from grade to grade, other courts have stated that services are not due beyond this bare minimum.[63]

Similarly, although the Supreme Court has not directly addressed what constitutes a "least restrictive environment," some circuit courts have. On the basis of the presumption that Congress had a preference for integrating disabled and nondisabled students in classrooms under the EACHA, the Sixth Circuit Court of Appeals created a "portability" test in *Roncker v. Walters* in 1983.[64] In this case, the court looked at "whether the services that made [a] segregated setting superior could be feasibly provided in a nonsegregated setting. If they could, the placement in the segregated setting would be inappropriate."[65] However, the Ninth Circuit Court of Appeals created a different test for determining whether a student is placed in the least restrictive environment, including a comparison of the benefits that the disabled student receives in different settings, a consideration of the impact of a disabled students' presence on teachers and students in a regular classroom, and a consideration of the costs of placement in a regular classroom.[66]

Other circuit courts have developed widely used tests for determining the extent to which a student must be "mainstreamed," or placed in a regular classroom. In the 1989 case *Daniel R. R. v. State Board of Education*, the Fifth Circuit Court of Appeals found that the EACHA reflected a strong congressional preference for mainstreaming.[67] In doing so, the court asked whether education in a regular classroom could be accomplished satisfactorily with supplementary aids, and whether students removed from regular classrooms were participating with nondisabled peers in academic and nonacademic activities to the appropriate extent. Other courts have widely looked to this legal test when considering the appropriateness of a student's placement. For example, the Third Circuit Court of Appeals emphasized in *Oberti v. Board of Education*, "Inclusion is a right, not a special privilege for a select few."[68] However, other courts, such as the Fourth Circuit Court of Appeals, have underscored a more limited approach based on the idea that the EACHA requires mainstreaming only to the extent that it does not prevent a child from receiving educational benefit.[69]

Congress has also clarified the EACHA repeatedly over the course of decades. The law was reauthorized in 1983, 1990, 1997, and 2004. The 1990 reauthorization renamed the law the Individuals with Disabilities Education Act (IDEA). Some of the changes made during the reauthorizations and through other amendments directly responded to court decisions. For example, after the Supreme Court ruled that parents who won lawsuits under the EACHA could not be reimbursed for attorney's fees, Congress amended the EACHA in 1986 to permit such reimbursement.[70] Congress also modified the law to fit better with other laws being implemented. As Chapter 7 details, the 2004 reauthorization of the IDEA was somewhat aligned with the accountability-based approach of the No Child Left Behind Act of 2001. Still, the core tenets of the law remained the same through 2010, and it continued to focus on ensuring that students with disabilities receive a free appropriate education in the least restrictive environment through detailed procedures revolving around the development and implementation of IEPs.

While much of the litigation under the EACHA has been aimed at clarifying the law's requirements and enforcing rights for individual students, some of this litigation has been more sweeping. *Jose P. v. Ambach* presents a high-profile example of this sort of litigation.[71] This class action lawsuit

was initiated in 1979 in a federal district court against the New York City
school district for failing to evaluate students with disabilities and properly place them quickly.[72] At first, the plaintiffs pursued an order requiring
the district to adopt a plan to remedy this problem. However, the district
court judge consolidated this case with *United Cerebral Palsy v. Board of
Education*, which included a significantly broader range of issues, including a lack of IEP procedures, poor preparation of IEPs, and the lack of
opportunities to "mainstream" disabled students. In 1979, Judge Eugene
Nickerson issued a consent decree aimed at instituting fundamental structural reforms to address these problems, including requirements for the
district to engage in a complex planning process for the implementation
of a new special education system and the development of procedures for
the Board of Education to evaluate the system. As of 2010, this case was
ongoing and supervised by district court judges.

Some commentators have highlighted positive outcomes from this litigation, such as the increased attention it has forced the school district to
pay to the education of disabled students and increased funding for programs devoted to those students. However, several critics have highlighted
the problems raised by the litigation. For example, the consent decree limited the flexibility of the district, the oversight of the court seems endless, and the decree has focused on hiring personnel and complying with
procedures instead of facilitating a high-quality education for disabled
students.[73] While most special education litigation is not of this structural reform variety, there have been a handful of similar cases, such as the
Corey H. litigation that was filed against the Chicago Board of Education
and ultimately settled.[74]

Despite such problems with litigation aimed at large-scale structural
reform, law and policy reform efforts aimed at equalizing educational
opportunities for students with disabilities are among the most successful by some measures. Under one recent count, approximately 13 percent
of the school-aged population has a disability.[75] However, the number of
children with developmental disabilities moved from more than ninety
thousand around 1970 to approximately thirty-five hundred in 1995.[76] In
addition, the number of students with disabilities seems to have increased in
postsecondary education. While 2.6 percent of college freshman reported
that they had disabilities in 1978, 8.8 percent reported that they had in
1991.[77] Still, the IDEA has been attacked for being overly procedural and
for its significant cost. In the 1999–2000 school year, special education
accounted for 19.1 percent of total national elementary and education
spending, which represented an increase of 13 percent from the 1977–8

school year (largely due to rising enrollment in special education and not per pupil costs).[78] Perhaps most significantly, minority students have constituted a highly disproportionate number of students who are identified as having disabilities.

In short, the law and policy efforts aimed at equalizing the educational opportunities for students with disabilities followed in the wake of desegregation litigation. As it was first conceived, this movement was partly rooted in the constitutional dimensions of the equal protection clause and almost wholly rooted in the politics of protecting a minority group carrying social stigma. The efforts to reform the education of disabled students, however, developed through significantly different governance arrangements. While these efforts found their first purchase in the courts, they soon moved to Congress and were very successful in putting at least procedural protections in place for students under federal law. And while courts continually fleshed out requirements of federal law, courts were not the driving force as they were in desegregation litigation.

In this context, the shape of the underlying idea of equality was very different from that in other education reform movements such as desegregation and school finance reform. Much governmental attention focused on instituting and defining rights-based procedural protections. Such a focus strongly contrasts with one aimed at discrimination and rooted in broad and slippery issues embedded deep within the social fabric, such as people's decisions about where to live and the effects of family wealth. Moreover, with a few exceptions like *Jose P.*, the courts largely focused on clarifying the rights of disabled students under federal law through very individualized tools such as IEPs; the courts were not focused on fundamentally reforming entire school systems to equalize educational opportunities for groups. Still, as discussed in Chapter 7, the direction of federal law focused on students with disabilities would later turn toward holding educational organizations accountable for their effectiveness at not just equalizing disabled students' educational opportunities, but increasing their achievement as well.

The Education of English Language Learners

In addition to the expanding into the education of students with disabilities, the push toward educational equality in law and policy also emerged in the area of English language learner (ELL) students in the late 1960s and 1970s. The issue of how education would be provided to ELL students in law and policy was not new. For example, in the early part of the twentieth century, the Supreme Court struck down laws prohibiting instruction in German and teaching foreign languages without a permit.[79] Yet, law and policy changes to address the equality of educational opportunities that ELL students receive were not strongly instituted until the 1960s. Over the course of the 1960s, the population of minority groups that spoke languages other than English significantly increased in the United States.[80] The Civil Rights Act of 1964 in part responded to this trend. Title VI of the Civil Rights Act specifically prohibited discrimination in federally funded programs on the basis of race, color, or national origin. Reformers and governmental officials quickly focused on the protection of citizens on the basis of national origin as a proxy for protection on the basis of language.

The Bilingual Education Act of 1968 soon provided additional protection for the rights of ELL students. Initially proposed by Senator Ralph Yarborough (D-TX), the Bilingual Education Act was incorporated into the ESEA as Title VII and included a competitive grant program aimed at incentivizing school districts to create innovative educational programs to meet "special educational needs of ... children of limited English speaking ability."[81] The law was specifically aimed at providing non-English instruction to ELL students until they were proficient in English. In order to accomplish this goal, the law provided funding for educational programs, training for teachers and aides, developing and disseminating materials, and projects spurring parental involvement. The law also prioritized low-income students. While the law only provided $7.5 million for bilingual education in 1969, its funding level rose to $35 million in 1974.[82] Indeed, although this funding increased during President Nixon' s presidency, which was generally hostile to the expansion of Great Society programs, the Bilingual Education Act fit with Nixon's broader political strategy of building a wider Republican majority by courting Latino votes.[83]

With this basic legal framework in place, much of the effort to protect the rights of ELL students shifted from the legislative branch to the executive and judicial branches. In 1970, the Office for Civil Rights in the Department of Health, Education, and Welfare (HEW) released a memorandum describing how it would enforce Title VI of the Civil Rights Act.[84] This memorandum was directed at school districts with more than 5 percent "national-origin minority group" children.[85] The memorandum specifically required any school district with high concentrations of national-origin minority group children to take "affirmative steps to rectify the language deficiency [of national-origin minority students who are not proficient in English] in order to open its instructional program to these students."[86] If school districts failed to comply with these require-ments, the Office of Civil Rights could assert its power to withhold federal funds.

With the Supreme Court's unanimous decision in *Lau v. Nichols* in 1974, the press to provide native language instruction to ELL students intensified.[87] In *Lau*, non-English-speaking students of Chinese ancestry sued the San Francisco school district for providing unequal educational opportunities.[88] California state law required English to be "the basic lan-guage of instruction in all schools," permitted a district to determine "when and under what circumstances instruction may be given bilingually," and authorized bilingual education "to the extent that it does not interfere with the systematic, sequential, and regular instruction of all pupils in the English language."[89] The plaintiffs believed that such provisions resulted in unequal educational opportunities. Although the plaintiffs urged the Supreme Court to decide the case under the Fourteenth Amendment, the Court instead found the district to be in violation of Title VI and the 1970 HEW guidelines because the district discriminated against students on the ground of national origin. The Court reasoned that under the state law, "there is no equality of treatment merely by providing students with the same facilities, textbooks, teachers, and curriculum, for students who do not understand English are effectively foreclosed from any meaningful education."[90] While the Court did not impose a specific remedy and explic-itly relied on the expertise of the school board to rectify the situation, the Court emphasized that school districts receiving federal funds must com-ply with Title VI and provide appropriate relief.

Given the ambiguity of the Supreme Court's mandate for an appropri-ate response, law and policy efforts soon focused on fleshing out what such a response actually requires. In the same year as *Lau*, Congress passed the Equal Educational Opportunity Act, which explicitly required educational agencies "to take appropriate action to overcome language barriers that impede equal participation by students in an instructional program."[91] This law defined a bilingual educational program as one providing instruc-tion in English and students' native language such that students could participate in a regular classroom as quickly as possible. The law also included provisions aimed at helping districts accomplish this goal though providing funds for expanding curricula and staff, and building exper-tise. In 1975, the Office for Civil Rights in HEW also focused on districts' responses with the release of guidelines known as the "*Lau* Remedies."[92] These guidelines provided criteria for evaluating whether districts serving at least twenty students of the same language group were complying with

Lau and properly developing plans for bilingual educational programs. In particular, the guidelines construed an appropriate response as including four phases in the preparation of a response: student identification, student language assessment, analysis of achievement data, and analysis of program offerings. However, the *Lau* Remedies were ultimately withdrawn in 1981 by the Reagan administration, which was overtly hostile toward bilingual education.[93]

Law and policy efforts to define the scope of *Lau* continued into the early 1980s. In 1981, the Fifth Circuit Court of Appeals decided *Castaneda v. Pickard* and directly addressed the scope of *Lau*.[94] In *Castaneda*, Mexican American children and their parents in Texas sued their school district for using an ability grouping system based on racially and ethnically discriminatory criteria and failing to implement an adequate bilingual education program. The plaintiffs sued on several legal grounds, including the Fourteenth Amendment, Title VI, and the Equal Educational Opportunities Act. Finding that the district was not taking appropriate action to overcome the students' language barriers, the Fifth Circuit ultimately established three criteria to define such action: a bilingual education program must be based on sound educational theory, must have sufficient resources and personnel, and must prove effective at teaching students English. Still, the court did not require districts to provide bilingual education programs. As some scholars have noted, such an approach to providing a bilingual education program has led to a tension between reconciling the goals of language appropriate instruction and integration – while language appropriate instruction may require separate classes in languages other than English, integration requires students to be in the same classroom.[95] The requirement for language appropriate instruction also raises the possibilities that some students may have to be transported to different schools in order to receive such instruction.[96] Although the Supreme Court never ruled on the *Castaneda* standard, courts around the United States have adopted this standard to evaluate school districts' approaches to ELL students.

Since the early 1980s, there have been several other modifications to this basic law and policy framework for providing ELL students with equal educational opportunities. Congress amended Title VII of the ESEA four times before it was allowed to expire in 2002 and was replaced with Title III, which focused on teaching English to ELL students. Amendments to Title VII have focused on a range of changes, including increasing funding for evaluation and program development, providing increased flexibility to schools and districts to develop their own programs, and training staff. The change to Title III particularly removed provisions allowing for native-language instruction for ELL students and required demonstrated annual improvements in English proficiency.

To be sure, there have been significant demographic shifts and changes in the politics of education for ELL students. During the 1990s, the number of immigrants entering the United States and the number of Spanish-speaking students rose dramatically.[97] Many of these students were from poor backgrounds, and the ELL population increased by 52 percent in the 1990s.[98] At the same time, sentiment against bilingual education swept through the United States, especially in areas with high proportions of ELL students. For example, states such as Arizona, California, Colorado, and Texas passed laws and propositions prohibiting illegal immigrants from taking advantage of public education.[99] Courts have generally been hostile to such requirements. The Texas Supreme Court struck down a law that prohibited undocumented students from receiving a public education as early as 1982 in *Plyler v. Doe*.[100] Sounding a familiar refrain of courts dealing with such issues of equality, the court wrote:

> Public education has a pivotal role in maintaining the fabric of our society and in sustaining our political and cultural heritage; the deprivation of education takes an inestimable toll on the social, economic, intellectual, and psychological well-being of the individual, and poses and obstacle to individual achievement.[101]

Other courts considering laws and propositions prohibiting education for undocumented students in the 1990s displayed similar stances, highlighting the persistence of ideas about the fundamental democratic and social mobility purposes of education, at least where an education would be completely denied.

In short, law and policy reform efforts focusing on bilingual education emerged during the 1960s and 1970s as yet another branch of the movement focused on providing students with equal educations. Although the equal protection clause did not provide the legal hook for this movement, it found a firm foothold in Title VI of the Civil Rights Act and Title VII of the ESEA. While Congress passed more laws directly affecting the education of ELL students, such as the Equal Educational Opportunities Act and modifications to Title VII, the reform efforts primarily proceeded in the context of federal agencies and courts. Grounded in this legal framework, these governmental institutions extended educational protections to ELL students and gradually fleshed out requirements for adequate governmental responses. Indeed, as these institutions delved more deeply into

ELL issues, their efforts focused not simply on defining and protecting individual rights but on structuring a system that would actively ensure educational opportunities. There is certainly much more that could be said about law and policy reforms focused on the education of ELL students and the implications of these efforts for educational equality, governance, and goals. Indeed, much strong research has been conducted on this issue throughout the years. However, as noted in Chapter 1, such reform efforts are not a focus of this book. Still, this brief discussion should serve as an overview of the major issues surrounding the ELL movement in law and policy and provide useful context for the discussion of other types of large-scale education reform efforts.

The Maturation of Title I of the Elementary and Secondary Education Act

While the concept of equality in major education laws and policies expanded to include areas such as the education of ELL students and students with disabilities in the late 1960s and 1970s, the concept continued to be fleshed out in the context of the ESEA as well. As discussed in Chapter 3, the original passage of the ESEA in 1965 was considered a legislative breakthrough. Given the politics surrounding the passage of the ESEA and concerns about expansion of the federal role, Title I spread funds widely and initially contained few requirements about how program funds had to be spent. States only approved and monitored local choices, and the federal government only provided approvals as well.[102] As such, Title I was large but had vaguely defined objectives.

Given the limited capacities of the institutions suddenly responsible for implementing the ESEA, the law faced immediate implementation challenges. The U.S. Office of Education (USOE) staff in HEW that was responsible for overseeing Title I was small and inexperienced.[103] State departments of education were also small and were not geared toward activities focused on compliance.[104] When Title I was first implemented, there was no written procedure, audit, or formal evaluation to reveal how or even whether Title I funds were being used by districts and schools. In this context, early looks at the implementation of the law found that Title I funds were being used for improper purposes. For example, a high-profile report written by Ruby Martin and Phyllis McClure of the NAACP Legal Defense Fund found that funds were being used for purposes such as buying color televisions instead of enhancing schools' instructional programs.[105] Because the program was so large, benefits were also spread very thinly – some early looks at Title I funding estimated that it added $9 to $120 per student annually, which ultimately accounted for very little additional funding for each student.[106]

Perhaps just as troubling, educational research was beginning to investigate the relationship between school funding and student performance and cast doubt on the strength of this relationship. Prior to such studies, most simply assumed that increasing school funding would inevitably improve education at the school and classroom levels. However, James Coleman and a group of other researchers published the Equality of Educational Opportunity Study in 1966 and began to weaken this widely held assumption.[107] While its findings were nuanced, the "Coleman Report" revealed that students' backgrounds and socioeconomic status are much more important than school funding for predicting students' performance. The Coleman Report also highlighted large gaps in academic performance between white and African American students. The report accordingly raised worries about the efficacy of Title I.

Despite such concerns about the basic funding mechanism of Title I and the broader political concerns about Great Society programs in the late 1960s and 1970s, Title I proved very durable. In addition to the law's political popularity, which owed to widely distributed funding, Title I persisted in large part because it matured through the years. During the 1970s, Congress modified the legal requirements of Title I in three major ways to ensure that funds were spent more appropriately. First, "maintenance of efforts" provisions required school districts to maintain the level of spending from state and local funding from one year to the next.[108] Second, "comparability" provisions required districts receiving Title I funds to provide services that were comparable to services provided in schools that did not receive Title I funds.[109] Third, "supplement not supplant" provisions required states, districts, and schools to ensure that Title I funds are not spent on costs that would otherwise be met by state and local funds.[110]

Changes other than those rooted in legal text improved the implementation of Title I as well. Prompted by concerns such as those raised by the Martin-McClure report, Title I staff grew in the 1970s and began to engage in audits and program reviews of state and local Title I administration.[111] As a result, the federal government issued reports recommending changes in administrative practice and the repayment of inappropriately spent Title I funds. Moreover, program regulations mandated that students served by Title I funding receive identifiable educational services.[112] In this context of focusing services on eligible students and an increased emphasis on financial compliance, many districts and schools adopted "pull out" programs, an approach that separated eligible students from their peers to provide instruction using Title I funds.[113] Such programs generally provided remedial instruction to smaller groups of students than in regular classes for thirty to sixty minutes per day.

Given the expansion of the ESEA and the continuing flow of money from the federal government into state (and ultimately local) governments, the power of states in education grew alongside that of the federal government. With states as the first stop for ESEA implementation, the federal government became one of the major funders of state education agencies.[114] Title V of the ESEA provided funds specifically for the development of the capacities of state departments of education to implement Title I effectively. Through the 1970s, Title V thus helped spur the growth of Title I offices in states with direct connections to the federal Title I office and provided improved guidance about how states and localities could comply with federal requirements.[115] By 1980, the administrative structures of state and federal agencies closely paralleled each other, even to the extent that state programs and federal programs operated in "silos" that were largely disconnected from other programs.[116]

Despite the growth of state and federal capacities and an increased focus on financial compliance, studies focusing on the implementation and effectiveness of Title I continued to raise concerns through the 1970s. For example, the 1968 "TEMPO" investigation found that student achievement tended to decline in Title I schools and that schools with 40–60 percent African American student enrollments showed the poorest response to Title I.[117] The "Sustaining Effects Study," conducted by the System Development Corporation in the 1970s, reinforced concerns about the efficacy of Title I funds to improve students' educational opportunities and close the achievement gap significantly.[118] This comprehensive study included a longitudinal national survey of 300 elementary schools and included ethnographic studies of 55 high-poverty schools and about 120,000 students.[119] While the study found that Title I participation was linked with some increased relative growth in student performance, this growth was not consistent across subjects or grades, and the shape of Title I programs varied dramatically at the local level. Moreover, the study found that Title I funding largely provided additional funds to local programs for more teachers, aides, and specialists, and that Title I students continued to receive educations focusing on basic skills. Indeed, although generally less rigorous than the Sustaining Effects Study, other early evaluations of Title I conducted around the same time yielded similar conclusions about the ability of Title I funds to improve students' educational opportunities.[120]

Despite such issues surrounding the implementation of Title I, the federal government strongly reinforced its commitment to education throughout the 1970s. Under Presidents Richard Nixon and Jimmy Carter, more than one hundred new categorical education programs were created.[121] In 1979, President Carter fulfilled his campaign promise to his liberal constituency and gave a "political payoff" to the National Education Association for the campaign support of its constituents with the creation of the cabinet-level U.S. Department of Education (ED).[122] In line with the limited approach that the federal government had traditionally employed to what happens in schools and classrooms, the authorizing legislation of ED explicitly prevented the U.S. secretary of education or any ED officers from exercising any control over the "instructional program" of any school.[123] Still, the creation of ED reflected a significantly diminished opposition to the role of the federal government in education, as several congressional conservatives supported the transfer of federal education programs to ED.[124] Indeed, ED oversaw approximately five hundred federal education programs by 1980.[125]

So, although Title I grew directly from the civil rights movement and was a key part of school desegregation (in connection with the Civil Rights Act of 1964), the program ultimately became a separate branch of equality in education law and policy. In part to strengthen its political viability, Title I began as a sweeping federal funding mechanism with vague requirements and few controls available to program administrators. This lack of control was largely rooted in the history of the federal government (and even state governments) as an institution that had little to do with education. But as Title I matured, the concept of equality embedded in the law became more precise and program specific in ways that channeled funds to poor students. Moreover, given the increasing commitment to the federal role in education, the managerial and administrative capacities of the agencies responsible for implementing Title I significantly grew in ways that fostered increased financial compliance and even support for implementing Title I. Despite such improvements, Title I remained rooted in the traditional role of the federal government in education and focus on educational equality largely in financial terms. In this context, there was significant variation in how Title I funds were used at the local level and little indication that Title I was having its intended effect on any consistent basis in improving the learning opportunities of low-income students.

CONCLUSION

The late 1960s and 1970s were a time of maturation for law and policy reform efforts focused on educational equality. Grounding their efforts in the logic and ostensible success of desegregation, reformers significantly expanded the idea of educational equality. In addition to primarily aiming at altering the demographics of schools attended by African American students, major law and policy efforts began to attempt to reform the educational experiences of ELL and disabled students, and school funding structures. Moreover, the federal executive and legislative branches became entrenched institutions in education, in stark contrast with their roles less than two decades earlier.

As educational equality expanded into new areas and became the core of new institutional arrangements, the concept inevitably took on new meanings. In the context of reform focused on students with disabilities, laws and policies focused on what constitutes "free appropriate public education" in the "least restrictive environment." In comparison to desegregation litigation, this formulation of equality was much more individualized; under this formulation, equal treatment means providing differentiated services for unique individuals. Still, familiar arguments about the meaning of equality in this context continued to emerge. For example, federal appeals courts underscored the ambiguous nature of equality when they differed over the level of services due to disabled students under *Rowley* and the extent to which the concept of a least restrictive environment requires mainstreaming. In the context of ELL students, the concept of educational equality developed differently. Both laws and court decisions treated students of the same minority language group much more as a homogeneous group. Yet, such treatment of ELL students was markedly different from the treatment of African American students in desegregation litigation. Law and policy efforts focused on ELL students often required different programs and practices for ELL students than those implemented in regular classrooms. In contrast, Title I continued to treat all students from low-income backgrounds as similar and simply funneled money toward them. Still, Title I became increasingly targeted and tightly regulated over time as constructions of educational equality were clarified in largely financial terms.

The governance structures created in the late 1960s and 1970s played a significant role in this development of educational equality in law and policy. Although the law and policy reform movement focused on students with disabilities originally reflected the logic of the desegregation movement, this movement truly took off with the passage of statutory protections centered on students' rights, such as section 504 and the EAHCA. This statutory framework developed over time through an interplay of judicial interpretations of key issues and congressional revisions that responded to both judicial decisions and other problems that emerged through the implementation process. Grounded in this framework, which became fairly isolated from other education law and policy movements, this type of equality-based reform was able to develop with a focus on the procedural protection of individuals and largely on the more concrete elements of an equal education instead of broader social issues.

The ELL movement in education law and policy was similarly grounded in the logic of desegregation, but it developed in law and policy through different governance structures. While the Bilingual Education Act and Equal Educational Opportunities Act were tied closely to ELL issues, Title VI of the Civil Rights Act applied much more broadly. Indeed, it was originally unclear from a legal standpoint whether Title VI even applied to ELL issues until administrative agencies and courts interpreted Title VI in this fashion. Grounded in this framework, governmental institutions also focused on the protection of rights, but in a way that mirrored other educational equality movements to a greater extent than the one focused on disabled students – with various statutory revisions, judicial decisions, and politically motivated administrators, this movement to improve the educational opportunities for ELL students was not simply focused on protecting the rights of individuals and groups; it was also moving toward the more difficult and amorphous goal of spurring educational systems actively to ensure the equality of educational opportunities.

Founded on the overtly social logic of the links between poverty and education, the ESEA highlighted the importance of a centralized, federal role, separated from local politics, for leveraging large-scale reform focused on equality. Although it is now clear that money alone cannot effectively leverage school reform at scale, the focus on channeling billions of dollars per year made much sense at the time – especially given assumptions about the effect of money on schools and the distance of HEW from local schools, a centralized reform needed to be focused on such a resource that could be easily regulated.[126] Yet, the first couple of decades after the ESEA was originally enacted showcased the difficulties of implementing large, equality-based reform from the "capitol to the classroom" through several governmental layers. Title I implementation problems stemmed from a variety of factors, including the lack of personnel, lack of skill among personnel, and political resistance to new programs. The program ultimately matured into one that operated more smoothly, especially as the federal role in education became increasingly accepted. But this maturation was unfortunately characterized by a silo structure and mentality that worked against any sort of holistic reform. Indeed, the *Milliken II* compensatory academic programs were plagued by the lack of an overarching plan as well.

The expansion of law and policy into school finance was perhaps the most natural extension of the desegregation movement because school finance reform extensively relied on litigation to address inequalities that clearly tracked racial lines. Despite the Supreme Court's refusal to recognize education as a fundamental right under the Constitution in *Rodriguez*, Justice Brennan's dissent underscored the conceptual links between education and a robustly functioning democracy. And although the Supreme Court also refused to extend the application of the Fourteenth Amendment to find that wealth is a suspect class, state courts around the United States looked on such arguments more favorably under state constitutions. Yet, the concept of equality proved malleable in school finance litigation as well. While equality was originally defined under concrete and easily quantifiable formulations like per pupil expenditures, this concept morphed over the course of decades to include a range of different elements that contribute to students' educational opportunities, including facilities, textbooks, and more slippery elements like teacher quality. On one hand, this way of formulating equality has proven very compelling. School finance litigation has appeared in almost every state and has remained a way to address unequal educational opportunities in school systems around the country. But, on the other hand, this type of reform effort has continued to operate without an overarching statutory framework shaped to the specific problems of school finance and has continually faced significant legal, political, and scientific problems since litigation in this area began.

Indeed, despite the expansion of law and policy efforts focused on equality, deep cracks in the very core of the idea of an equal education were beginning to emerge. As discussed previously, equality can be defined in an almost limitless number of ways. While some of these constructions are relatively concrete, such as the sameness of money or buildings, these constructions are ultimately limited. Especially as Title I revealed, fundamentally changing students' educational opportunities seems to require addressing what ultimately transpires in schools and classrooms – even when Title I actually overcame its initial problems of misappropriated funds and lack of administrative capacities to operate effectively, the law still did very little in 1970s for actually enhancing the educational opportunities of low-income students.

Unfortunately, directly changing these opportunities is not something that any high-level governmental institution is well equipped to do. While courts and legislatures proved fairly effective at structuring rights-based protections, they were not nearly as effective at leveraging system-level change. Representatives of these institutions (and especially of the courts, which already had decades of experience with desegregation) accordingly began to express their reluctance to engage in system-level change as it became clear that each reform only required a more fundamental reform in order to be truly effective – such reform increasingly seemed to require both deep changes in the schooling process and attention to even more diffuse social issues, such as demographic changes and the factors impacting where people live. This was precisely the sort of thinking powering the growing public hostility to the Great Society programs that became reflected in the agenda of the Nixon administration and the Supreme Court justices appointed by Nixon. In the realm of law and policy, this pushback was concretely manifested in the ascendancy of the notion of local control. If educational equality meant anything, it was that certain differences across local sites needed to be at least substantially mitigated, if not completely erased. In order to accomplish this end, some sort of centralized governmental institution needed to intervene. At least at first glance, extreme local control appears to be the antithesis of this concept.

Given their grounding largely in the vague constitutional demands of the equal protection clause, desegregation and school finance litigation became natural sites for the concept of local control to take root. *Milliken I* was decided by a Supreme Court with a quickly changing political composition and focused on a large, metropolitanwide remedy involving structural changes in the education system. By the time *Milliken I* was decided, busing was already growing unpopular in many sectors, and the Court heavily underscored the value of local control when it refused to find that such a remedy was warranted. Notably, the Court did approve academic compensatory remedies as a valid response in *Milliken II*, but such remedies appeared short-lived and isolated. And after the *Milliken* cases, the Court largely withdrew from deciding desegregation cases for years.

The Supreme Court acted similarly in the area of school finance with its decision in *Rodriguez*. Citing the importance of local control and deferring to state-level decision making, a changing Court stated that the equal protection clause does not require absolute equality and refused to find that centralized requirements to equalize educational resources are warranted. As such, school finance litigation has proceeded on a state-by-state basis and under state constitutions. But even in this context of more local, state-level reform efforts, familiar problems continued to arise. Given vague legal mandates, often resistant state legislatures, and a growing awareness that money alone cannot deeply change students' educational opportunities, courts still had trouble defining equality and often found that the law offers little help. Even when state courts did order changes and legislatures actually complied with modifications to school finance systems, very little change consistently occurred at the school level.

Taken together, such governmental responses reflect the resiliency and appeal of educational equality – a concept at the heart of the American polity grounded in the basic requirements for a democracy and the dream of social mobility. With courts increasingly unwilling to push reform forward by themselves, legislatures and agencies often took up the fight after initial judicial involvement and sporadic judicial interpretations of laws and regulations. While this type of statutory-based reform left less room for principles of equality to cross reform efforts and focused disputes over particular statutory provisions that were much more narrow than sweeping constitutional clauses, it did facilitate the longetivity of certain reform efforts. Still, the era also reflects deep tensions within the concept of educational equality that became apparent as it continually played out in concrete, real-world settings fraught with harsh politics, inevitable implementation problems, and a never-ending wave of new and unexpected issues that tested the integrity of the concept. For better or worse, the concept could expand eternally to include different groups and elements of an education and would seemingly require an eternal deepening of reform efforts under some sort of centralized authority to realize its promise. With fundamental social, technological, and economic changes bearing down hard on the United States, the concept of educational equality was ripe for change.

5

The Turn to Adequacy, Outcomes, and Systemic Change

In the 1980s and 1990s, education law and policy efforts to improve schools transformed dramatically. While large-scale reform efforts in the 1970s aimed at cementing and expanding an agenda focused on educational equality for various groups, cracks in this agenda also started to emerge in both legislative and judicial spheres during this decade. Reformers won battles in federal courts establishing protections for English language learner (ELL) students and students with disabilities, but the Supreme Court began to withdraw from pursuing desegregation and essentially moved litigation involving school finance reform from federal to state courts. Although implementation of the Elementary and Secondary Education Act (ESEA) was increasingly smooth, serious doubts about the effectiveness and efficacy of federal education policy also began to emerge. It was in this context of doubt about the education reforms centered on equality that education law and policy became ripe for fundamental changes.

The election of Ronald Reagan to the presidency in 1980 marked the beginning of many of these changes. The Reagan administration pushed for several shifts in education policy: from equity to excellence, from needs and access to ability and selectivity, from regulations and enforcement to deregulation, from common school to parental choice and institutional competition, and from social and welfare concerns to economic and productivity concerns.[1] While the Reagan administration was not able to accomplish many of its goals in education, it was at least successful in changing the overarching rhetoric of the education law and policy debate for decades to come. Galvanized by the publication of *A Nation at Risk*, a report drafted by a federally appointed panel in 1983, an explosion of state-level efforts aimed at educational "excellence" quickly appeared. By the mid-1990s, many states had begun to enact standards – written specifications of what all students should know and be able to do – as major policy levers for fundamentally restructuring state education systems. Under the Clinton administration, the federal government became deeply involved in pushing and shaping the "standards-based reform" movement as well. At the same time, school finance litigation and state legislative responses to it focused increasingly on the "adequacy" of educational resources instead of simply equality, and later iterations of school finance litigation directly involved state standards.

Although equality remained an important and driving concept in education law and policy, the ascendancy of adequacy marked fundamental shifts in both the underlying logic and practical details of governmental decisions aimed at improving schools. While much of the large-scale education law and policy in the years following *Brown v. Board of Education* framed schooling as a vehicle for social mobility and the creation of democratic citizens, the focus of rhetoric about schooling shifted to highlight the links between education and international economic competitiveness in a quickly globalizing world. In this context, legal and policy decisions increasingly focused on the actual skills and knowledge that students should demonstrate instead of sameness of treatment. As governmental decision makers came to believe, such a shift required more than enhanced protection of group rights and support for "disadvantaged" groups that tinkered at the margins of schooling; fundamental changes in the structure of educational institutions and governance were needed as well.

This chapter traces the transformation of equality in education law and policy from the beginning of the 1980s through the end of the 1990s. The emergence of the ideas of educational excellence, standards, and adequacy in the legislative and judicial spheres is particularly discussed. This examination focuses on the growth of legislation at both state and federal levels aimed at boosting students' skills and knowledge, often in relation to written standards about what students should know and be able to do. Moreover, related changes in the direction of school finance reform litigation are analyzed. In contrast to early school finance efforts, this new wave of litigation emphasized not only the equalization of funding but also the adequacy of funding, educational outputs, and the ways in which educational institutions and governance accordingly should be restructured. Together with the following chapter on desegregation and the growth of the school choice movement during the 1980s and 1990s, this chapter discusses the ways in which shifts in educational purposes, governance, and visions of equality interacted to lay the foundation for the modern era of school reform.

THE REAGAN ADMINISTRATION AND EDUCATION
REFORM IN THE 1980S

The election of Ronald Reagan to the U.S. presidency in 1980 marked a turning point in education law and policy. President Reagan was elected in a time of political and social tumult that generally made U.S. law and policy ripe for reform. By the end of the 1970s, the United States had experienced severe economic problems, such as the Organization of petroleum Exporting Countries (OPEC) oil embargo, recession, and stagflation.[2] Western countries, including the United States, were becoming less competitive with Pacific Rim countries in manufacturing. Amid these economic problems driven largely by global economic competition, the per capita gross national product (GNP) of the United States had dropped from second to fifth in the world, and primarily because of its trade deficit, the United States had become the largest debtor in the world.[3] With the growth of modern computing technology and rapid intercontinental transportation, the U.S. economy had also begun to center on information.[4] At the same time, both liberal and conservative politicians had already begun to attack the Great Society social programs for being ineffective and inefficient and encouraging dependency upon the state.[5] President Reagan's election built on growing public concerns about the role of the U.S. government in both international and domestic spheres.

During his campaign and throughout his presidency, Reagan espoused a neoliberal economic philosophy centered on free market principles and opposed to a strong governmental role in policy. President Reagan specifically reversed much of the rhetoric that had characterized education law and policy during the previous decades and reframed both the goals and the strategies of education reform: in contrast to reform efforts centering on educational equality, social concerns, individual and group needs, governmental regulations, and common schooling, the Reagan administration advanced the notions of educational excellence, economic productivity, individual ability, deregulation, parental choice, and institutional competition.[6] Indeed, during his presidential campaign, Reagan called for a deregulation by the federal government of public education and the elimination of the recently created U.S. Department of Education (ED).[7]

With the passage of the Omnibus Budget Reconciliation Act of 1981 (OBRA), the Reagan administration formally began to implement this philosophy by cutting funding across a range of domestic spending areas.[8] The Education Consolidation and Improvement Act of 1981 (ECIA), a component of the OBRA, made changes to the federal government's approach to education.[9] The ECIA renamed Title I of the ESEA as "Chapter 1"and relaxed its regulatory requirements, consolidated twenty-eight federally funded categorical programs into a single block grant while reducing funding by approximately 12 percent in its first year, and introduced limitations on ED and state agencies to regulate the use of federal funds by schools.[10] Along similar lines, the Reagan administration enforced federal civil rights requirements less robustly than its predecessors and called for stronger support of private schools through educational vouchers – a policy tool that would allow parents to use funds that would be given to public schools for their child's education as tuition at private schools.[11] While Congress passed amendments to the ECIA in 1983 that restored many of the targeting and reporting requirements of Title I, it was clear that the federal approach to educational equality was beginning to undergo a marked change.[12]

The publication of *A Nation at Risk* by the Reagan administration in 1983 built on public concerns that had catapulted President Reagan into office and set the tone for education law and policy efforts for the decades that followed.[13] The report was drafted by the National Commission on Excellence in Education (NCEE), a bipartisan committee appointed by U.S. Secretary of Education Terrell Bell, the first secretary of education under the Reagan administration. The primary aims of the NCEE were to examine the quality of education in the United States and make recommendations for educational improvement. The report cited several statistics reflecting students' low educational performance and criticized the U.S. education system for its low standards and expectations, limited use of instructional time, and poor quality of teachers. *A Nation at Risk* also employed fiery rhetoric to frame its findings. As the report stated:

> The educational foundations of our society are presently being eroded by a rising tide of mediocrity that threatens our very future as a Nation and a people. What was unimaginable a generation ago has begun to occur – others are matching and surpassing our educational attainments. If an unfriendly foreign power had attempted to impose on America the mediocre educational performance that exists today, we might well have viewed it as an act of war.... We have, in effect, been committing an act of unthinking, unilateral educational disarmament.[14]

In order to address these problems, the report called for several improvements to U.S. schools, including the strengthening of graduation requirements, the adoption of more rigorous and measurable standards, more time in school, and increasing the quality of teaching.

Although researchers have criticized *A Nation at Risk* in the years following its publication for its overly strong rhetoric and misleading use of
statistics to depict the quality of U.S. schools, the report had an immediate effect on the dialogue surrounding education.[15] More than six million
copies of the report were distributed, and major newspapers excerpted the
report and repeatedly included references to it.[16] Galvanized by the report,
both the public and policy makers began to make links between the quality
of schooling and the international economic competitiveness of the United
States, and public confidence in public education precipitously declined.[17]
Although the Reagan administration originally did not anticipate the findings of the report or the way in which it would focus public attention on
education, the administration quickly embraced the opportunities that it
raised.[18] The Reagan administration particularly made use of the "bully
pulpit" as an impetus for reform. For example, Secretary Bell developed the
"Wall Chart" – a visual representation ranking states' educational attain-
ments with student outcome indicators such as ACT and SAT scores.[19]
While the Wall Chart was originally controversial among state educational
leaders, the Council of Chief State School Officers ultimately accepted the
idea that comparisons on the basis of educational outcomes would not
disappear. Similarly, President Reagan's second secretary of education, Bill
Bennett, traveled across the United States and made speeches criticizing
the ineffectiveness of the federal involvement in education and calling for
a more limited federal role.[20]

In this climate, business leaders became increasingly convinced that
education could provide a capable workforce and engaged in education
reform.[21] As the education researcher Lee Anderson argued, the corporate sector embraced education reform with a "messianic fervor" immediately after the release of *A Nation at Risk*.[22] A slew of articles in business
publications, such as *Business Week*, *Forbes*, and *Fortune*, reflected the
idea that the business community could effectively reform education. By
the early 1990s, corporate panels had issued approximately three hundred reports on education. Several business groups, like the Committee
for Economic Development, forged alliances with advocacy groups that
supported the education of poor and minority students.[23] The U.S. business community further created the Business Coalition for Education, an
umbrella organization representing a range of business groups, including
the Business Roundtable, U.S. Chamber of Commerce, National Alliance
for Business, and Committee for Economic Development.[24] With such
shifts in the dialogue surrounding education, the entrance of the business
community, and the resumption of education's place under the political

spotlight, the excellence movement in education blossomed. Under this movement, the state role in education quickly expanded as states initiated a significant amount of reforms largely based on standards, monitoring, and assessments.[25]

Such efforts were not altogether new. For example, building on the intelligence testing movement that had emerged during World War I to predict the performance of soldiers at various tasks, the College Entrance Examination Board began to administer the Scholastic Aptitude Test (SAT) in 1926 to predict the readiness of high-school students for college. By the 1950s, the use of this test had become widespread.[26] In a climate of increased political attention to education in the wake of drops in student performance on the SAT in the late 1960s and early 1970s, many states enacted minimum competency tests (MCTs) throughout the 1970s. Responding to critiques that the awarding of academic diplomas reflected unjustified social promotion and low academic standards, MCTs measured basic skills in subjects such as reading, writing, and mathematics.[27] Given the release of studies such as the Coleman Report and Title I evaluations in the 1960s and 1970s, the use of MCTs also reflected the growing concern that reformers could not improve the quality of schooling by simply increasing the level of resources or inputs provided to schools. By 1979, thirty-six states had adopted some form of MCT, and eighteen states required students to pass these tests to receive diplomas. As these types of "high-stakes" testing practices were implemented through the 1980s and beyond, they proved highly controversial and politically explosive.[28] Because students from underserved groups (such as minority students and students with disabilities) often failed these tests at disproportionate rates compared to their white counterparts who were not from underserved groups, high-stakes testing practices were repeatedly challenged in court.[29]

The excellence movement that emerged in the wake of *A Nation at Risk* intensified this sort of approach to education reform around the country. By the first anniversary of the publication of *A Nation at Risk*, 275 state-level task forces on education had been convened around education reform.[30] During the mid-1980s, forty-one states increased high-school graduation requirements, and twenty-nine states required prospective teachers to pass a standardized test before entering teacher training or as a condition for certification.[31] Moreover, forty states put new testing provisions into effect.[32] A range of other state-level reforms also emerged during this time, such as the institution of career ladders and incentive pay systems for teachers, enrichment and academic recognition programs for students, changes in state funding formulas for schools, and changes in the academic calendar.[33] There was a general increase in different types of educational standards during this time, including those involving behavior (such as attendance) and academic work in core subjects.[34] While most of these reforms were enacted through sweeping state legislation (sometimes in the form of single laws that spanned one hundred pages or more), state boards of education also instituted many of these reforms through rules and regulations.[35]

Largely in response to these sorts of centralizing policies, a second wave of reforms swept through the country in the mid- to late 1980s. This wave of reforms emphasized the concepts of decentralization, professionalism, and bottom-up change.[36] In contrast to the earlier state-level reforms, these second wave reforms focused on the actual processes of educational change and the school building as the primary site of reform, with local educators as the designers and implementers of change. But as in the previous wave, the second wave also included a focus on outcomes as a mechanism to hold local educators accountable for instituting change. Although it appeared as if the second wave of reforms resulted in some increased learning opportunities in schools, critics stressed that such school-by-school reforms yielded no evidence of the potential for leveraging widespread change.[37]

Despite such fast and pervasive developments at the state level, federal education policy remained largely unchanged in the years immediately following the publication of *A Nation at Risk*. As noted previously, the ECIA made some modifications to the federal role in education by shifting options to states and localities through the replacement of categorical grants with block grants, but Chapter 1 ultimately maintained its narrow, categorical focus on the education of low-income students.[38] Indeed, instead of the large-scale elimination of federal education programs, incremental changes to these programs largely took place within the existing range of federal categories.[39] As a result, the effect of Chapter 1 on students' educational opportunities continued to be marginal at best. Chapter 1 funds continued to be spent on traditional educational resources, such as teachers, aides, administrators, instructional materials, and tests.[40] Under Chapter 1, students were still exposed to instruction in mathematics and reading in "pullout" classes that drew on available staff in a school or district.[41] As such, the quality of students' learning opportunities was strongly dependent on the setting in which they occurred, and fiscal accountability (instead of accountability for program quality) continued to dominate the implementation of Chapter 1.

While far less entrenched than Chapter 1, state education policies following *A Nation at Risk* in the 1980s similarly had a limited effect on the educational opportunities available to students. Although quite varied, these policies generally had a centralizing and standardizing effect by strengthening the state role in education reform.[42] These policies were also largely based on the assumption that the educational system only needed to be intensified instead of fundamentally changed.[43] As at least a partial result, these policies often suffered the same fate as many other centralizing education policies in the second half of the twentieth century – without adequately accounting for the range of factors that influence the implementation of policy on a local level, these reforms had little overall effect on teachers' and administrators' practices.[44] State education systems generally absorbed these reforms without significant changes for student learning opportunities, as many reforms had been similarly absorbed in the past.[45] At the very most, these policies reinforced traditional views of teaching and learning, centered around the notion that teaching consists of telling, learning, and restating, and that learning consists of mastering knowledge from external sources.[46]

So, in the context of growing concerns about international competitiveness and the role of the government, large-scale education law and policy began to take a sharp turn. While improving the opportunities available to particular groups was still important, equality had also begun to refer to the improvement of educational opportunities for *all* students and was no longer simply about access – educational outcomes had become an important element of conceptualizing equality as well. Reflecting this shift, a wave of centralizing state-level policies, partly driven by the activity of the business community, aimed at broadly increasing the quality of schooling instead of focusing on more narrowly targeted services. Although the Reagan administration had not succeeded in significantly modifying the federal role in education, it had succeeded in fundamentally changing the rhetoric surrounding education. While the Reagan era policies were ultimately ineffective at changing educators' practices and ultimately increasing learning opportunities for students, they accordingly laid the conceptual foundation for the reforms that would soon follow.

STANDARDS, TESTING, AND ACCOUNTABILITY IN THE LATE 1980S AND EARLY 1990S

During the late 1980s and early 1990s, momentum steadily built toward education policies centered on standards, testing, and accountability. A handful of state governors became a leading force for this sort of reform by emphasizing actual school performance and decreasing regulatory burdens on schools. Lamar Alexander (R-TN), Richard Riley (D-SC), and Bill Clinton (D-AR) led high-profile campaigns for education reform policies centered on the enactment of student learning standards and assessments and limiting the reach of governmental authority in the schooling process.[47] In 1986, these governors worked together to produce the report *Time for Results*, published by the National Governors' Association (NGA). In the report, Governor Alexander wrote, "The Governors are ready for some old fashioned horse-trading. We'll regulate less, if schools and school districts will produce better results."[48] Similarly, Governor Alexander emphasized that while state leaders would not bargain away minimum standards, they were also learning that excellence could not be imposed from a distance; according to Governor Alexander, local school leaders, teachers, parents, and citizens are the real drivers of excellent schools.[49] Amid this push for results in education policy, eight states agreed to administer the same test, the National Assessment of Educational Progress (NAEP), to a representative sample of students in their states in 1986.[50] In doing so, these states underscored their willingness to focus on student achievement data to ensure that state reforms were actually spurring progress.

The push for accountability continued to strengthen during the 1988 reauthorization of the ESEA with the passage of the Hawkins-Stafford Amendments.[51] Under this legislation, Congress modified Chapter 1 to require states to define the levels of academic achievement that students in Chapter 1 schools should attain. Moreover, Congress required states to collect and publish student test scores, identify the schools that were failing to make substantial progress toward their performance goals, and set out the steps that districts and states needed to take to assist schools that failed to perform adequately. Under the law, these steps were required to include the institution of school improvement plans and eventually state intervention in schools that continued to perform inadequately. However, these requirements generally were not implemented or enforced robustly, and many states failed to comply with these requirements.[52]

Swept up in the movement toward standards and accountability, those interested in education outside the formal policy making sphere became involved as well. In 1989, the National Council of Teachers of Mathematics (NCTM) – a professional organization of mathematics teachers, researchers, and administrators – drafted a comprehensive set of student learning standards to establish "criteria for excellence" usable by the public and policy makers when considering mathematics reform efforts.[53] The

NCTM standards specified what students should know and be able to do in different grade levels in mathematics and called for changes in the way that mathematics is taught and learned. The NCTM standards specifically emphasized that students should engage each other in discussions about different mathematical concepts, make conjectures, and provide explanations for their thinking. Under this formulation, students would become mathematical problem solvers who could reason and think mathematically. In order to facilitate this sort of learning, teachers should facilitate discussions between students and probe for ideas in ways that develop students' thinking. This vision of mathematics teaching and learning stood in stark contrast to that underlying many education policy reform efforts in the educational excellence movement that focused simply on intensifying the time spent teaching and learning rather than changing it.

The 1988 election of President Reagan's successor, President George H. W. Bush, proved to be an important turning point in the federal government's role in education. Although President Bush was not always known as an education reformer, he stressed his commitment to improving education from the beginning of his primary campaign and repeatedly indicated his desire to be the "Education President."[54] At the beginning of his term, President Bush told a group of 250 teachers that "education is the key to our competitiveness in the future as a nation and to our soul as a people."[55] While there was little indication at this time that President Bush had in mind a vision of centralized standards or goals as a reform direction, he soon convened the Charlottesville Education Summit of 1989, a meeting of the nation's governors to discuss the state of education in the nation as a whole. Indeed, although the federal government had funded projects that developed curricula, it had never drafted legislation or regulations detailing how or what students should be taught, and it had never required states to set minimum levels of student achievement.[56]

The group at the Charlottesville Education Summit generally criticized then current educational practices and published a report listing six goals for the entire American education system to achieve by the year 2000:

> (1) all students must arrive at school ready to learn; (2) the nation's high-school graduation rate must be at least 90 percent; (3) students must be competent in English, history, geography, foreign languages, and the arts; (4) American students must lead the world in math and science; (5) all adults must be literate; and (6) all schools must be drug free.[57]

This vision also stood in sharp contrast to the large-scale reform efforts of previous decades. Instead of focusing on providing funds for disadvantaged students and ensuring that civil rights were preserved, this vision focused on boosting the quality of education for all students.[58] Moreover, this vision continued to emphasize the importance of student learning standards and outcomes and, by crafting national goals, reframed the federal government as an entity that could provide a shared, centralized direction to the states. As a joint statement issued by President Bush and the governors indicated, "We believe that the time has come, for the first time in U.S. history, to establish clear, national performance goals, goals that will make us internationally competitive."[59] Solidifying his commitment to this vision of education reform, President Bush established the National Education Goals Panel (NEGP) in 1990 to monitor the nation's progress toward these national goals formally.

In 1991, President Bush attempted to follow up on the ideas set forth at the Charlottesville Education Summit with the proposal of the America 2000: Excellence in Education Act (America 2000).[60] Announcing the proposal at a White House meeting, President Bush repeated the national goals and indicated that America 2000 would help the United States reach them.[61] In order to reach these goals, President Bush indicated that the bill would enable the creation of national "world-class standards" for schools, teachers, and students in mathematics, science, English, history, and geography. President Bush also indicated that the bill would support the development of assessments to measure student performance against these standards. However, mindful of the politics that would accompany such a change in the federal role, President Bush emphasized the limited influence that America 2000 would actually exert over states: "We will develop voluntary – let me repeat it – we will develop voluntary national tests for fourth, eighth, and 12th graders in the five core subjects."[62] By making the national tests voluntary, President Bush had carefully attempted to frame America 2000 as an acceptable political balance between the states and the federal government in education.

In order to effect the sorts of changes America 2000 called for, the plan also involved the creation of America 2000 communities.[63] A geographical area could gain the distinction of being an America 2000 community if it embraced the national education goals, created strategies for reaching the goals, devised report cards for measuring progress, and agreed to support the "new generation of America's schools." In order to further innovation around the nation and create this new generation of schools, Bush announced the creation of the New American Schools Development Corporation (NASDC). This private sector research and development corporation would be chaired by Paul O'Neil, the CEO of the Aluminum

Company of America, and would devote approximately $150 million to generate innovation in education. President Bush also pledged that he would urge Congress to provide $1 million in start-up funds for each of 535 "break-the-mold" New American Schools once he had the results of NASDC research in hand. In addition to spurring education reform with national standards and New American Schools, America 2000 would institute educational choice among both public and private schools.

Although observers generally received America 2000 enthusiastically at first, the bill did not fare well after it was submitted to Congress. Republicans particularly criticized it for its inclusion of reform strategies aimed at instituting national standards and assessments, while Democrats criticized the school choice provisions in the bill.[64] As a result, neither the House nor Senate version of America 2000 made it out of congressional committees. Still, another education bill being considered at the same time fared slightly better – the Strengthening Education for American Families Act, a bill proposed by Senator Edward Kennedy (D-MA) and aimed at codifying the six national education goals. This bill would have given the NEGP the responsibility for establishing a process for developing and certifying voluntary national content standards and "school delivery standards" – a vague concept generally referring to the types of inputs, such as funding, that would be needed for schools to help students meet content standards.[65] Although this bill also included a choice program, it would have allowed educational choice among only public schools. While the House of Representatives and Senate ultimately passed the bill, it died in the reconciliation process amid criticisms about the expansion of the federal role, the school choice provisions, and the requirement to develop school delivery standards.[66]

Although America 2000 and the Strengthening Education for American Families Act were ultimately not enacted, their political support and lengthy consideration highlight fundamental shifts in the conception of the federal role in education. Long focused on providing funding and protecting the rights of minority groups, the federal government had begun to center its efforts on education policies aimed at improving education for all students, especially under the logic that such reform was needed for international economic competitiveness. Building on policy efforts throughout the 1980s, the federal government had similarly begun to focus on educational outcomes. However, especially given lack of political consensus about the distribution of educational decision-making authority – whether located in the federal government under reforms involving standards or in parents under reforms involving school choice – a comprehensive education reform policy was never enacted during President Bush's time in office.

The Theory of Standards-based Reform

Despite the failed efforts to pass a federal law centered on standards in the beginning of the 1990s, the idea of standards-based reform was becoming pervasive, and several theories about standards-based reform had begun to emerge. During this time, many used the term "systemic reform" to refer to standards-based reform. Although this term is rarely used now, the logic of this concept still underlies standards-based reform policies. As education law and policy reform efforts since *Brown* highlight, the United States has maintained a multilayered and fragmented system of educational governance.[67] In this system, policy mandates, guidelines, incentives, sanctions, and programs at federal, state, and local levels have interacted with each other to create uncoordinated and sometimes conflicting demands for educators and administrators. Under theories of systemic reform, standards or curriculum frameworks can provide an anchor for the design and implementation of more coherent educational governance, law, and policy. In particular, standards or curriculum frameworks can provide a substantive anchor for a host of other aspects of educational policy, including teacher training, teacher certification, continuing professional development, school curriculum, and assessment.

Although different researchers, policy makers, and organizations have defined standards-based reform differently, the fundamental tenets of increasing coherence and the quality of what students should know and be able to do generally persist across theories.[68] Drawing on state reforms in the 1980s and concepts from the "effective schools movement," Marshall Smith and Jennifer O'Day crafted perhaps the most influential version of system reform in the early 1990s.[69] Under their theory, O'Day and Smith identified three primary components of systemic reform:

1. Curriculum frameworks that establish what students know and be able to do would provide direction and vision for significantly upgrading the quality of the content and instruction within all schools in the state ...
2. Alignment of state education policies would provide a coherent structure to support schools in designing effective strategies for teaching the content of the frameworks to all their students. Novice and experienced teachers would be educated to understand and teach the new challenging content, and teacher licensure would be tied to demonstrated competence in doing so. Curriculum materials adopted by the states and local districts, as well as state assessments of student performance, would reflect the content of the curriculum

frameworks. The integration of these and other key elements of the systems would act to reinforce and sustain the reforms at the school building level.

3. Through restructured government system, schools would have the resources, flexibility, and responsibility to design and implement effective strategies for preparing their students to learn the content of the curriculum frameworks to a high level of performance. This flexibility and control at the school site is a crucial element of the system, enhancing professionalization of instructional personnel and providing the basis for real change in the classroom.[70]

So, largely mirroring the NCTM standards, Smith and O'Day underscored that standards should reflect high-level cognitive goals that emphasize complex thinking skills and help students actively draw connections between areas of knowledge.[71] Such a change would entail significant shifts in teaching and learning at the classroom level. Under this formulation, standards represent the floor of what students should learn – while O'Day and Smith underscored that standards should reflect a high-quality vision of teaching and learning, they still represent the minimum threshold below which all students should not fall. Moreover, while O'Day and Smith focused on states as the primary drivers of educational change, they also emphasized the importance of local decision making.

In addition to positing the benefits of coherent educational policy anchored in rigorous standards, Smith and O'Day emphasized the importance of a handful of other policy tools. Perhaps most notably, they stressed the need for "opportunity-to-learn" (OTL) standards specifying the resources that must be in place to enable teachers and schools to implement coherent education policies around challenging content. The authors particularly stressed that OTL standards were important to ensure that systemic reform improves the educational conditions of *all* schools and of *all* students, including poor and minority students. Moreover, Smith and O'Day argued for some form of accountability system based on standards. Although the authors were not clear about exactly what such a system should look like and cited several potential problems in using standards for accountability purposes (such as conceptualizing and measuring standards and deciding who should perform assessments), the authors were clear that such a system was crucial for the fair and effective implementation of the systemic reform policy. While there were several other competing theories of systemic (or standards-based) reform that emerged around the same time, federal and state policy efforts in the late 1980s and 1990s were generally enacted and implemented in relation to these principles.

The Growth of Standards-based Reform and Accountability
Policies in the 1990s

Reflecting insights from various theories of standards-based reform and the excellence movement, standards-based reform and accountability policies emerged around the United States beginning in the mid-1980s and increasingly throughout the 1990s. California is widely considered to be the first state to enact a formal standards-based reform policy with its adoption of challenging curriculum frameworks in the mid-1980s.[72] Texas similarly adopted a set of "Essential Elements" in twelve core areas of knowledge in the 1980s, and Connecticut adopted the Common Core of Learning, which specified general skills and outcomes for education.[73] Moving into the 1990s, many other states began to develop and adopt standards, and some states began to implement accountability sanctions tied to how well school or student performance on tests aligned to standards.[74]

During this time, the business community became involved in the standards movement as well. Having become deeply enmeshed in education reform at the state level since the publication of *A Nation at Risk*, business groups pushed for the creation of standards and testing to ensure that students could succeed in the workplace after they left high school. Those groups, which included the Business Roundtable, U.S. Chamber of Commerce, and National Association of Manufacturers, which created the Business Coalition for Education Reform, lobbied Congress in support of national standards and federal education reform.[75] In 1996 the nation's governors and corporate leaders formed Achieve, Inc., a nonprofit education reform organization devoted to helping states develop and raise standards, improve assessments, and strengthen accountability.[76] So, by the mid-1990s, a significant political push for standards-based reform had emerged around the country.

The Clinton Administration and Standards-based Reform

Building on the increasing political emphasis on standards-based reform and momentum for increased federal involvement in education, the federal role in education significantly changed again in the mid-1990s. In the 1991 presidential race, Governor William Clinton defeated President George H. W. Bush with the strong backing of the nation's two largest teachers' unions, the National Education Association and the American Federation of Teachers. Employing a "third way" style of governing that involved both liberal and conservative approaches, President Clinton embraced the

ideas of standards favored by both the business community and some educational researchers, such as Marshall Smith, who was appointed under
secretary of the U.S. Department of Education in 1993. Given such ideas,
the Clinton administration developed the Goals 2000: Educate America
Act (Goals 2000), which was ultimately passed by bipartisan votes in both
the House and the Senate.[77] By signing Goals 2000 into law in March
1994, President Clinton cemented the federal role in providing direction
to the standards-based reform movement.

The core provisions of Goals 2000 provided grants to states to develop
their own sets of standards and aligned assessment systems. States were to
use this funding to align curricula and instructional materials with these
standards and develop OTL standards. In addition to providing funding
for the development of standards, Goals 2000 required the federal government to create national content and OTL standards that would serve as a
model for states and could be adopted voluntarily. The law also required
the federal government to create the National Education Standards and
Improvement Council (NESIC) to "certify" state and national content
standards and OTL standards. Moreover, states that received grants were
required to present plans to ED stating how Goals 2000 funds would
be used.

On the basis of the standards-based reform framework established
by Goals 2000, Congress passed the Improving America's Schools Act
(IASA) later in 1994 to reauthorize the ESEA.[78] In addition to restoring
the original Title I name to the ESEA, the IASA conditioned the continuing
receipt of Title I funds on the development of the standards, assessment,
and accountability systems addressed by Goals 2000 in every state. The
IASA also required states to hold schools accountable for the performance
of all students – under the IASA, states were required to test students at
least once in grades three through five, once in grades six through nine,
and once in grades ten through twelve. The IASA further required states to
determine whether schools and districts were making adequate yearly progress (AYP) in raising student performance on state assessments to state
standards, to identify schools that failed to make AYP for two consecutive years for school improvement, and to implement corrective action if
needed. As Goals 2000 was to provide the federal direction for education
reform, Title I of the IASA was to provide the push.

Both Goals 2000 and the IASA, however, faced a series of complex
implementation problems. Soon after the passage of Goals 2000, conservative groups like the Christian Coalition assailed the law for the

unjustified expansion of federal control in education.[79] Particularly after Republicans gained control of both houses of Congress in the beginning of 1995, several conservative members of Congress decried the expanded federal involvement in education and introduced several bills that would either repeal Goals 2000 entirely or eliminate some of its key provisions.[80] A handful of states similarly objected to the strong federal push for the implementation of standards-based reform and accountability policies and threatened to refuse Goals 2000 funds.[81] In this hostile political climate, President Clinton proved unwilling to implement and enforce key Goals 2000 provisions – the Clinton administration failed to convene NESIC and allowed states to continue receiving Goals 2000 funds even if they had not submitted plans to ED.[82] In the face of continuing political pressure centering on the improper expansion of the federal role, President Clinton ultimately signed into law an appropriations bill that set the permanent 1996 budget and eliminated the most controversial language from Goals 2000, including the requirement that states submit school improvement plans. The bill also eliminated NESIC and removed all references to OTL standards from Goals 2000.

With such political pressure and the withdrawal of the federal support for Goals 2000, states failed to meet many of the law's primary require-ments. For example, states used their Goals 2000 funds for a variety of uncoordinated educational activities, such as educational technology, and devoted only a minimum of funding to the development of standards and assessments.[83] As at least a partial result, states lagged far behind their statutory timelines for the development of standards, testing, and account-ability systems under the IASA.[84] Congress ultimately allowed the autho-rization for Goals 2000 to expire in 1999 as the attention of the Clinton administration shifted from Goals 2000 to the upcoming reauthorization of the ESEA and unrelated categorical programs, such as the Reading Excellence Act.[85] But given a heightened climate of partisan politics, Congress failed to reauthorize the ESEA on schedule for the first time in its history, ultimately leaving the reauthorization to the following Congress and the administration of President George W. Bush.[86]

The Implementation of Standards-based Reforms in States in the 1990s

Despite the problems plaguing federal standards-based reform policy under the Clinton administration, states developed their own standards-based reform systems throughout the 1990s. By the end of the 1990s almost all states had begun to engage in standards-based reform in at least some respects, and many had codified a standards-based reform system into law with requirements for testing and accountability. By 1999, forty-eight states plus Puerto Rico and the District of Columbia had developed content standards for student learning.[87] By the 1999–2000 school year, thirty-three states had also set performance goals for schools or districts and were holding them accountable for meeting these goals.[88] Still, the implementation of standards-based reforms in the 1990s proved slow and difficult at best. The quality of standards was inconsistent from state to state and sometimes quite low.[89] Despite the emerging presence of these standards, market pressures generated by the largest textbook buyers, such as Texas and California, largely drove the construction of curricula through the 1990s.[90] The alignment between standards and curricula thus remained uncertain as well.[91]

During this time, the professional development of educators also proved difficult to align with standards. Under the logic of standards-based reform, strong professional development is critical – teachers have often had difficulty altering their instructional practices to conform with the principles and content embodied in standards, and high-quality professional development aligned to standards can arguably facilitate this process.[92] However, various studies have revealed that teachers did not consistently receive high-quality learning opportunities through professional development. As a result of factors such as the range of professional development providers, the professional development opportunities accordingly available to teachers, and teachers' expansive freedom to choose their professional development, teachers generally experienced a range of professional development.[93] As at least a partial result, professional development did not prove sufficient to leverage changes in teachers' practices consistently.[94]

Despite the explosion of standards-based testing and accountability systems, the robust implementation of such systems also proved very difficult during the 1990s. Although almost every state was using a statewide assessment for standards-based reform purposes by 2000, state testing practices raised several concerns. Many state tests were poorly aligned with state standards and, because of the difficulty and expense of developing complex tests, also tended to focus on basic skills instead of the higher-order skills included in some state standards.[95] Many states also faced significant challenges implementing high-quality testing practices for ELL students or students with disabilities – despite the presence of "accommodations," such as additional time to complete a test, it proved difficult to assess the knowledge and skills of such students accurately.[96]

The performance goals for schools under standards-based accountability systems varied widely across states as well – the percentage of students in a school expected to meet basic or proficient standards varied significantly, and schools in some states had to meet multiple performance thresholds (such as maintaining sufficient performance on tests and a sufficient graduation rate). The sanctions for failure to meet these goals similarly varied. For example, state sanctions included mandatory development of improvement plans, mandatory technical assistance, on site audits or monitoring by state officials, probationary status or placement on a state warning list, loss of state accreditation status, transfer or replacement of instructional or administrative status, mandatory provision of options for students to transfer schools, state takeover or reconstitution, and school closure. In the context of developing accountability policies, many states failed to hold districts and schools to the same standards.

Given the difficulties states faced in implementing standards-based reform and accountability policies in the 1990s, classroom practices of teachers proved very resistant to change as well. Although there is some evidence that teachers responded to standards-based reform policies in isolated cases, many teachers' instructional practices remained unaligned to state standards.[97] Indeed, factors such as teachers' prior knowledge, experiences, and orientations, and the collective attitudes toward learning held by educators in schools, have strongly influenced how teachers engage with policies involving new instructional practices.[98] Moreover, although accountability policies appeared to focus educators' attention on student performance and in some cases focused teachers on the performance of minority students (where accountability systems explicitly accounted for minority performance), these policies raised several concerns of their own.[99] For example, these polices often focused teachers on decontextualized test preparation, especially in high-poverty schools where pressure from accountability systems to increase student performance was at the highest.[100]

In line with the inconsistent design and implementation of standards-based reform policies in the 1990s, evidence about the impact of these policies on student performance was very mixed. While nationwide NAEP scores rose slightly in both reading and mathematics during this time, long-term NAEP trends indicate a persistent widening of the achievement gap between high- and low-poverty schools.[101] Still, some statewide assessments seem to support the conclusion that student performance increased under teachers who received high-quality professional development under standards-based reform policies.[102] But at the same time, researchers have drawn very inconsistent conclusions about the impact of accountability systems on student performance on achievement tests during this time. For example, upon examination of test results in Texas and North Carolina, both of which instituted strong accountability systems with consequences for schools and districts in the early 1990s, some researchers found that these states made much larger gains on the NAEP between 1992 and 1996 than other states.[103] However, focusing on the technical aspects of test construction and dropout rates in the particular case of Texas, some researchers concluded that the "Texas Miracle" was nothing more than a myth and that the achievement gap and dropout rate were in fact increasing.[104] Similarly, researchers have disagreed about high-profile achievement gains under high-stakes accountability policies in Chicago.[105] And while the education researcher Brian Jacob found that these achievement gains were real, he also found that student performance gains generally occurred on test items that reflected mastery of basic skills.[106] Indeed, much of the mixed evidence on the effectiveness of standards-based reform and accountability policies likely reflects their uneven implementation through a multilevel governance system and the potentially negative effects of overly strong accountability measures.

In short, building on the wave of reform of the 1980s and the political focus on education as a lever for international economic competitiveness, the federal government and almost every state were swept up in the standards-based reform and accountability movement during the 1990s. Under this movement, the federal and state governments enacted policies aimed at systemically refashioning their education systems around standards that apply to all students and assessments tied to these standards. Yet, in the context of a strong political response to the centralization of educational authority and multilevel federalist governance system that has proven resistant to sudden and consistent change, the design and implementation of these policies varied dramatically. Moreover, as the original emphasis on opportunity to learn the content embodied in standards faded from the political discourse, the focus on student standards and outcomes remained. In this context, the effectiveness of standards-based reform and accountability policies for both equalizing and increasing learning opportunities and ultimately student achievement appears to have been limited at best. Still, the very enactment of policies around standards for all students and the concerted attention that they still receive reflect a transformation in the fundamental principles of education law and policy that continued to underlie almost every major education law and policy reform effort through 2010.

SCHOOL FINANCE REFORM POLICY AND LITIGATION

In the years following the publication of *A Nation at Risk* in 1983, significant shifts were emerging not only in the areas of state and federal legislation, but in state-level litigation as well. School finance reform litigation (and the legislative reforms that responded to this litigation) similarly evolved, often in ways that complemented and even converged with shifts in other education law and policy areas. By the time that the 1990s drew to a close, the underlying focus of school finance reform litigation had dramatically shifted to incorporate issues directly relevant to standards-based reform policies and the underlying idea that all students should receive at least an adequate education.

As discussed in Chapter 4, school finance litigation originally piggybacked on the logic of desegregation litigation and focused on whether school funding should be equalized across school districts. In the first wave of school finance litigation, reformers brought equal protection claims in federal courts. However, in *San Antonio Independent School District v. Rodriguez*, the Supreme Court refused to find that the equal protection clause constitutes a viable basis for equalizing differences in education funding.[107] As also discussed in Chapter 4, plaintiffs in the second wave of school finance continued to rely on arguments based on the idea of equality after *Rodriguez*, but they shifted the venue and legal basis for their arguments. Relying on equal protection clauses in state constitutions, education clauses in state constitutions, or both, plaintiffs continued to argue in state courts that interdistrict spending disparities were unconstitutional. Still, the effectiveness of second wave school finance lawsuits was also limited for equalizing educational funding and ultimately creating more equal learning opportunities for students.

In direct response to these problems, broader changes in the political and economic climate, and new policy initiatives appearing around the country, the third wave of school finance litigation emerged in the late 1980s. In the third wave, plaintiffs continued to bring their claims in state courts but restructured their arguments. Plaintiffs particularly shifted the emphasis of their arguments from educational equality to adequacy and focused litigation to a much greater extent on the education clauses of state constitutions. In addition to arguing that students were due equal educational opportunities, third wave plaintiffs often argued that state education clauses require states to provide the level of funds (or other educational resources) necessary to ensure that students receive adequate or minimally sufficient educational opportunities.

To be sure, the logic of adequacy was present in several school finance cases to some degree through the 1970s and 1980s. As the education law researcher William Koski highlighted, courts in many high-profile school finance lawsuits have long slipped between the logic of equality and adequacy.[108] For example, the logic of adequacy emerged as early as *Robinson v. Cahill*, the school finance case originally decided by the New Jersey Supreme Court in 1973.[109] Moreover, this logic became increasingly prevalent in school finance cases decided subsequently, such as in Washington and West Virginia.[110] Still, *Rose v. Council for Better Education*, decided by the Kentucky Supreme Court in 1989, is generally considered the beginning of the third wave, in which the concept of adequacy truly took off.[111]

Rose v. Council for Better Education

Rose v. Council for Better Education was a turning point for school finance litigation and provided a model of how adequacy arguments could be effectively employed in subsequent school finance cases.[112] *Rose* was filed in a Kentucky state court in 1985 in response to what appeared to be one of the worst state educational systems in the United States.[113] During the 1980s, Kentucky ranked fiftieth among the states in adult literacy and adults with high-school diplomas, forty-ninth in the rate of students continuing to college, and forty-eighth in per pupil expenditures in public schools. Only 68 percent of ninth graders in Kentucky were graduating from high school in four years, and more than 48 percent of the state's population in the Appalachian counties was functionally illiterate. In addition to the apparently low-quality education that Kentucky schools were providing to students, the schools were provided funding in an extremely disparate fashion. The highest-spending district had per pupil spending levels that were approximately two and a half times the per pupil spending levels of the lowest spending district.

The litigation itself was driven by a mobilization of diverse stakeholders that rarely exists at the state level.[114] In 1983, Edward F. Prichard, a high-profile Kentucky businessman, led the formation of the Prichard Committee for Academic Excellence (Prichard Committee), a nonprofit, independent volunteer citizens advocacy organization. This group included a mix of former governors, business leaders, and parents, and it aimed at stimulating a statewide public dialogue among citizens, educators, and the business community on school improvement. To this end, the Prichard Committee studied educational issues and issued recommendations for reform. At the same time, the broader business community in the state was becoming increasingly involved in education. Large businesses in the state and the Kentucky Chamber of Commerce publicly articulated links between education and the poor state of the Kentucky economy and framed the situation in Kentucky as a crisis that needed to be immediately addressed. Media organizations in Kentucky, including the state's two major newspapers, similarly highlighted educational problems and publicized messages from the Prichard Committee. Kentucky Educational Television also broadcasted a statewide forum on education convened by the Prichard Committee that was attended by nearly twenty thousand people. The Prichard Committee further disseminated information to interested individuals across Kentucky with the purpose of enabling recipients to speak in their communities. Building on this momentum, sixty-six poor rural school districts formed the Council for Better Education, which ultimately filed the lawsuit in *Rose* in 1985.

Given the state of education across Kentucky, arguments addressing a minimum sufficient level of education and not just equality seemed to make sense. The plaintiffs in *Rose* accordingly argued that the state was not providing students with adequate educations and that the state's actions were therefore unconstitutional. The plaintiffs based their central arguments on the education clause in the state's constitution: "The General Assembly shall, by appropriate legislation, provide for an efficient system of common schools throughout the State."[115] Because the education clause was vague about exactly what level of education is constitutionally required, the courts needed to articulate a more precise standard. The case wound through the state court system and was eventually decided by the state supreme court in 1989. After considering state constitutional history and expert testimony, the court defined a constitutionally adequate education under the state's education clause by listing seven capacities that Kentucky must provide students with a sufficient opportunity to obtain:

(i) sufficient oral and written communication skills to enable students to function in a complex and rapidly changing civilization; (ii) sufficient knowledge of economic, social, and political systems to enable the student to make informed choices; (iii) sufficient understanding of governmental processes to enable the student to understand the issues that affect his or her community, state, and nation; (iv) sufficient self-knowledge and knowledge of his or her mental and physical wellness; (v) sufficient grounding in the arts to enable each student to appreciate his or her cultural and historical heritage; (vi) sufficient training or preparation for advanced training in either academic or vocational fields so as to enable each child to choose and pursue life work intelligently; and (vii) sufficient levels of academic or vocational skills to enable public school students to compete favorably with their counterparts in surrounding states, in academics or in the job market.[116]

In constructing this definition, the Kentucky Supreme Court had done something remarkably important: it primarily focused not on equality of resources but on the substantive characteristics of an adequately educated student. Moreover, while stating the importance of education for traditional purposes such as promoting democracy, the court anchored its definition of adequacy in the principle of competition in a quickly globalizing world. Indeed, the articulation of the skills and knowledge that an adequately educated student should have was grounded in the type of reasoning present in *A Nation at Risk* and tracked the logic of curriculum frameworks that were beginning to emerge in states like California.

To determine whether Kentucky was providing students with this sort of adequate education, the court not only examined the financial inequities across districts, but also curricula, facilities, student-teacher ratios, and achievement test scores. On the basis of such evidence, the court ruled that Kentucky's system of public schools was not complying with its duty to produce the kind of student required by the state constitution and ordered the state legislature to fix this deficiency. The response of the legislature to the court's order seized upon the possibilities offered by this sort of legal reasoning. In 1990, less than a year after *Rose* was decided, the legislature enacted the Kentucky Education Reform Act (KERA).[117] On one level, KERA looked much like legislation that other states had enacted in response to school finance decisions. KERA provided for many changes in the state funding system to equalize and increase educational funding. On another level, KERA mandated fundamental education reform in the areas of curriculum and school governance. KERA required Kentucky to develop learning standards, a model curriculum framework based on these standards, assessments of student progress in relation to the standards, and accountability measures following the assessments.

KERA particularly provided that the state must develop a performance-based assessment for students in grades four, eight, and twelve, and group student scores on the assessment into the categories of novice, apprentice, proficient, and distinguished. The state was also required to hold schools accountable for the performance of students by creating an "accountability index" for each school. This index was to change annually on the basis of student test scores and several other factors, such as a school's ability to increase attendance rates, decrease dropout rates, decrease retention rates, and increase the proportion of students who make a successful transition to adult life. If a school's accountability index failed to exceed its performance requirement in any given year, a host of consequences potentially awaited a school. Possible sanctions included producing a school improvement plan, receiving the services of an outside "distinguished educator" to assist with planning requirements and implementation, placing certified staff on probation, instituting public school choice, and possibly dismissing all or some of the school's staff.

So, in the context of quickly shifting political rhetoric about the fundamental purposes of education, the Kentucky Supreme Court underscored the importance of economic competitiveness and the skills and knowledge accordingly needed by students. In doing so, the fundamental logic of the *Rose* decision mirrored that underlying much of the standards-based reform movement. Moreover, the *Rose* decision destabilized the educational status quo in Kentucky and provided a sort of political cover for the state legislature to act in a political context that was already ripe for education policy change.[118] Riding this momentum and framed in the broad logic laid out by the *Rose* court, the Kentucky state legislature enacted one of the first standards-based reform and accountability systems in the United States with almost unprecedented speed. In this instant, all the moons seemed to align as governmental institutions, political understandings, and policy advocacy movements embraced the logic of educational adequacy as a core state function.

School Finance Litigation after Rose

In the years immediately following *Rose*, courts ruling in school finance cases in other states quickly adopted the legal logic used by the Kentucky Supreme Court. For example, state supreme courts in Massachusetts and New Hampshire struck down their state school finance systems after explicitly looking to the *Rose* decision and defining adequacy in relation to the capacities articulated in *Rose*.[119] These courts similarly laid out broad orders to which their state legislatures needed to respond. As the legal researcher William Koski noted, three different judicial strategies centered on adequacy have emerged throughout the course of such litigation.[120] First, some courts have articulated a vague and broad qualitative standard tied to producing democratically capable and economically competitive individuals but have provided little guidance to state policy makers. Second, some courts (like the *Rose* court) have identified specific, though abstract, capacities and skills students should have and then ordered their state legislature to provide the necessary resources. Third, as discussed further later, some courts have explicitly tied adequacy with state content standards. In employing these different types of strategies grouped around adequacy, courts have examined a wide array of educational resources, such as funding, qualified teachers and staff, books and supplies, facilities, and lower student-teacher ratios, in addition to prevalent outputs such as student test scores and graduation rates.[121]

In comparison to second wave lawsuits focused on equality, third wave lawsuits focused on adequacy have fared fairly well. According to one count, twenty-one of the twenty-six states in which courts considered adequacy claims had rulings that were favorable to plaintiffs.[122] This comparative success is attributable to several factors. Adequacy arguments are not as politically explosive as equality arguments.[123] The rhetoric of ensuring that all students have minimally sufficient educational opportunities does not directly threaten wealthy districts and undermine local control to the same extent as equality arguments. Along similar lines, adequacy arguments do not immediately raise the concerns about equality-based judicial activism that surrounded federal courts' treatment of equality-driven cases after the initial surge of desegregation litigation in the 1960s.[124] Adequacy arguments additionally are based on constitutional text that explicitly articulates states' duties to provide education systems that function in particular ways.[125] At least at first glance, adequacy also appears easier to define than equality in the school finance litigation context. Some courts, such as the *Rose* court, have examined the constitutional history of education clauses and expert testimony to determine the content of an adequacy standard. Moreover, given that litigation centered on adequacy arguments flowered in the late 1980s and 1990s, some courts hearing adequacy arguments have had legislatively mandated content standards available to flesh out the definition of educational adequacy even more precisely.

Still, school finance litigation centered on the logic of adequacy has entailed several limitations that have limited its power ultimately to change educational conditions in schools. As in second wave litigation, some states under court order to provide students with adequate educations have failed to pass strong legislation restructuring school funding even after years of attempts.[126] Although adequacy litigation appears to have resulted in some increases in educational funding and narrowing in spending disparities among districts, there is little evidence that student learning has consistently improved as a result of court orders to increase spending.[127] Indeed, as adequacy cases were being litigated throughout the states in the 1990s, debates about how and whether "money matters" for improving student learning opportunities raged in the pages of academic journals.[128]

The definitional problems plaguing equality-based school finance litigation have also weakened the effectiveness of adequacy litigation. Adequacy is, by nature, an ambiguous concept that can be defined in any number of ways.[129] As discussed previously, the *Rose* court defined an adequate education in relation to seven primary capacities that students must attain. However, the North Carolina Supreme Court defined an adequate education in terms of four such capacities.[130] On the basis of this definitional ambiguity, some courts have found that adequacy does not involve judicially manageable standards and have therefore labeled determinations of adequacy a "political question" that should be addressed by other governmental branches, such as state legislatures.[131] As some courts particularly argued, it is unwise for judges who lack educational expertise to rule in such a highly complex area without precise guidelines.[132] So, although adequacy litigation has proven more successful than second wave litigation in court, its ultimate effectiveness at addressing the fundamental problem of increasing the learning opportunities of poor and minority students, and students more generally, has been limited.

The Convergence among Adequacy, Standards, and Accountability

In many cases since the 1990s and continuing into the 2000s, school finance litigation directly converged with the standards-based reform and accountability movement. Much of this convergence has been due to a judicial recognition of some of the problems persistently facing adequacy litigation and the implementation of judicial decisions after litigation ended. This convergence has occurred in a couple of different ways. First, faced with the ambiguity of the concept of adequacy and what a state education clause concretely means, courts have looked to state standards for definitional help and ultimately as an anchor for decisions about the adequacy of resources. Second, courts have looked to standards-based reform and accountability policies as tools for ensuing that states spend educational funds effectively when funding changes are instituted. Together, both of these trends reflect not only the shared ideological underpinnings of various reform movements during the 1990s but the beginnings of new institutional arrangements that cut across courts and legislatures as well.

Using standards and aligned assessments to help determine whether students are receiving adequate educations has been the most common way in which the school finance and standards movement have converged.

Although courts have generally shied away from explicitly equating adequacy and state standards, state courts hearing school finance cases have often looked to standards and assessment data linked to standards since the 1990s. For example, in *Leandro v. State of North Carolina*, various North Carolina state courts paid close attention to the meaning of test scores to flesh out whether the state was providing students with an adequate education.[133] The case moved through the state court system in the 1990s, and the state supreme court issued a decision in 1997 just as the "ABCs" system – a statewide standards-based accountability system – was being adopted. While the state supreme court did not decide whether the state had met its duty of providing students with adequate educations, the court gave explicit guidance to lower courts about how this issue should be approached. Emphasizing the greater institutional capacity of the legislature to deal with technical educational issues, the court stated that the "[e]ducational goals and standards adopted by the legislature," the "level of performance of the children of the state and its various districts on standard achievement tests," and "the level of the state's general educational expenditures and per pupil expenditures" are "factors which may be considered on remand to the trial court for its determination as to whether any of the state's children are being denied their right to a sound basic education."[134]

The lower courts complied with the state supreme court's decision and deeply considered these factors. Although Judge Howard E. Manning of the Wake County Superior Court did not explicitly equate standards and adequacy, he did find that student performance on state exams aligned to standards was "highly probative" of whether students were receiving adequate educations. Furthermore, Judge Manning determined that "academic performance below grade level [as defined by Level III on the state test] is a constitutionally unacceptable minimum standard."[135] Given such evidence, Judge Manning ultimately found that North Carolina's education system was unconstitutionally inadequate and that the state needed to ensure that schools had sufficient personnel and instructional programs to provide students with such opportunities. Reviewing the case after Judge Manning's decision, the state supreme court specifically upheld Judge Manning's ruling about Level III as the proper standard for determining adequacy and found that North Carolina had failed to provide its students with adequate educations after examining statewide test score data.[136]

In line with such reasoning, standards have proven particularly useful to courts for determining how much money is required to provide students with adequate educations. Courts in several school finance cases since the 1990s have particularly looked to state standards and accountability systems as anchors for "cost studies" conducted by legislatures or independent consultants. Cost studies are generally aimed at determining the amount and types of resources necessary to provide students with adequate educations. By 2006, more than thirty cost studies had been completed in almost thirty states.[137]

Cost studies have employed four primary methodologies.[138] The "professional judgment" method relies on educational professionals (such as teachers) to determine the resources necessary to produce a specified level of achievement. After determining what resources are needed from these experts, the cost of these resources is determined. The "expert judgment" method relies on literature specifying "effective models" of school reform on the basis of empirical evidence, as recommended by panels of experienced educators and researchers. After determining what school reform strategies are needed, the cost of implementing these strategies is determined. The "successful school districts" method relies on statistical modeling to analyze resources deployed in school districts that are deemed successful via various performance measures. The cost to provide resources to all districts to be successful is then determined. Finally, the cost function method involves econometric modeling of the resources a district needs to spend to reach a performance target, given the characteristics of the school district and student body. This method is arguably the most rigorous of the four methods employed in cost studies, but it requires extensive statewide data sets that are often not available.

Although cost studies are aimed at increasing the scientific rigor of making determinations about school funding and anchoring these determinations in concrete articulations of the skills and knowledge that student should attain, cost studies in education have yielded few clear or consistent answers. Different methods of conducting cost studies have generally resulted in different outcomes.[139] Even cost studies that employ the same general method can entail different assumptions that significantly impact the outcomes of the studies. For example, different cost studies employing the successful school districts method have used different standards for determining what constitutes a successful district, and these differences have in turn influenced recommended increases in financial resources for the same state.[140] Because each state has its own accountability system and set of standards that can dramatically differ from those of other states, the definition of adequacy employed in cost studies has differed significantly across states as well.[141] Indeed, the academic debate about cost studies reflects such inconsistencies. As the school finance expert Deborah

Verstegen argued, "Cost studies provide a rational basis for determining the amount of funding necessary for all children to have a meaningful opportunity for an adequate education. They raise the level of discussion and are a vast improvement over the political decision making and residual budgeting practices of the past."[142] But several researchers have strongly criticized the methods employed in cost studies and have labeled them as unscientific and politicized.[143]

So, using standards to help define adequacy has entailed many advantages for courts in school finance suits. Having concrete standards at hand has helped mitigate persistent judicial fears that creating standards from scratch is not a task that judges have the capacities to manage effectively or should manage, especially given the argument that school finance decisions should be considered political questions.[144] Moreover, because these standards are supposed to be aligned to state assessments, results from these assessments have appeared directly relevant to analyses of whether students have received adequate educations. Instead of examining a seemingly random array of educational inputs and outputs, courts can examine educational outputs that are directly tied to the definition of educational adequacy.[145] The growth of cost studies centered on student performance highlights the utility of this use of standards in school finance litigation.

However, some scholars have highlighted the disadvantages of courts using standards in such a fashion. For example, researchers have criticized this trend because legislatures may not actually intend for standards to be used as proxies for adequacy.[146] In addition, even where state standards have been used, courts still lack the technical and scientific capacities to analyze school finance policies and craft remedial orders effectively.[147] This lack of scientific capacities has proven especially problematic when courts have been presented with competing cost studies – they have had little scientific basis for assessing the merits of different studies. Still, the emergence of standards in school finance litigation at least represents a new judicial approach aimed at improving the courts' role in this litigation. And on a broader level, the convergence of standards-based reform and school finance reform underscores both the restructuring of institutional arrangements between courts and legislatures, and the growing centrality of standards and the idea of adequacy as a dominant force in educational reform.

In addition to using standards to help define adequacy, courts hearing school finance cases have looked to standards-based accountability systems as tools for making school funding more effective. *Campaign for Fiscal Equity v. State of New York*, litigated throughout the 1990s and early 2000s, reflects this sort of convergence between state standards and school finance litigation.[148] In this case, a New York trial court heavily leaned on the state's standards to flesh out the definition of adequacy. While the court declined to base the definition of adequacy entirely on state standards, it deeply examined student data from tests aligned to the standards. Stressing the comparatively greater expertise of other governmental branches in education, the court also ordered the state to decide how to fix the problems. However, upon considering the difficulties involved with simply ordering the state to fix its school finance system, the state's highest court, the Court of Appeals, stated:

> We are, of course mindful – as was the trial court – of the responsibility, underscored by the State, to defer to the Legislature in matters of policy-making, particularly in a matter so vital as education financing, which has as well a core element of local control. We have neither the authority, nor the ability, nor the will, to micromanage education financing. By the same token, in plaintiffs' favor, it is the province of the Judicial branch to define, and safeguard, rights provided by the New York State Constitution, and order redress for violation of them. Surely there is a remedy more promising, and ultimately less entangling for the courts, than simply directing the parties to eliminate the deficiencies, as the State would have us do.[149]

In terms of such reasoning, the Court of Appeals ordered the state to reform the state's system of school funding and management and implement an outputs-based accountability system tied to these reforms.[150] This accountability system was specifically to ensure that students were provided the opportunity for an adequate education.

As the Court of Appeals noted, New York already had in place an accountability system that required the state to identify schools in need of improvement. Moreover, because the Court of Appeals decision came down in 2003, the federal No Child Left Behind Act (NCLB) was already in place, and the state had already begun to implement the standards-based accountability system required under NCLB.[151] Still, the court refused to rule that this accountability system was sufficient to meet the state's constitutional burden – the court indicated that the state must determine the extent to which the accountability system was tied to the definition of an adequate education and modify the system accordingly. Although a panel convened by the state ultimately found that New York's existing accountability system was sufficient, courts hearing school finance cases in at least two other states have also required the implementation of standards-based accountability systems.[152]

In *Williams v. State*, a school finance case originally filed in California in 2000, the litigation concentrated on the accountability system and governance system underlying the state's funding system even more intensely.[153] Given that California was one of the first states to implement standards-based reforms, the state was already implementing a standards-based accountability system. In addition to focusing on traditional sorts of resource disparities, the plaintiffs argued that California had failed to establish minimum standards not for student learning but for educational personnel, instructional materials, and school facilities. Framing the case through an order in the early stages of litigation, the court stated:

> The lawsuit is aimed at ensuring a system that will either prevent or discover such deficiencies going forward. The specific deficiencies that take up so much of the Complaint are evidence of an alleged breakdown in the State's management of its oversight responsibilities ... this case will deal with the oversight and management systems the State has in place to determine if they are legally adequate and whether they are being properly implemented.[154]

Because the case was settled before its conclusion, the court never had an opportunity to issue a formal ruling. Still, under the settlement, California passed laws establishing minimum standards for teacher quality, instructional materials, and facilities, along with an oversight and accountability system to enforce these standards.[155]

This accountability system required the state to perform several new functions. The system required evaluations of school compliance with the standards on instructional materials, facilities, and teacher misassignments and required the results of these evaluations to be published in annual School Accountability Report Cards. The accountability system also included a Uniform Complaint Process that enabled parents, students, teachers, and other individuals to file complaints if they believed that schools were not meeting these standards. Upon implementation, this accountability system appeared to have at least some modest effects on ensuring that students received sufficient textbooks, facilities in good repair, and fully credentialed teachers.[156] So, although no court issued a decision in *Williams* that ruled on the merits of the plaintiffs' arguments, the *Williams* litigation centered on school governance and essentially on creating and enhancing OTL standards as well.

School Finance Litigation beyond Standards and Accountability

In addition to focusing on standards and accountability systems to address problems that have historically plagued school finance litigation, courts began considering a range of other reform strategies in the 1990s. As discussed previously, school finance litigation had dragged on for years in some states, and even where courts had ordered changes in states' funding structures, there was little indication that such orders consistently augmented students' learning opportunities. Specifically stating that they wanted to prevent decades of litigation and more directly boost educational quality, some courts began to consider new strategies in school finance lawsuits – instead of focusing their attention only on funding, courts in at least eight states have ordered the implementation of class-size reduction programs, whole school reforms, and free preschool programs to ensure that additional funding is used effectively.[157]

School finance cases involving the preschool remedy in New Jersey and North Carolina in the 1990s broadly reflect how courts ruling in school finance cases have addressed these types of strategies.[158] In both of these cases, the litigation focused on the adequacy of school funding. However, trial court judges also heard extensive testimony from educational researchers about the value of preschool and deeply examined the scientific evidence underlying preschool.[159] In addition to ordering funding changes, these judges ordered their states to implement free preschool for certain groups of poor or "at-risk" students to ensure that they would receive adequate educations. On one hand, ordering the very specific remedy of free preschool for certain groups of students appeared to be a well-targeted response to problems that school finance litigation has historically faced – this remedy requires funds to be channeled to a promising educational strategy, supported by educational research, that directly affects students' learning opportunities.[160] Moreover, this approach entails precise orders about what states should do, thus arguably avoiding one of the major pitfalls historically plaguing school finance reform.[161]

On the other hand, the preschool remedy appears to have raised some significant concerns. The research base underlying preschool, especially with regard to the capacity of the program to be effectively implemented at scale, is very complex, and researchers disagree about many conclusions that this research offers.[162] Moreover, the courts in New Jersey and North Carolina that considered the preschool remedy ignored many of these complexities when they crafted their decisions and remedies and considered preschool programs very inconsistently. For example, while the trial court in New Jersey ordered full-day preschool for three- and four-year-olds, the New Jersey Supreme Court found that half-day preschool was sufficient. And while the trial court in North Carolina determined that preschool must be implemented in the state to ensure that students receive adequate educations, the North Carolina Supreme Court found that "a single or definitive means for achieving constitutional compliance ... has yet to surface from the depths of the evidentiary sea." [163]

Given both the state of the evidence underlying preschool and the problems courts have faced considering this evidence, similar issues have likely been present when courts have considered other types of particular educational reforms in school finance litigation. Compared to the other specific reforms ordered in school finance lawsuits, preschool has the most extensive research base. [164] There is room for courts to act even more inconsistently when they examine other educational interventions, such as class-size reduction. Indeed, even though some of the most ardent critics of the idea that there is a strong relationship between funding and student performance have concluded that money likely matters if it is spent wisely, the educational researcher Stephen Raudenbush has specifically argued that our knowledge about how to use educational resources is "woefully lacking." [165]

Moreover, there remains very little consensus about the cost-effectiveness of popular educational reform strategies. While some "model" programs, such as preschool programs implemented with unusually high levels of resources and staff expertise, have been found to be effective for boosting students' learning opportunities, it is very difficult to scale up such programs because similar levels of resources and expert staff are not widely available. [166] And while researchers have underscored that we are learning more about the various types of strategies that can increase educational opportunities, [167] they have also emphasized that there are few studies analyzing cost-effectiveness or the comparative cost efficiency of such strategies. [168] As a result, several prominent educational researchers have argued that we need a significantly better research base for constructing productive education policy. [169] So again, although the detailed consideration of scientific evidence and experimentation with new institutional arrangements seems to have held promise for making more effective educational funding decisions, the convergence of several familiar issues has continued to pose serious problems. Courts' limited abilities and dispositions to consider scientific evidence, along with the state of the evidence and ambiguous legal frameworks in school finance cases, limited courts' potential to govern educational funding effectively throughout the 1990s and beyond.

CONCLUSION

The 1980s and 1990s marked a pivotal period for the concept of equality in education law and policy and for large-scale education reform more broadly. In the preceding decades, the concept of equality in large-scale education law and policy largely centered on equal educational opportunities to provide for a more robust democracy and enhanced social mobility. While this vision of equality focused on the education of African American students in the early days of desegregation, it expanded to encompass other racial minorities, in addition to other groups such as students with disabilities. Given its roots in the civil rights movement, this vision of equality specifically centered on protecting educational rights, providing financial support for the education of underserved groups, and mobilizing centralized governmental institutions to take such actions.

However, the early 1980s marked the ascendancy of adequacy. Like equality, adequacy is a concept focused on all students. But instead of ensuring sameness of students, adequacy involves some sort of minimum level that all students must at least meet. Also like equality, adequacy can be construed in an almost limitless number of ways. Throughout the 1980s and 1990s, adequacy came to mean several things, including a very minimal level of sufficiency, excellence, and the varying qualities of educations embodied in standards. But unlike equality, adequacy could arguably be attained through less top-down and centralized methods of governance. Instead of ensuring that all students receive exactly the same opportunities, adequacy permits large differences between opportunities or outcomes so long as they do not fall below a certain threshold. At least in theory, centralized control is not quite as necessary to accomplish this goal.

Several factors appear to have influenced the rise of adequacy across governmental institutions. Adequacy is a concept that blurs into equality at a number of different points, and several education law and policy reform efforts throughout the 1980s and 1980s reflect persistent devotion to a traditional logic of equality. During this time, the improvement of learning opportunities for poor and minority students continued to provide much of the impetu s for school finance reform. Indeed, this logic has never come close to disappearing completely from school finance reform litigation and has particularly surfaced with the consideration of reform strategies aimed at low-income or "at-risk" students. And although the notion of OTLs eventually disappeared from federal education policy in the mid-1990s, it played an essential role in the early theories of standards-based reform and accountability. As O'Day and Smith emphasized, requiring students to perform at specific levels without ensuring they had the opportunities to do so would be unfair and possibly harmful.

The significant economic and technological changes during the late 1970s and early 1980s also played a significant role in the rise of adequacy.

In light of such changes, U.S. politics in the 1980s increasingly focused on the neoliberal strategy of decentralized governance and the goal of economic international competitiveness. This emphasis strongly drove the political framing of major education law and policy reforms. In the 1980s, high-profile governmental institutions articulated links between education and the economy in communications such as *A Nation at Risk* and the decision in *Rose v. Council for Better Education.* Instead of focusing on equalizing students' opportunities, reform efforts increasingly concentrated on driving up student learning across the board to increase economic productivity of states and the United States as a whole. In line with the growing influence of business principles on education law and policy, accountability for performance against standards to ensure results also emerged as a dominant blueprint for reform. Given the rhetorical implications of education for the U.S. economy as a whole, the federal government began to focus states on this sort of reform in even Title I of the ESEA, which has historically been the flagship law federal law for addressing civil rights era concerns.

At the same time, other factors appear to reflect reasoned responses to problems that plagued educational reform in the past. Especially given the promise of specificity in standards, adequacy (whether a minimal level of sufficiency or excellence) appeared to have a more concrete definitional anchor than equality. Accountability mechanisms seemed to have the promise of making decisions about educational funds more effective and efficient by focusing school systems on outputs and providing incentives that could overcome weak political will to engage in reform. Judicial orders to states to enact specific reforms in the context of school finance litigation similarly appeared able to increase efficiency and sidestep the political intractability of state legislatures when they were not given specific orders.

The reordering of governance arrangements similarly seemed to respond to the historical problems of federally centered mandates, rights-based protections, and increasingly tight regulations that had dominated the previous decades. The focus on reform at the state level in the excellence movement, standards movement, and school finance movement made sense as a move that entailed centralized governance at a level that could theoretically still adapt to local conditions. The reordering of horizontal governance arrangements between courts and legislatures in school finance litigation responded to institutional weaknesses that courts had explicitly identified, such as courts' lack of scientific expertise. Indeed, these new institutional relationships appeared to offer much promise for leveraging more effective education reform because they accounted more effectively for the strengths and weaknesses of federal and state courts and legislatures. Where courts act as destabilizing institutions that broadly manage reform and rely on other governmental branches to craft more concrete standards, they are arguably at their most effective.

The dramatic expansion of the federal role in education during the late 1980s and 1990s further reorganized traditional governance arrangements. Building on the wave of reform of the 1980s and the political focus on education as a lever for international economic competitiveness, the nation's governors created the national education goals, and Congress passed laws such as Goals 2000 and the IASA. Indeed, although the federal role had long been expanding, education became more of a national priority under the Clinton administration as these laws focused on facilitating the creation of standards in every state to ensure that all students could perform adequately. To be sure, these laws were enacted and implemented in a political and legal system that has traditionally been hostile to federal control in education. As such, the adoption of national model standards was made voluntary under Goals 2000, and in the context of a hostile political climate, key provisions of Goals 2000 and the IASA were not robustly implemented. Still, such moves reflect the increasing political legitimacy of standards and the concept of adequacy more generally, as well as the notion that education reform at the broadest level needed to move closer to the educational core of schools and classrooms.

Indeed, a focus on teaching and learning appeared to be a cure for the seemingly ineffective focus on raw inputs that had dominated education law and policy reform efforts through the 1970s. Standards by nature focus on student learning. As a result, they at least implicitly entail visions of effective teaching. This focus on classroom practices emerged in both federal and state policy. Laws such as Goals 2000 and the IASA reflected a fundamental shift away from the federal government's traditional role of providing resources and rights-based protections to focusing states on student learning and performance. School finance litigation similarly drove closer to the classroom level. Especially given the problems with primarily financial solutions to improving student learning and the lack of state responsiveness to court orders, courts began to focus on particular reform strategies that seemed to hold some promise of more effectively improving student learning. Such moves highlight a recognition that, while deep attention to inputs far from the educational core of schools is likely a necessary component of effective education policy, such attention has proven to be insufficient.

Yet, this new emphasis on adequacy opened up a new set of even more difficult problems. Instead of moving students from place to place, ensuring that students have books, and modifying cash flows, many education law and policy reforms shifted to ultimately requiring changes in teachers' practices. This type of change involved influencing not only teachers' skill and will, but also their disposition toward reform. Moreover, this change was to occur not just in a handful of selected local sites but at scale. So, laws and policies focused on this sort of reform did not deal directly with individuals but flowed through a large multilayered governance system, sometimes crossing the vast distance from the capitol to the classroom. In this context, standards-based reform unsurprisingly yielded huge variability in teachers' practices.

The emphasis on adequacy entailed several other new problems as well. The implementation of testing practices at scale proved very costly and was riddled by issues affecting their validity. In addition, the knowledge base underlying specific educational reforms aimed at leveraging adequacy is often very complex, contested, and ultimately limited, as highlighted by the research on the reforms ordered by courts in school finance cases. As a result, laws and policies resulted in devoting significant time and money to reforms that ultimately had little impact. Complicating such matters, most governmental decision makers (including but not limited to courts) lack the educational expertise to understand the strengths and weaknesses of such reforms. As these problems have emerged, the focus on OTLs largely faded from the political discourse. Many large-scale education reforms accordingly were based on an overly narrow focus on outputs. As such, while there appeared to be some promise for effective reform by the end of the 1990s, there was no indication that deep reform was happening at scale in classrooms and some evidence that reforms heavily focused on outputs were in fact having negative effects.

Nevertheless, much of the education reform that happened during the 1980s and 1990s simply could not have emerged under a regime focused purely on equality. It is very difficult to equalize various factors that contribute to student learning opportunities, such as per pupil expenditures and textbooks. But given the almost limitless influences that are situated outside schools, it is virtually impossible to equalize "softer" factors, such as the teaching that transpires in the classroom and ultimately student learning. Even if construed as a very minimal level of sufficiency, adequacy may be unreachable at scale. But this notion inherently allows room for many different types and levels of student performance.

So, like equality, the concept of adequacy is a creature of its history. On one hand, it grew from the cracks that had opened in the equality regime in the 1970s. Adequacy bled into the concept of equality at several junctures and directly responded to problems that laws and policies centered on educational equality had historically faced. On the other hand, adequacy was shaped by the shifting politics and broad understandings of educational purposes that characterized the early 1980s and beyond. Adequacy thus became a concept that involved an overlapping but ultimately different set of possibilities than a more traditional version of equality for education reform. In practice, the rise of adequacy not only meant that education law and policy needed to involve different requirements for school systems; it also meant that the fundamental governance structures of education needed to shift as well.

6

Developments in Local Control

While the rise of standards-based reform and third wave school finance litigation in the 1980s and 1990s represented a fundamental change in large-scale law and policy reforms involving educational equality, another change was lurking at the same time – one built around the notion of local control. As discussed in Chapters 3 and 4, local control has often been positioned against the idea of equality in education law and policy. In the early stages of desegregation, southern states and districts employed "freedom-of-choice" plans, ostensibly empowering parents to decide where their children attended schools, to avoid integrating schools. The Supreme Court explicitly cited the value of preserving local control when it began to withdraw from desegregation in *Milliken v. Bradley*, and the Supreme Court and state courts emphasized the value of local control when refusing to overturn states' school finance schemes. In doing so, these governmental institutions backed away from the centralized governance structures that appeared necessary to effect greater educational equality.

In the 1990s, however, the principle of local control began to intersect with equality in education law and policy in several different ways. On one hand, local control continued to serve as a central justification for courts to back away from traditional notions of educational equality. Driven by a trio of cases decided by the Supreme Court in the 1990s, the value of local control served as a primary legal reason for federal courts to withdraw from desegregation cases around the country. As at least a partial result, the levels of segregation in many schools returned to those at the time when *Brown v. Board of Education* was decided. Yet, local control has also served as one of the fundamental principles driving the movement in law and policy for school choice that began to sweep through the United States in the 1990s, primarily under the banners of charter schools and tuition voucher programs.

While charter school policies ultimately became much more common than those authorizing vouchers, they have key features in common. Charter school laws are generally passed at the state level and enable governmental institutions to contract with (or grant a charter to) an independent school operator.[1] Charter school operators then receive a specified sum of money for each student who attends the school and, in exchange for meeting goals specified in their charters, have significant control over key issues such as personnel, budget, and curriculum. Laws or policies authorizing vouchers provide students with publicly funded tuition certificates that may be redeemed at participating public and private schools, which often include both religious and nonreligious private schools.[2] Both charter school and voucher policies accordingly allow students and their parents some degree of choice over which school to attend and place a significant amount of power at the individual and school levels. Given that there are a variety of other governance structures that emphasize local control and choice, such as policies authorizing magnet schools, structures focusing on school choice have become highly visible and widespread.

Despite this emphasis on local control in school choice efforts, these reforms are deeply rooted in the idea of educational equality. The school choice reforms are based partly on the idea that a politically unresponsive, centralized bureaucracy cannot respond effectively to serious educational problems facing underserved groups. Under this logic, the only way to provide more equal and high-quality education is by decentralizing education. This decentralized structure arguably empowers and encourages educators to employ their expertise without the challenges of the traditional public school administrative and regulatory environment. Moreover, this theory relies on the market rather than governmental institutions (such as school districts) to improve weak schools through competition. While school choice has been cited by politicians and advocates as promoting important public values like international competitiveness, the school choice movement is also founded on empowering private individuals to take control of their own fate.

In order to examine local control in education law and policy in the 1990s and beyond, this chapter first examines the emergence of school choice strategies as a major type of large-scale education reform. To this end, the movement to institute voucher programs in various states is first examined. This examination focuses on the spread of laws involving vouchers, the underlying politics of this movement, the judicial treatment of voucher programs, and the empirical evidence on the effectiveness of vouchers. The discussion of voucher policies closely attends to *Zelman v. Simmons-Harris*, a case decided by the Supreme Court that addressed the constitutional issues raised by public institutions providing funds for students to attend private, religious schools.[3] This chapter then turns to the spread of policies focused on the authorization of charter schools in states, with a similar focus on the politics of the charter school movement, the judicial treatment of charter schools, and empirical evidence of their effectiveness. Finally, the cases decided by the Supreme Court in the 1990s and 2000s that relied on the logic of local control to justify the almost complete judicial withdrawal from desegregation are discussed to show how the notion of local control has continued to operate in a more traditional fashion.

THE EMERGENCE OF SCHOOL CHOICE

In the 1990s, tuition voucher programs and the authorization of charter schools emerged in states as major education reform strategies. While voucher programs had most of the momentum in the beginning of the decade, it quickly became clear that the creation of charter schools was a much more politically and legally feasible reform. Throughout the 1990s, charter schools accordingly proliferated around the United States as a decentralizing brand of reform that served as a counterpoint to the standards-based reform and accountability movement spreading through the states at the same time. By 2010, charter schools were present in a large majority of states and highlighted by President Barack Obama as one of the most promising types of education reform strategies.[4]

Despite this surge of school choice strategies in law and policy, some forms of school choice had long been present in the United States.[5] For example, students had long attended private schools without public support, and magnet schools for academically gifted students had provided public school options to students and parents besides traditional neighborhood schools for decades. Magnet schools were an especially prevalent form of public school choice before the 1990s. These types of schools generally have specialized elements that differ from those of traditional public schools, including different curricula or pedagogical approaches. In response to court orders to desegregate (or to avoid judicial oversight), various districts created magnet schools in the 1970s and 1980s to attract students from other neighborhoods to attend magnet schools in racially homogeneous neighborhoods.

Beginning as early as the 1960s, calls to decentralize increasingly large and consolidated school districts arose in several sectors. Grassroots groups supporting minority rights called for decentralized decision making over schools to restore power to parents and communities, and business groups called for decentralizing school authority to increase efficiency and innovation. These two forces visibly joined in 1988 with a policy that created "local school councils" (LSCs) in Chicago Public Schools.[6] Each public school in Chicago had its own LSC, which assumed a significant amount of governance authority over issues such as principal hiring and school budgeting for its school. Moreover, both the business and grassroots communities supported the initial creation of LSCs, and eight of eleven members of each LSC were to be parents and community representatives.

Since the 1980s, business groups and neoliberal political organizations have driven the public discourse surrounding school choice and particularly charter schools.[7] For example, the Democrats for Education Reform (a political action committee supported largely by hedge fund managers) and the Progressive Policy Institute (the policy arm of the Democratic Leadership Council) have consistently pushed for school choice. Groups that provide services like charter school management and alternative training for teachers and school leaders have similarly pushed for school choice, including New Leaders for New Schools, Knowledge Is Power Program (KIPP), Green Dot charter networks, Teach for America, and the New Teachers' Project. While these organizations have generally associated themselves with liberal politics, right-leaning groups have heavily supported school choice as well. In line with the sort of deregulatory approach espoused under the Reagan administration, right-leaning think tanks that espouse free-market philosophies, such as the American Enterprise Institute, Cato Institute, and Hoover Institution, have proliferated and generated policy papers that consistently support school choice. With continuing support from different fronts, school choice became one of the most high-profile education reform strategies in the 1990s and continued to expand through 2010.

School Vouchers

When voucher policies first began to appear as a viable sort of education reform, they reflected a seemingly unlikely fusion of political ideas. On the most basic level, voucher policies are a form of school choice that entails alternative mechanisms for funding students' educations. Under a voucher system, students and their parents can choose which school to attend, and the government (generally a state government or school district) routes funding to follow the student to that school. Under the least restrictive voucher systems, students can choose to attend public, nonreligious private, and religious private schools and the government pays for at least a certain amount of the tuition. However, some voucher programs have limited the types of schools that are eligible to receive vouchers. Because of the difficult legal and political issues raised by including religious private schools in public voucher programs, these more limited programs have excluded religious private schools.

Although voucher systems gained most of their traction in the early 1990s and beyond, voucher proponents attempted to institute these systems at the state level from at least the 1950s. Many of the freedom-of-choice schemes enacted in southern states in the wake of *Brown v. Board of Education* provided students with tuition grants that could be spent at nonreligious private schools.[8] Although the Supreme Court effectively deemed such schemes insufficient for desegregation purposes in *Green v. New Kent County Board of Education*, new coalitions of voucher proponents emerged by the late 1960s.[9] Grounded in a distrust of the government's capacity to guard the interests of underserved groups, these proponents supported vouchers as a way to protect minority students from failing bureaucratic big city school systems. These efforts particularly focused on the value of community control over schools. Such logic intersected with that of free-market enthusiasts who supported the idea of vouchers because of the market that would be created by treating students and parents as consumers who could make choices between public and private schooling options.[10]

In the 1970s, voucher policies also began to gain support from leaders of religious dominations such as Catholicism who aimed at providing educations that accorded with their religious beliefs.[11] Such support for voucher programs was particularly strong in states such as New Hampshire and Wisconsin. Although these efforts ultimately did not gain a strong political foothold, vouchers began to look increasingly viable in the wake of the political changes of the early 1980s. As discussed in Chapter 5, the support for deregulation, individual freedom, and private markets dramatically increased in the early 1980s and provided fertile political soil for vouchers to take hold.[12]

By the late 1980s, voucher policies accordingly began to gain significant political traction as reform options in various states legislatures. In 1988, Governor Tommy Thompson (R-WI) spearheaded the introduction of the first comprehensive private school voucher proposal in the Wisconsin state legislature.[13] The program was eventually passed on the second attempt in 1990 when Governor Thompson worked with a Democrat, Representative

Annette Williams. In 1991, this program began as the Milwaukee Parental Choice Program (MPCP). The program was limited to students in Milwaukee, restricted student attendance to nonreligious private schools, and was quite small when it began – in its first year, the program served only ten schools and 341 students. Moreover, the program provided grants only to students in families with incomes that did not exceed 175 percent of the federal poverty line and capped student participation at no more than 1 percent of total district enrollment. However, state legislation expanded the program in 1995 to include religious schools and raised the student participation cap to 15 percent of district enrollment. As a result, this program radically expanded by the end of the decade. In the 1998–9 school year, 6,085 students participated in the program.[14]

Comprehensive voucher systems that provided tuition grants for students to attend religious private schools also emerged in two other major locations during the 1990s. In 1995, the Ohio state legislature enacted the Cleveland Scholarship and Tutoring Program (CSTP).[15] This program was enacted after Republicans took control of the state House of Representatives, which put Republicans in control of both houses of the state legislature and the governorship (under the Republican governor George Voinovich). The implementation of CSTP began in the 1996–7 school year and applied only to students entering kindergarten through second grade who lived inside the boundaries of the Cleveland school district. CSTP eventually expanded through eighth grade as the students initially enrolled in the program progressed from grade to grade. Students and their families were given tuition vouchers of either 75 percent or 90 percent of private school tuition, with the larger amount reserved for families with incomes below 200 percent of the federal poverty level. Both private schools in district boundaries and public school districts surrounding Cleveland could apply to participate, and tuition vouchers were awarded by lottery with priority given to low-income families. Notably, fifty-three private schools in Cleveland participated during the first year. Most of these schools were religious Catholic schools. By the 1999–2000 school year, the program included fifty-six schools and more than thirty-seven hundred students. The program also included a tutoring component that provided assistance to any students who chose to remain in public school and similarly provided more funds for students from families with greater financial needs.

In 1999, Florida adopted the other major voucher policy of the 1990s, the Opportunity Scholarship Program (OSP). This program was the country's first voucher program implemented on a statewide basis, and it provided tuition vouchers to students who attended schools that failed to perform adequately on the basis of student test scores. If a school was labeled as failing for any two years during a four-year period, the students in the school became eligible to receive tuition vouchers that could be redeemed at private schools. Efforts to enact vouchers during the 1990s emerged in several other states as well, such as Pennsylvania and New Mexico. However, these efforts were ultimately defeated in state legislatures.[16] Bills were also proposed in the U.S. House of Representatives and Senate that would have involved federal support for students to attend religious private schools through devices such as tax-free educational savings accounts.[17] However, in part because of the issues raised by public support of religious institutions, Congress refused to adopt these proposals. Still, given the popularity of vouchers, some states (such as Maine and Vermont) have enacted voucher policies that allow students to attend only nonreligious private schools.

Zelman v. Simmons-Harris and the Aftermath

Although vouchers gained significant political support throughout the 1990s, they also attracted vocal critics. While some critics focused on vouchers' potentially negative effects on the public school system (such as the potential to siphon money away from public schools and undermine social cohesion promoted by public schools), others focused on the problems arguably raised by the public funding of religious organizations. This hostility toward vouchers quickly led to litigation. Immediately after the passage of the Cleveland voucher program in 1996, a group of Ohio citizens challenged the law authorizing the program in state court. When the Ohio Supreme Court eventually considered the case, it found that the program violated certain procedural requirements of the Ohio state constitution.[18] In response, the Ohio legislature remedied these problems and left the basic structure of the program intact. In 1999, reformers sued again in federal court in *Zelman v. Simmons-Harris* on the grounds that the program violated the establishment clause of the First Amendment of the U.S. Constitution. The establishment clause provides, "Congress shall make no law respecting an establishment of religion" and has generally been used as the basis for litigation aimed at enforcing the "separation of church and state."[19] Both the district court and the Sixth Circuit Court of Appeals found that the voucher program was unconstitutional because it violated the establishment clause.[20] However, the Supreme Court held that the program was constitutional by a 5–4 vote in 2002.[21]

In order to analyze the constitutionality of the voucher program under the establishment clause, the Supreme Court looked to precedent from several earlier establishment clause cases it had decided. On the basis of an analysis of such cases, the Court found that the establishment clause prevents a state from enacting laws that do not have a secular purpose or have the effect of advancing or inhibiting religion. According to the majority, there was no dispute that the voucher program was enacted "for the valid secular purpose of providing educational assistance to poor children in a demonstrably failing public school system."[22] The Court accordingly turned to the question of whether the program had the proscribed effect of advancing or inhibiting religion. After conducting an analysis of establishment clause cases involving school funding issues, the Court found that a governmental aid program is constitutional under the establishment clause where it is "neutral with respect to religion, and provides assistance directly to a broad class of citizens who, in turn, direct government aid to religious schools wholly as a result of their own genuine and independent private choice."[23]

Having articulated this test, the Supreme Court proceeded to an analysis of whether the Cleveland voucher program offered "true" private choice. To answer this question, the Court noted several aspects of the program: the program provided assistance to a broad class of individuals (parents who reside in Cleveland) without reference to religion; the program permitted the participation of all schools in the district; adjacent public schools had the opportunity to participate; program benefits were available to parties regardless of their religion; the only state preference in the program was for low-income families, who would receive more assistance; and there were no financial incentives to skew the program toward religious schools. On the basis of this evidence, the majority of the Court found that the voucher program in fact offered individuals "true" choice. Justice Souter notably disagreed in his dissent. He pointed out that because 82 percent of participating private schools were religious and 96 percent of scholarship recipients enrolled in religious schools, the program favored religious schools. However, Justice Rehnquist countered in the majority opinion that 81 percent of private schools in Ohio were religious as well and that there were several factors driving these statistics that were not related to religious favoritism in the program. Moreover, emphasizing his view of the efficacy of Cleveland's program, Justice Thomas stated in his dissent that vouchers would enhance the life prospects of African American students who want to escape failing inner city schools.[24] On the basis of such legal and policy reasoning, the Court found that vouchers are constitutional under the establishment clause.

The Supreme Court's decision in *Zelman* elicited strong responses from critics and supporters. Critics focused on the public funding of religious schools assailed the Court's logic and broader shifts in establishment clause jurisprudence that prefigured its opinion in *Zelman*.[25] Other critics voiced arguments about how the decision would destroy public schools by allowing market-based education policies to channel money toward private schools.[26] However, others celebrated the Court's decision and predicted that vouchers would quickly spread across the nation. U.S. Secretary of Education Rod Paige favorably compared *Zelman* with *Brown v. Board of Education* because it encouraged a "new civil rights revolution and usher[ed] in a 'new birth of freedom' for parents and their children everywhere in America."[27]

Despite such praise, states enacted school voucher laws only to a very limited extent after *Zelman*. Laws permitting students to attend private schools with tuition vouchers on a statewide basis were passed in Arizona, Colorado, Indiana, Ohio, and Utah, and laws permitting students in particular cities to attend private schools were passed in Washington, D.C., and Louisiana (permitting vouchers only in New Orleans after Hurricane Katrina devastated public school facilities).[28] These laws mirrored the major characteristics of the voucher laws that had been enacted in the 1990s – they generally focused funding on families with low incomes. While only some of these laws included caps on the number of students who were eligible to participate, very few students in the United States actually used vouchers. In 2006, only about fifty thousand students across the country used them.[29]

There are several reasons that vouchers did not spread as some had predicted. Implementing voucher programs entails several administrative and financial burdens for school districts due to factors such as the need for districts to engage in monitoring processes and provide information to the public, the need to provide students with transportation services, and the lack of available seats in schools that accept vouchers.[30] Voucher programs also failed to generate strong and widespread political support. In 2005, at least sixteen states considered bills authorizing voucher programs, but only two states passed such bills (with one of these bills focused on expanding the Cleveland voucher program throughout Ohio).[31] This political opposition proved especially strong in suburban areas because voucher laws made it possible for low-income students to enter wealthy suburban districts, thereby arguably decreasing the competitive advantage held by students whose families reside in those areas.[32] Even voucher laws that were successfully enacted faced strong political opposition. For example, Utah voters repealed the state's voucher law before its implementation began.[33]

The language of state constitutions has also presented significant barriers for the spread of voucher laws. Several state constitutions include "Blaine Amendments," or provisions that explicitly prevent the government from providing funds to religious schools. According to one count, sixteen state constitutions prohibit direct or indirect aid to religious schools, while fourteen more states prohibit direct aid without explicitly referencing indirect aid (such as aid provided through the provision of tax credits for educational expenses).[34] Focused on the language of this type of provision in its state constitution, the Arizona Supreme Court found its statewide voucher program unconstitutional.[35]

At least fourteen state constitutions also have provisions that require the establishment of a "uniform" system of public schools.[36] This type of provision was at the center of litigation in *Bush v. Holmes*, a case decided in 2006 by the Florida Supreme Court.[37] In this case, the court considered the legality of Florida's OSP and found that the program was unconstitutional under the state constitution's uniformity clause. The majority indicated that because the OSP funded schools subject to less regulation than public schools, the program prevented the school system from being uniform. The court particularly focused on the fact that the OSP permitted public funds to be allocated to private schools that did not receive direct oversight from the state and were not required to implement standardized state curricula and teacher certification requirements. Although the Wisconsin Supreme Court reviewed a similar argument and found that the Milwaukee voucher program was permissible under the Wisconsin constitution, commentators have argued that the reasoning of *Bush v. Holmes* could be replicated by other courts in states that have uniformity provisions.[38] Finally, at least six state constitutions contain provisions that delegate authority to control public schools to local school boards and districts.[39] The Colorado Supreme Court found its state's voucher law unconstitutional under this type of provision in 2004 in *Owens v. Colorado Congress of Parents*.[40] In at least a partial response to such barriers (legal and otherwise), a handful of states have implemented "neo vouchers," which support families that send their children to private schools through the provision of tax credits for educational expenses.[41]

Despite the significant attention vouchers have received, there has been little compelling empirical evidence about their effectiveness at equalizing or improving students' educational opportunities at scale. Much of the ultimately limited research on vouchers programs has found that vouchers have a very small and limited benefit at most on student achievement.[42] Although vouchers may increase competition among public and private schools and facilitate greater parental engagement, the focus of increased competition and engagement is often on school features other than academic quality.[43] In contrast to the claims of many critics, vouchers also do not appear to segregate students or "skim the cream" of the top students from low-performing schools.[44] So, although voucher programs do not appear to harm students and schools, these programs also do not appear to be effective at leveraging equal educational opportunities or performance.

In short, voucher programs emerged in states in the early 1990s by capitalizing on favorable political sentiments toward the free market and the value of the individual that flowered in the early 1980s, as well as the potential to equalize educational opportunities by removing schooling from centralized bureaucracies. Strongly reflecting the values of local control and the empowerment of individuals who had been poorly served by the schools, vouchers held promise as a policy tool under which traditionally opposed political groups could rally. Indeed, voucher programs were continually advocated by proponents (and criticized by opponents) largely on the basis of political preferences rather than empirical evidence. However, especially given the ways in which vouchers programs resulted in the channeling of public funds to religious institutions, these programs ultimately faced strong political and legal pushback, and their spread has been limited at most. By 2010, only Louisiana, Ohio, Wisconsin, and Washington, D.C., operated traditional voucher programs.[45] Still, the fundamental emphasis of voucher programs on decentralizing educational authority to improve the education of underserved students held significant political promise that would be integrated into other reforms.

Charter Schools

As it became clear that vouchers did not have the political backing to spread across the United States, the charter school movement quickly emerged as a major reform effort with similar philosophical underpinnings. Like the voucher movement, the charter school movement focused on decentralizing educational decision-making authority. As noted in the beginning of this chapter, state laws authorize the operation of charter schools. As a result, the legal requirements governing charter schools can differ significantly across states.[46] Still, charter schools are generally created when a governmental entity contracts with, or grants a charter to, an independent school operator under a state's charter school law.[47] Although rules for attending charter schools are also inconsistent across states, students generally decide whether they want to attend a charter school and choose which school to attend.[48] Charter schools then receive a certain amount of money for each student who attends the school, and these schools maintain significant control over key issues, such as personnel, budget, and curriculum, in exchange for meeting goals detailed in the charter.[49] Charter schools generally receive funds from the school districts in which students reside but ultimately receive less money per pupil than public schools in the same areas. Many states also have caps on the number of charter schools allowed.

A wide range of constituencies has supported state legislation authorizing charter schools.[50] As a result of the choice and flexibility inherent in charter school policies, business-oriented proponents (including both conservatives and the "New Democrats" of the 1990s) have argued that charter schools lead to innovation and efficiency. As a result, charter schools arguably generate competitive effects that drive up the quality of both charter and traditional public schools.[51] After it became clear that voucher policies would not be enacted at a federal level, many conservatives also supported charter school policies as a second-best option. As discussed previously, a range of conservative, market-oriented think tanks and service-oriented education groups have strongly supported charter schools. As with vouchers, some liberal advocacy organizations have also supported charter schools because they arguably empower minority groups through the decentralization of authority away from unresponsive governmental entities. Albert Shanker, the president of the American Federation of Teachers, supported charter schools because he believed that they could increase teacher professionalism and autonomy by removing burdensome administrative oversight from these schools. Given the presence of independent school operators, the increased flexibility given to these operators, and the extent to which the logic of charter schools draws from that of privatization, charter school laws arguably blur the distinctions between public and private schools, and charter schools have been accordingly labeled as "quasi-public."[52]

Once legislation authorizing charter schools appeared, charter school laws spread quickly around the United States. Minnesota enacted the first law authorizing the creation of charter schools in 1991; California soon followed in 1992. By 1996, more than half the states and Washington, D.C., had charter school laws in place.[53] The federal government also became formally involved in the charter school movement with the enactment of the

Public Charter Schools Program, spearheaded by the Clinton administration. This discretionary grant program was integrated into the Elementary and Secondary Education Act (ESEA) in 1994 and originally appropriated $6 million to support the planning, development, and initial implementation of charter schools in states with charter school laws.[54] In 1998, Congress reauthorized this program with the Charter School Expansion Act, which was appropriated $145 million for FY 2000.[55] By 2011, there were more than fifty-four hundred charter schools serving more than 1.7 million students in forty-one states.[56] However, charter schools continued to be funded at the lower rate on average of 61 percent of their traditional public school counterparts.

Despite the popularity and political viability of charter school laws, the debate surrounding charter schools has been highly politicized. Because charter schools can be seen as a direct threat to traditional public schools, several critics have argued that charter schools represent an unjustified and harmful privatization of education.[57] Moreover, conflicting research of suspect methodological quality about the effectiveness of charter schools has been reported in major news outlets and cited by both charter school proponents and opponents in policy debates.[58] As such, the political scientist Jeffrey Henig argued that advocates at each extreme of this debate "wave studies to support their position and claim that their proponents are willfully perverting the canons of social science methodology."[59] Yet, many policy makers have continually framed charter schools as engines for social mobility and international economic competitiveness.

Further highlighting the extent to which charter school legislation has proven controversial among different sectors, several interested parties have challenged the legality of charter schools through litigation. Courts in states including California, Michigan, and New Jersey have considered whether charter schools are in fact "public" schools under state constitutions and whether charter school laws unconstitutionally authorize the allocation of public funds for private purposes.[60] In these cases, state supreme courts have universally found that charter schools are indeed public and laws authorizing charter school funding are constitutional.[61] Plaintiffs in Ohio alternatively argued that the state's charter school legislation violates the education clause of the state constitution, which requires a "thorough and efficient" system of common schools throughout the state.[62] However, emphasizing the benefits of local control of schools, the Ohio Supreme Court found that the state's charter school law appropriately emphasizes flexibility, choice, customization, and experimentation to ensure that children receive an adequate education. At least one federal court has also upheld the constitutionality of a charter school law resulting in a school district's decision to close a noncharter public school with a large Hispanic population because it could not find any discriminatory intent.[63] In addition to ruling on the fundamental legality of charter schools, some courts have addressed the power of authorizing bodies to govern charter schools. Courts have found that inadequate instructional materials, fiscal mismanagement, unsafe conditions, or an inability to deliver an adequate educational program should be overseen and remedied by authorizers.[64] Courts have also upheld the rights of authorizing bodies to refuse, revoke, or authorize charter schools for similar reasons.[65] On the basis of such decisions, it appears unlikely that courts will invalidate charter school legislation.[66]

As with vouchers, the significant political support received by charter schools has appeared to outstrip the available evidence.[67] Empirical research on the effectiveness of charter schools to boost student performance has revealed that some charter schools have produced students with high test scores, such as those in the high-profile national charter school network Knowledge Is Power Program.[68] But at the same time, many charter schools have been riddled with organizational and personnel problems and have produced students with very low test scores.[69] When examined in the aggregate, it appears that charter schools have produced students who, on average, perform the same as or slightly lower than traditional public school students on standardized tests.[70] Still, parents who send their children to charter schools generally have been happier with their schools than parents who send their children to traditional public schools.[71] Despite such evidence, it has remained very difficult to make robust comparisons between charter schools and traditional public schools on the basis of student achievement. A variety of statistical issues, such as the selection bias related to differences among students who attend charter schools and those who do not, have proven very difficult to eliminate conclusively from most large-scale analyses of charter schools.[72]

The evidence has been similarly mixed about the extent to which charter schools facilitate innovation in schools. Given charter schools' comparative autonomy, charter school proponents have argued that these schools will change the basic operations of schools.[73] As a result, charter schools will arguably create competition among schools, which in turn will increase the overall quality of schooling.[74] While charter schools have emphasized certain innovations, such as extended time in school and the use of technology to facilitate distance learning, there in fact has been little going on in charter schools that has not been piloted within the traditional public school system.[75] Although some researchers have found that charter schools have positive competitive effects, other researchers have found that there are negligible effects.[76] And although some have criticized charter schools for screening out racial and ethnic minorities and poor students, and for contributing to increasing segregation in schools, empirical research generally has not reflected these claims in the aggregate.[77]

In short, charter school legislation appeared at approximately the same time as voucher legislation but has spread much more widely. Like vouchers, charter schools strongly reflect the values of local control and the empowerment of individuals to act as consumers to make their lives better. And although charter schools receive public funding, they are free from traditional methods of democratic control over schooling. However, charter school legislation has proven to be a much more politically feasible brand of reform that can garner the support of liberals and conservatives without running into the pitfalls raised by including truly private and religious schools in school choice programs. Yet, especially given the way in which charter school policies blur the distinction between public and private schools, the charter school movement has faced significant pushback in the public sphere and even in court. And although the empirical evidence on the effectiveness of charter schools has been mixed at best, charter school legislation has only spread and strengthened. So, while charter school policies have proven to be a politically appealing reform strategy, there is little evidence that they can serve as a "magic bullet" for dramatically improving learning opportunities for individual students around the United States as many of its proponents claim.

THE SUPREME COURT RETURNS TO DESEGREGATION

Although school choice policies such as charter school and voucher programs have relied on the principle of local control to effect educational reform, this principle has also been used to halt federal court oversight of desegregation in the 1990s and beyond. Returning to desegregation litigation after largely withdrawing since the 1970s, the Supreme Court decided a series of three cases in the 1990s that clarified when a desegregating school district should be declared unitary – *Board of Education v. Dowell*, *Freeman v. Pitts*, and *Missouri v. Jenkins*. In doing so, the Court repeatedly highlighted the notion of local control, which had played a prominent role in *Milliken v. Bradley* and *San Antonio Independent School District v. Rodriguez*. Moreover, the Court's 2007 decision in *Parents Involved in Community Schools v. Seattle School District No. 1* made it very difficult for districts that were deemed unitary or never under a desegregation decree to diversify their student bodies. Together, these cases have freed school districts from continuing oversight by district courts and have allowed significant resegregation in schools around the country.

Board of Education v. Dowell, decided by the Supreme Court in 1991, marked the Court's reinsertion into desegregation litigation.[78] Like many other desegregation cases of the 1990s, *Dowell* had been going on for decades. The case began in 1961 when African American students and their parents sued the Oklahoma City school board to end de jure segregation in its public schools. In 1972, a federal district court ordered the school board to implement a busing plan to desegregate the school district. In 1977, the district court stopped enforcing the plan when it found that the school board had complied with the plan, the plan had worked, and the school district had achieved unitary status. Although this decision of the district court was not appealed, the school board passed a new student assignment plan in 1984 that relied on neighborhood assignments for students and weakened busing requirements. Reformers returned to court, arguing that the district had not in fact achieved unitary status and that the new student assignment plan would actually resegregate schools – under the plan, eleven of sixty-four elementary schools would have had greater than 90 percent African American enrollment, twenty-two schools would have had greater than 90 percent white enrollment plus other minorities, and thirty-one schools would have been "racially mixed."[79]

After the case moved back and forth between the district court and the Tenth Circuit Court of Appeals, the Supreme Court decided its first major desegregation case in more than a decade in 1991. In a 5–3 decision (with one justice taking no part in the decision), the Court underscored that federal supervision of school systems was intended only as a temporary measure for past discrimination. In doing so, the Court heavily emphasized the importance of local control over schools and cited cases where this principle had also played an important role, such as *Milliken* and *Rodriguez*. On the basis of this logic, the Court stated that the Constitution does not require the "Draconian result" of "judicial tutelage for the indefinite future" and that the vestiges of past discrimination only needed to be eliminated "to the extent practicable."[80] Once a district had complied with this requirement, the district should be declared unitary and local control should be restored by dissolving judicial oversight.

In *Freeman v. Pitts*, the Supreme Court continued to clarify the requirements for districts to be declared unitary.[81] This case was first decided in 1969 when a district court ordered the DeKalb, Georgia, school system to desegregate. In 1986, the district court found that the school system had successfully met four of the *Green* factors through strategies such as shifting attendance zones and the strategic placement of magnet schools – the court found that the school system was unitary with regard to student assignments, transportation, facilities, and extracurricular activities.[82] When the court made this finding, there was still significant racial imbalance in many DeKalb schools. For example, 50 percent of the African American students attended schools that were more than 90 percent African American, while 27 percent of the white students attended schools that were more than 90 percent white. However, much of this racial imbalance appeared due to demographic change. In 1969, 5.6 percent of the students in the DeKalb school system were African American, while 47 percent of the students in the school system were African American by 1986. Reasoning that such imbalances were due to demographic change and stating that the school system had accomplished the maximum practical desegregation, the district court ruled that it would order no further relief in those areas. However, the court stated that the vestiges of a dual school system remained in the areas of resource allocation and teacher and principal assignments.

After reviewing the logic of the district court's decision, the Eleventh Circuit Court of Appeals found that the district court had erred by considering the *Green* factors as separate categories. According to the Eleventh Circuit, a school system must achieve desegregation with regard to all of the *Green* factors at the same time in order to be considered unitary and a school system may not shirk its duties by pointing to racial imbalance in the district.[83] However, in an 8–0 decision, the Supreme Court concluded in 1992 that school districts do not need to satisfy all the *Green* factors at the same time. Once a district has satisfied a *Green* factor, partial and final withdrawal of judicial control with regard to that factor is warranted. The Court particularly highlighted that racial balance is not to be achieved for its own sake but only pursued when it has been caused by a constitutional violation. Thus, school districts are not required to cure racial imbalance caused by demographic factors. Likewise, federal district courts are not required to make annual adjustments to the racial composition of student bodies once the original duty to desegregate has been accomplished (unless another violation is found). The Court reasoned that it is "beyond the authority and beyond the practical ability of the federal courts to try to counteract these kinds of continuous and massive demographic shifts. To attempt such results would require never-ending supervision by the courts."[84] Building on this analysis, the Court framed the return of school districts to the control of local authorities as the ultimate objective.[85] In doing so, the Court reemphasized the notion from *Dowell* that courts must evaluate whether school systems have complied in "good faith" with desegregation decrees and that segregation in districts must be "eliminated to the extent practicable."[86]

Missouri v. Jenkins, the last of the three major desegregation cases decided by the Supreme Court in the 1990s, also focused on ending judicial oversight over school districts.[87] This case had been before a district court since 1977 and centered on the efforts of the Kansas City, Missouri, school district to desegregate its schools. In 1985, the district court determined that segregation had caused a systemwide reduction in student achievement in Kansas City schools and ordered the implementation of a wide range of education programs for all students in the district. For example, the court ordered the school district to reduce the student–teacher ratio, implement full-day kindergarten, expand summer school offerings, and implement a state funded "effective schools" program that consisted of annual cash grants to each school in the district.

Because the district enrollment was 68.3 percent African American and there was no interdistrict violation, the court aimed at attracting white students into Kansas City schools instead of ordering additional student reassignments. To this end, the court approved a comprehensive magnet school and capital improvements plan in 1986. Under this plan, every senior high school, every middle school, and one-half of the elementary schools were converted into magnet schools to provide greater educational opportunities to students in the district and draw nonminority students from private schools and the suburbs. Beginning in 1987, the court also ordered salary increases for instructional and noninstructional staff in the district. From the time these plans were implemented through the early 1990s, the cost ran into the hundreds of millions of dollars for the district and state.

Given these expenditures, Missouri challenged the ongoing implementation of these programs. The state particularly argued that it had achieved partial unitary status with respect to the quality of education programs already in place. The district court rejected the state's argument, largely because it found that student achievement scores had not risen enough to warrant a finding that the school district had achieved partial unitary status with regard to the quality of education programs. The Eighth Circuit Court of Appeals affirmed the district court's opinion and looked favorably on its reasoning that the success of the quality of education programs must be measured by their demonstrable effects on student test scores and not the mere implementation of these programs.[88]

However, in a 5–4 decision, the Supreme Court found that the district court had improperly decided. Reviewing the history of major Supreme Court desegregation decisions and especially highlighting *Dowell* and *Freeman*, the Court reiterated that the ultimate inquiry is whether the school district and state have complied in good faith with the desegregation decree and whether the vestiges of past discrimination have been eliminated to the extent practicable. The Court again highlighted the value of local control and emphasized that federal supervision of local school systems was intended as a temporary measure. Framed by this logic, the Supreme Court found that the district court acted improperly by trying to attract nonminority students into the school district through salary increases that would theoretically boost the quality of Kansas City educational programs – in line with *Milliken*, the district court was not justified in ordering programs designed to attract students from outside the school district because there was no interdistrict violation.

Given the combination of *Dowell, Freeman,* and *Jenkins,* district court supervision of desegregation districts began to disappear quickly in the 1990s and continued to do so through the 2000s. For example, eighty-nine school districts in the southern states of Alabama, Florida, Georgia, Louisiana, Mississippi, North Carolina, and South Carolina had their desegregation decrees lifted from 2004 to 2009 alone.[89] As a partial result, schools and districts began to resegregate rapidly.[90] While the share of African American students in majority white schools around the United States was about 44 percent in 1988, it fell to about 30 percent by 2001.[91] In the 2003–4 school year, 38 percent of African American students and 39 percent of Latino students attended schools that had at least 90 percent minority enrollment.[92] Some states had much more highly segregated school systems. For example, 41 percent of African American students in California attended schools that had at least 90 percent minority enrollment at this time, and the average Latino student attended a school with a 19 percent white population.[93] This rapid resegregation was occurring just as the Latino population in the United States was quickly growing. As of 2000, Latino public school enrollment was more than seven million: almost triple what it was in 1968.[94] Indeed, as the data discussed earlier reflect, Latino students have been facing similar patterns of segregation to African American students.

Such resegregation has arguably had serious undesirable effects. In 2007, the National Academy of Education prepared a comprehensive report analyzing a range of research on racial diversity in schools into inform the Supreme Court's decision in *Parents Involved in Community*

Schools v. Seattle School District No. 1, which is discussed later.[95] This report concluded that while white students are generally not hurt by desegregation efforts, African American student achievement can be enhanced by integrated schooling (although the magnitude of this influence can dramatically vary). Moreover, diverse environments are likely to support improved intergroup relations, and under some circumstances and over the long term, experience in desegregated schools increases the likelihood of greater racial tolerance and intergroup relations among adults. So, while the research is complex and nuanced and does not simply indicate that desegregation by itself is an effective strategy for equalizing or increasing students' educational opportunities, the research does suggest that desegregation can yield substantial educational and social benefits.

Parents Involved in Community Schools v. Seattle School District No. 1

While *Dowell, Freeman,* and *Jenkins* heavily emphasized the value of local control to hasten the dissolution of court oversight of desegregation, the Supreme Court doubled back on this reasoning in *Parents Involved in Community Schools v. Seattle School District No. 1 (PICS)*, a case decided in 2007.[96] In an effort to combat the school resegregation that was occurring around the country as a result of the desegregation plans that were being lifted and shifting housing patterns in school districts that were never under desegregation decrees, many school districts implemented a range of strategies aimed at integration. These strategies included carefully constructed attendance zones, plans allowing students to transfer to a school in which they are not of the majority race, plans allowing students to transfer to a school on the basis of their socioeconomic status, and the creation of magnet schools to attract students of different races.[97]

PICS involved two school districts that adopted such strategies. The school districts of Seattle, Washington, and Jefferson County, Kentucky, voluntarily adopted student assignment and school choice plans that involved students' race to diversify the racial makeup of schools. The Seattle school district, which had never been subject to court-ordered desegregation, had a series of four "tiebreakers" to allocate slots to high schools if the schools were oversubscribed. The first tiebreaker was whether a student had a sibling in the desired school. The second tiebreaker was based on race. The Seattle plan classified students as "white" or "nonwhite" and used these racial classifications to ensure more integrated schools if the racial composition of a school differed significantly from the overall composition of the district. The third tiebreaker gave priority to students who lived closer to the school, and the fourth tiebreaker was a lottery.

The Jefferson County school district used a similar student assignment plan involving a racial classification. The school district had been under court-supervised desegregation until a federal district court declared the school district unitary in 2000. The school district then adopted a plan heavily involving school choice and magnet schools. A fundamental requirement of the plan was that all nonmagnet schools must maintain a minimum African American enrollment of 15 percent and a maximum African American enrollment of 50 percent. At the elementary school level, a student could not be assigned to a school if the school had reached the "extremes of the racial guidelines."[98] Although different federal district and circuit courts decided the cases involving Seattle and Jefferson County, the cases were consolidated when they went before the Supreme Court because of their similar issues.

The Supreme Court's decision about the use of race in the choice systems was highly divided but ultimately struck down the plans used in both districts. A four justice "plurality" opinion, written by Chief Justice John Roberts, was accompanied by two concurring opinions and two dissenting opinions. The plurality opinion applied the equal protection framework at play in cases such as *San Antonio Independent School District v. Rodriguez* to decide whether the use of a racial classification in the school choice plans was constitutional.[99] The plurality particularly employed strict scrutiny to decide whether the plan was "narrowly tailored" to effect a "compelling governmental interest." The opinion first concluded that "diversity" was not a compelling governmental interest. The opinion here notably differed from the Court's decision in *Grutter v. Bollinger*, a case focused on the constitutionality of affirmative action programs that was decided a few years earlier in 2003.[100] In *Grutter*, the Court found that diversity can be a compelling governmental interest in the higher education setting. However, according to the plurality in *PICS*, diversity is more important in higher education because this setting requires expansive "freedoms of speech and thought" and occupies a "special niche in our constitutional tradition."[101]

The plurality further found that the choice plans in *PICS* were not tailored to "achieving a degree of diversity necessary to realize the asserted benefits."[102] According to the plurality, the plans were only designed to achieve racial balancing; they were not designed to achieve any concrete educational or social goals that flow from racial diversity. The Court further articulated explicit concerns that racial balancing has "no logical stopping point."[103] Notably, Justice Kennedy only joined part of the plurality's opinion and thus left key issues unresolved. Justice Kennedy particularly joined the plurality's conclusion that the choice plans were not narrowly tailored because he was concerned about the mechanical formula used to classify students. However, Justice Kennedy also concluded with four dissenters that diversity could be a compelling governmental interest.

After the Supreme Court decided *PICS*, it was quickly criticized by several observers. Some focused on the Court's treatment of empirical research in the case. For example, the education law researcher Michael Heise highlighted that Justices Thomas and Breyer discussed the same empirical research referenced by the litigants and *amicus curiae* briefs on the educational and social effects of diversity, but they did so to reach very different legal points.[104] Moreover, as the education law researcher Danielle Holley-Walker noted, *PICS* "represents a marked detour from the local control of schools as an important theme championed by the Supreme Court in previous K-12 desegregation cases."[105] In this case, the Court decided to strike down the decisions made by local school districts instead of ensuring that they were provided with more control over education.

Taken together, the Supreme Court's decisions in the 1990s virtually signaled the end for federal court oversight of desegregation. As *PICS* reflects, the Supreme Court also made it more difficult for districts to take active steps to integrate racially schools that are not under court supervision. As at least a partial result, schools have begun to resegregate rapidly across the country. Grounded in cases like *Milliken* and *Rodriguez*, the Court relied heavily on the idea of local control to justify the withdrawal of federal courts in this area. While the concept of local control was also central to the school choice movement of the 1990s at exactly the same time, the judicial treatment of local control in these cases sharply contrasts with the school choice movement – where local control was used to justify school choice reforms, this concept was used to block continuing education reform in the case of desegregation as opposition to seemingly never-ending judicial oversight grew. So, at least in the context of desegregation, the notion of local control and perceived value of decentralized governance brought a halt to the most long-standing type of large-scale education reform focused on equality.

CONCLUSION

The principle of local control drove both the expansion and the contraction of large-scale law and policy reforms involving educational equality in the 1990s and beyond. On one hand, some governmental institutions in the 1990s framed local control as the enemy of efforts to leverage greater educational equality. In *Dowell, Freeman,* and *Jenkins,* the Supreme Court repeatedly cited the principle of local control as the primary reason to lift judicial oversight over school districts' desegregation efforts. In these cases, the Court faced the issue of how difficult it is to desegregate schools sustainably when they are located in racially isolated neighborhoods. Indeed, as the costly implementation of desegregation plans for a seemingly unlimited amount of time appeared necessary to achieve long-standing integration in many schools, the Court subtly shifted its focus to whether districts had complied in "good faith" and "to the extent practicable" with the duty to desegregate.

In sharp contrast to the logic underlying the Supreme Court's treatment of desegregation in the 1990s, the school choice movement was partly founded on the idea that greater local control can enhance educational equality. Grounded in the logic of neoliberal politics that flowered in the 1980s, the school choice movement was based on the idea that schools can offer innovative programs if they are freed from bureaucratic control. Parents and students can then choose to attend these schools if the schools' offerings meet their needs. Under this structure, traditional public, private, and charter schools would compete with each other, and the quality of all schools would rise as the weak schools shut their doors. It was precisely this logic and the promise of greater educational equality that bound advocate groups for minority rights with more market-oriented groups in support of both vouchers and charter schools. Although vouchers never spread to the extent their supporters had hoped in the wake of *Zelman* (largely because of vouchers' religious implications), some of the core political underpinnings of vouchers propelled the quick spread of charter schools. This focus on the potential of greater local control to improve schools for minority students was in fact a major focus of Justice Thomas's concurring opinion in *Zelman.*

Despite the convergence of desegregation and school choice around the principle of local control, the institutional arrangements and concrete approaches to reform in both movements were quite different. Desegregation was never an easy reform to implement effectively. There were strong political, legal, administrative, and financial barriers to overcome, to name but a few. However, the problem at hand was ultimately the concrete one of educational access through populating school buildings with students of certain races. At certain points in time (such as the late 1960s and early 1970s), governmental institutions were quite effective in their desegregation efforts. And when the federal courts began to withdraw from desegregation as a result of changing Supreme Court jurisprudence, segregation in schools increased. Although modern empirical evidence about school and neighborhood demographics has revealed that desegregation litigation was largely a failure in creating sustainably integrated schools, desegregation has been a reform focused on educational equality at least involving major outcomes that are fairly concrete.

School choice, however, is ultimately aimed at improving the quality of what actually goes on in schools and classrooms. Like reforms such as standards, accountability systems, and modern school finance lawsuits, school choice is focused on improving teaching and learning at scale. Where many of these other strategies increase governmental control over what goes on in districts and schools, school choice strategies treat education reform as more like a "black box" that can arguably avoid the difficulties other reforms have faced. Instead of directly changing what students learn and how teachers teach, school choice reforms are founded on the notion that individuals and local organizations can and will innovate if given space and freedom from governmental oversight. Given the difficulty of directly instituting reforms in a variety of differently oriented schools at scale, treating schooling as a black box that will naturally adapt to local context is attractive. However, as with other reforms, there is very limited evidence that school choice strategies have consistently had their intended effects and equalized the learning opportunities that students receive. These strategies have even been criticized for exacerbating existing inequalities through processes such as "skimming the cream" from public schools by attracting the best public school students to private or charter schools.

While there is not strong evidence that school choice strategies have in fact diminished the equality of learning opportunities for students of different races or socioeconomic classes, such criticisms point to perhaps the most fundamental difference between school choice and other large-scale reform strategies aimed at educational equality. Most of the other strategies discussed throughout this book reflect the idea that education is a public good. These strategies clearly differ with regard to the content of this good. For example, some strategies frame education as supporting democracy, while others frame education as supporting international economic competitiveness. School choice draws in part from such logic, but this type of reform also reflects the idea that education can be a private good. Charter schools and private schools that students attend through tuition vouchers are free from traditional methods of democratic control and at least in part treat education as a good to be attained by individuals that can help them economically or otherwise as they compete with each other throughout their lifetimes. This philosophy is precisely what drove some of the litigation aimed at school choice, as plaintiffs argued that charter schools were not actually public. Indeed, many have argued that charter schools are "quasi-public" schools at best.[106] This type of private good logic lies at the heart of the very theory of action of school choice and drives a vision of educational equality that accordingly differs from that of many other large-scale reforms.

Notably, the focus on individuals instead of groups in *PICS* reflects this conception of education as well. At first glance, *PICS* does not seem to square with the logic of local control espoused by the Supreme Court in cases like *Milliken* or *Rodriguez*. Given the value the Supreme Court has placed on local control, one might have expected the Court to support locally crafted strategies to integrate schools, such as the racially weighted school choice plans that were at issue in *PICS*. However, *PICS* also involved the new legal and conceptual wrinkle of dealing with school districts that were no longer or never were under court order to desegregate. And although the *PICS* decision was sharply fragmented, it ultimately reflects a view of educational equality that is more focused on the equality of individuals without regard to their race – unlike earlier desegregation decisions that were focused on equal educations for groups of students and often for sweeping public purposes, *PICS* was focused on erasing the construct of race from the treatment of educational placement decisions and did not clearly recognize the value of the public purpose of diversity.

So, the large-scale educational reforms of the 1990s and beyond that are explicitly rooted in the notion of local control reflect a quickly changing relationship between conceptions of governance structures and the notion of equality. Grounded in the neoliberal politics that flourished in the 1980s, decentralized governance and individual competition powered the ascendancy of local control as a core concept in educational reform strategies focused on equality. In the hands of the Supreme Court, this concept followed the well-trod path that had been laid decades earlier to dismantle the centralized judicial oversight of desegregation – perhaps the most fundamental governmentally driven reform focused on educational equality. But this concept also drove the quick rise of school choice as a pervasive educational reform strategy built on the theoretical power of decentralized authority, competition, and the ability to adapt to local conditions. While the fundamental theory of action and philosophical underpinnings of school choice dramatically differ from those of other major reforms of the 1990s (such as standards-based reform), its implementation has proven similarly problematic as it has demonstrated little capacity to improve schools significantly at scale. Moreover, the legislative focus on actually improving the quality of educational institutions and not simply protecting the rights of individuals and groups accords with that of other concurrent education reforms. In this way, educational reforms emerging in the 1990s and beyond reflect the changing conception of equality as one focused on the difficult challenge of fundamentally transforming schools and districts into highly performing educational institutions.

7

The Continuing Expansion of the Federal Role

The beginning of the twenty-first century marked another period of significant expansion for the federal role in education law and policy. With the passage of No Child Left Behind (NCLB) in early 2002 and the American Recovery and Reinvestment Act (ARRA) in 2009, Congress built on the reforms of the 1990s to intensify the federal focus on education reform. While the federal role had been expanding for decades, the president and Congress became perhaps the most influential drivers of large-scale education reform in the United States during the early 2000s. In doing so, federal education reform intensely focused on instituting structural changes in educational governance arrangements through tools such as standards, testing, accountability, and school choice.

Underlying this expansion in the federal role was a fundamental shift in educational politics that positioned the federal government as a broadly acceptable and even appropriate institution for increasing the academic quality of schools. Several factors drove this political shift, including recognition of some problems that had faced federal involvement in education in the past, the continuing rhetoric of international economic competitiveness, and changing attitudes toward the efficacy of the federal government in education. On the basis of such logic, federal education reform became increasingly centered on student performance on standardized tests and strong sanctions for schools if student performance was not sufficiently high. At the same time, federal law also began to embrace strategies aimed at enhancing schools' capacities to improve, such as increasing teacher quality and attempting to ground education reform more strongly in scientific knowledge and evidence. Still, federally driven education reform remained tied to more traditional notions of equality and the preexisting educational governance system. Indeed, the laws and policies that structured the U.S. education system in 2010 and beyond have continued to reflect a hybridized approach toward adequacy, equality, and the governance system needed to support such goals.

This chapter examines large-scale education reform in federal law and policy from the early 2000s through 2010. First, the passage, design, and implementation of NCLB are discussed, with a particular emphasis on the changing relationship between the state and federal governments, the accountability mechanisms aimed at improving school quality, and the implementation problems NCLB has faced. Next, the federal education policies enacted in the wake of NCLB are discussed, including the reauthorization of the Individuals with Disabilities Education Act (IDEA) and the Education Sciences Reform Act (ESRA), which has required certain educational decisions to be grounded in "scientifically based evidence." Building on these discussions, this chapter turns to the ARRA and focuses on the increasing specification of school reform strategies by the federal government and changes in the policy instruments used to leverage such reform. Together, this constellation of reforms depicts a much changed landscape of education law and policy that has been primarily defined not by individual and group rights but by the educational systems and structures that were built to promote the demonstrated academic performance of all students.

NO CHILD LEFT BEHIND

On January 8, 2002, President George W. Bush signed into law NCLB, a reauthorization of the Elementary and Secondary Education Act (ESEA). While the underlying logic of NCLB was grounded in the standards-based accountability systems enacted by states in the 1990s and federal laws such as Goals 2000 and the IASA, NCLB entailed more stringent demands on states than its predecessors. In exchange for the continuing receipt of Title I funds, NCLB required states to enact standards, implement annual tests aligned to these standards, and subject schools that did not perform adequately to a range of potential sanctions. NCLB thus represented a significant expansion of the federal role in education and the basis for a more centralized education system focused on educational outcomes and adequacy. Given the persistent conservative objections to the expansion of the federal government into schools, one would not necessarily expect such a law to have been enacted under the watch of a Republican president. Yet, the Republican president George W. Bush led the charge to pass NCLB and forged a bipartisan consensus about the desirability of the law. As such, the passage of NCLB reflects a much changed understanding of the federal role in education reform.

The Passage of No Child Left Behind

The end of the 1990s and early 2000s reflect significant shifts in perceptions about the appropriateness and effectiveness of the federal government to leverage large-scale educational change. Although the ESEA was due to be reauthorized in 1999 while President William Clinton still held office, partisan divisions prevented the passage of a law. Following the highly politicized problems surrounding the implementation of Goals 2000 and the IASA, the attention of the Clinton administration largely turned to the enactment of unrelated categorical programs and the ESEA reauthorization.[1] The Clinton administration succeeded in spearheading the passage of policies such as a class size reduction program and the Reading Excellence Act, which provided grants to states to improve reading instruction in poor and low-performing districts and schools.[2] However, the Clinton administration's proposal for the reauthorization of the ESEA, which focused on reforms such as decreasing class sizes and modernizing classrooms, failed to gain traction.[3]

Several other bills aimed at reauthorizing the ESEA and containing ideas that were eventually co-opted for the design of NCLB were also proposed in Congress under the Clinton administration.[4] Republicans sponsored or cosponsored many of these bills. After Bob Dole's defeat by President Clinton in the 1996 presidential campaign, many Republicans realized that the electorate did not strongly support their position on the federal role in education.[5] Indeed, the ideas underlying the bills subsequently proposed by both congressional Republicans and Democrats overlapped on several points as many of their ideas stemmed from politically savvy think tanks that had begun to emerge as important voices on the policy scene, including the Progressive Policy Institute (the policy arm of the Democratic Leadership Council) and the conservatively oriented Heritage Foundation.[6] These bills generally focused on the need to increase school accountability in order to make the U.S. education system more efficient and support U.S. economic international competitiveness. The bills were also based on several common strategies, such as including disaggregating test score data for different subgroups of students, setting performance goals for schools with sanctions for poor performance, and allowing students to transfer out of low-performing schools. Still, Congress failed to reauthorize the ESEA under the Clinton administration and simply extended funding for the IASA without changing its requirements.

The election of President George W. Bush in 2000 provided the needed push for forging a bipartisan consensus about the federal role in education.

Before becoming president, Bush was the governor of Texas. As governor, Bush oversaw the continuing implementation of education reform policies focused on standards, annual testing of students, disaggregation of student data on the basis of race and ethnicity, and consequences for students and schools that failed to perform adequately. As these policies were being implemented, student test scores for African American and Latino students quickly increased, prompting some to label the Texas school reform as a "miracle."[7] While some observers cited reasons other than the reforms for the increases in test scores and labeled increased educational performance in Texas a "myth," Bush's ostensible success politically positioned him as a successful education reformer.[8] Building on this reputation, Bush articulated a vision for a strong federal role in education throughout his presidential campaign.[9] He decried the "soft bigotry of low expectations" in education and trumpeted reading as the new civil right. Bush particularly argued that Title I had failed poor and minority students and that there needed to be more accountability in education to remedy this problem. Bush also successfully lobbied to eliminate language from the 2000 Republican platform calling for the abolition of the U.S. Department of Education (ED). Still, Bush adhered to some conservative principles in education, such as enhancing school choice and local spending flexibility.

Immediately after Bush won the 2000 presidential election, he began to fulfill his promise of making education one of his top priorities by releasing an outline of his education reform plan, titled No Child Left Behind.[10] This blueprint reiterated that the federal role needed to be reformed – it emphasized the disappointing results of spending billions of federal dollars on education while falling short in increasing and equalizing student performance. It also called for a federal role centered on holding schools accountable for improving student performance to boost the efficiency and effectiveness of schooling. Congressional debate on the reauthorization of the ESEA soon commenced on the basis of this blueprint and continued even in the months following the terrorist bombing of the World Trade Center in 2001. Throughout this debate, several members of Congress reiterated the need for a more efficient federal role and a strong education system to support U.S. international economic competitiveness.[11] Significant debate in line with traditional partisan positions occurred as well. For example, Democrats pushed for dramatically increased funding, while Republicans worried about unwarranted federal intrusion and the setting of a de facto national curriculum.[12] Still, the Bush administration was able to discipline the far right wing of the Republican Party effectively and forge an agreement focused on trading accountability for flexibility and increased financial resources.[13] As a result, NCLB was passed by an overwhelming bipartisan consensus that would lead to a new era of federal involvement in education reform.[14]

The Design of No Child Left Behind

As a reauthorization of the ESEA, NCLB was a sweeping law that broadly set the federal direction in education reform. NCLB was explicitly designed "to ensure that all children have a fair, equal and significant opportunity to obtain a high-quality education and reach at a minimum, proficiency on challenging State academic achievement standards and state academic assessments."[15] NCLB thus embraced the principles of standards, assessment, and accountability that had emerged in state reforms through the 1990s, Goals 2000, the IASA, and various bills that had surfaced in Congress at the end of the 1990s and early 2000s. NCLB accordingly conditioned states' receipt of Title I funds on states' agreements to adopt standards and assessments aligned with these standards, and to hold schools and districts accountable for their performance on these assessments.[16]

NCLB particularly required states to adopt standards in reading, mathematics, and science that described at least three levels of student achievement – basic, proficient, and advanced.[17] States were required to administer tests in reading and mathematics at least once annually to students in grades three through eight and one grade in high school.[18] The law also required states to report the results of student performance on these tests for every school publicly and disaggregate the student performance data by certain subgroups, such as low-income students, students from major racial and ethnic groups, students with disabilities, and students with limited English proficiency.[19] Schools receiving Title I funds were further required to make "adequate yearly progress" (AYP).[20] In order to comply with this requirement, states defined for themselves what constitutes an acceptable annual increase of student performance on state assessments in schools.[21] This annual increase was required for all identifiable subgroups. Reflecting the name "No Child Left Behind," the law also required states to ensure that each of these student subgroups reached proficiency by 2014. While states were given much latitude to decide for themselves what constitutes AYP, the law required the annual increase of student proficiency to include separate objectives for all subgroups of students.

When schools failed to make AYP, they faced a range of possible sanctions. The sanctions that flowed from failure to make AYP were markedly more demanding than any type of accountability sanctions that had been prescribed previously by a federal law. If a school failed to make AYP for two consecutive years, it was required to be identified for school improvement, and the district in which the school was located was to provide all students in the school with the option to transfer to another public school.[22] If a school failed to make AYP the following year, it was required to offer supplemental educational services to all of its students.[23] These services were to be administered by a provider with a demonstrated record of effectiveness that was selected by parents and approved by a state agency.

If a school failed to make AYP after its second year of identification for school improvement status, NCLB required the school to be identified for corrective action. Once a school was identified for corrective action, the school's district was required to implement at least one of several demanding actions, including replacing the school's staff, instituting a new curriculum, significantly decreasing management authority at the school level, appointing an outside expert to advise the school, extending the school year or day, or restructuring the internal organization of the school.[24] If the school continued to fail to make AYP while in corrective action, it was required to implement at least one of a set of even more demanding reforms, including reopening as a charter school, replacing all or most of the school staff, entering into a contract with an external entity to run the school, turning over the operation of the school to the state, or undertaking another major restructuring of the school's governance arrangement.[25]

Although the primary focus of NCLB was on measuring and holding schools accountable for their performance, the law devoted some attention to increasing schools' capacities to improve student achievement. NCLB required states to place a "highly qualified teacher" (HQT) in every public school classroom by the end of the 2005–6 school year.[26] NCLB also authorized ED to provide grants to states for implementing sanctions and for states in turn to provide subgrants to districts.[27] Moreover, NCLB provided that states must establish a system of intensive and sustained support for improving schools, provide support to districts with schools that failed to make AYP, and create school support teams to help such schools.[28] NCLB aimed at ensuring that high-quality support was provided to schools by requiring several programs to be based on "scientifically based research." – this phrase appeared in NCLB 111 times to describe the evidence that must underlie a range of programs, including those involving reading, teacher training, drug prevention, and school safety.[29]

Perhaps most notably, Congress provided for large increases in education funding to boost the capacities of states, districts, and schools to meet the requirements of the law. Upon NCLB's passage, the discretionary budget of ED was increased to $48.9 billion.[30] This figure represented an increase of 15.9 percent – the largest in the history of ED. NCLB funds were also authorized at higher levels than ever before in ESEA history. For example, NCLB was authorized at $26.4 billion in its first year, $29.2 billion in its second year, and $32 billion in its third year.[31] Reflecting persistent concerns among Congress about the cost to implement NCLB, the law further included the "unfunded mandates provision," which prohibited federal officers or employees from mandating states and localities to spend funds for costs not paid for by NCLB.[32] So, while NCLB included requirements for states and ultimately schools that were unprecedented in strength and scope, the law also included some focus on building the capacities needed to comply with NCLB and flexibility at the state and local levels.

The Implementation of No Child Left Behind

After NCLB was passed, it faced an array of significant implementation problems. States, districts, and schools had much difficulty implementing NCLB testing and accountability requirements, and support to implement the law was limited as pressure mounted to ensure that an increasing number of students in different subgroups would be considered proficient. Given such difficulties and the range of unintended consequences that resulted, many evaluations of the law's effectiveness were extremely negative. In response, critics launched a series of harsh attacks against NCLB and reinvigorated the debate about the appropriate federal role in education.

The lack of adequate funding for NCLB testing and accountability mandates was one of the highest-profile implementation problems. As states began to implement NCLB, they were experiencing one of the worst fiscal crises since World War II.[33] In this climate, congressional appropriations repeatedly fell short of NCLB authorization levels.[34] Partly as a result of insufficient appropriations, states experienced much difficulty implementing central NCLB provisions, such as those governing testing and assessments.[35] Especially given that sophisticated testing systems can cost billions of dollars to implement, many states indicated that NCLB funds were insufficient for developing state assessments.[36] States similarly lacked the financial capacities to implement fully the consequences for failure to make AYP, such as school choice, supplemental services, and the range of sanctions required when schools were marked for corrective action.[37] Exacerbating these funding issues, states faced several other problems affecting their abilities to implement NCLB sanctions fully. For example, many states had difficulties implementing public school choice sanctions because there were an insufficient number of receiving schools, an insufficient amount of space in schools, tight time frames, and existing state class size restrictions.[38] Similarly, given states' inability to monitor the quality of supplemental services providers adequately, the quality of the supplemental services students received differed dramatically across states and localities.[39]

Several problems also plagued the implementation of the law's requirements surrounding AYP determinations. Given states' flexibility to adopt standards and assessments of their choice, the quality of states' standards was sometimes low and varied significantly.[40] Because states also had flexibility when constructing their definitions of AYP, these definitions varied widely across states in areas such as starting AYP goals, the rate at which student performance was required to increase, and the minimum size of subgroups needed for inclusion in AYP calculations.[41] Many states also administered assessments that likely did not provide valid interpretations of what students know and are able to do because constructing well-designed assessments is very costly and technically difficult.[42] Indeed, creating testing systems that could yield valid interpretations proved especially challenging for assessing students with disabilities and English language learner (ELL) students.[43] As a result of such problems, several educational researchers have argued that AYP determinations lacked validity.[44]

States faced further difficulties implementing provisions aimed at ensuring that schools had the capacities to provide students with the needed learning opportunities for performing adequately on state assessments. The HQT provisions proved particularly difficult to implement. Immediately before NCLB was passed, only slightly more than half of U.S. secondary teachers could be considered highly qualified under the law's definition.[45] However, teacher shortages in high-need subjects and difficulties constructing information systems for tracking teacher qualifications data hampered efforts to improve the number of highly qualified teachers.[46] As a result, several states developed low standards for defining an HQT.[47]

States also implemented the school support and assistance provisions of NCLB in a range of ways that had largely unknown efficacy and effectiveness. Many state strategies lacked strong empirical bases and included approaches such as assigning a state-approved school support team to make recommendations to schools, providing grants for school improvement, using universities and private providers to assist schools, and assigning distinguished educators to work with schools.[48] Many schools did not even receive any such support when required by NCLB.[49] And although states and districts having difficulty raising student performance were often required to implement strategies grounded in "scientifically based research," many had difficulty doing so as well. ED had verified few strategies based on such research, and states and districts generally lack the expertise to judge the scientific rigor of educational research effectively.[50] Given the lack of a concrete knowledge base and weak federal enforcement of the scientifically based research requirements, diverse programs with a range of evidentiary bases were implemented around the country.[51] Compounding such issues, representatives of several states simply argued that the federal government did not provide them with sufficient funds to ensure that all students could reach proficiency on state assessments.[52]

In the context of these concerns about the design and implementation of NCLB, the effect of NCLB on teachers, classrooms, and students sparked hot debate. Because NCLB included strong accountability requirements, the law appeared to focus educators on state standards and the performance of students in relation to these standards.[53] But it also intensified the pressure on schools and students to the extent that they felt overwhelmed and forced to "teach to the test" by engaging in practices such as teaching students how to fill in answer sheets and focusing almost solely on test-taking skills.[54] These pressures were most intense in high-poverty schools that faced a significant risk of failure to make AYP, and several high-profile accusations of teachers facilitating cheating to raise test scores surfaced in these places.[55]

Changes in test scores during the implementation of NCLB reflected a similarly mixed and ambiguous record. Results from the 2005 administration of the National Assessment of Educational Progress (NAEP) indicated that nine-year-olds had their best scores in reading and mathematics in the history of the test's administration, and the Bush administration concluded that NCLB "is working" on the basis of these results.[56] However, some analysts attacked this claim by focusing on other trends in student achievement.[57] As the Center on Education Policy argued, any increases in achievement may have been due to factors other than the law.[58] And despite some increases in achievement, a quickly increasing number of schools in large urban districts with large numbers of high-poverty schools continued to fail to make AYP.[59] Given the range of influences on student learning, it has proven very difficult to ascertain the impact of NCLB accountability mechanisms on students' learning opportunities and achievement.

At least in part because of such problems, NCLB became the subject of heavy political attacks soon after its passage. Governors sent letters to

ED criticizing the new federal requirements under NCLB and appealed for more flexibility implementing the law.[60] Bills or resolutions to opt out of or limit NCLB funding were introduced in at least twenty-one states, and at least thirty bills calling for changes in NCLB were proposed in Congress.[61] In response to this pressure, ED loosened some key NCLB requirements and regulations, such as those governing the way in which AYP was calculated (particularly for subgroups such as ELL students and those with disabilities) and the definition of an HQT. Perhaps most prominently, ED implemented a pilot program that allowed several states to implement "growth models" to determine AYP, which were based on increases in student performance instead of whether student performance simply rose above a particular threshold.[62] Still, ED generally enforced NCLB more robustly than it had enforced Title I in the previous decade through actions such as withholding federal funds for states that had failed to comply with NCLB.[63] As a result, the pressure to improve school performance without a major increase in school capacity remained in place throughout 2010 as NCLB continued to be implemented.

Litigation Aimed at No Child Left Behind

Perhaps most clearly signaling the controversies and concerns raised by NCLB, the law faced a wave of litigation. Mirroring much education litigation since *Brown*, reformers aimed several lawsuits at NCLB to mitigate the perceived harms of education policy. For example, the Education Law Center, a nonprofit legal advocacy organization that has historically fought for the rights of minority students, ELL students, and students with disabilities, filed a lawsuit to ensure that NCLB testing practices yield better interpretations of what students know and can do.[64] Similarly, schools and districts threatened by NCLB sanctions sued to halt the application of sanctions in locations where it was very difficult for certain schools to make AYP because of factors such as poverty and a high number of subgroups.[65] In such cases, plaintiffs challenged several aspects of NCLB's design and implementation, ranging from the technical method of calculating minimum subgroup size to a state's failure to administer assessments in the native languages of students and the funding required to implement sanctions. Still, courts in all these cases ultimately refused to halt the implementation of NCLB.

Some plaintiffs attempted to use the courts in a very different way that aimed at enforcing the law more robustly. To these plaintiffs, the identification of low-performing schools and application of sanctions were precisely the point of the law because they appeared to be well-founded tools for spurring effective school reform. As such, some groups that had historically defended minority rights, including the National Association for the Advancement of Colored People (NAACP) and Lawyers' Committee for Civil Rights under Law, publicly expressed support for NCLB.[66] Following this logic, ACORN, a community organization primarily composed of low- and moderate-income families devoted to social justice, employed litigation to enforce the school choice and supplemental services sanctions in areas that were not implementing them when required.[67] Although these efforts to use the courts to influence NCLB implementation ultimately failed as well, the presence of such litigation reflected support for accountability-focused school reform from groups that had focused historically on protecting students' rights.

A third type of litigation carved a path down the middle of enforcing NCLB and halting its implementation. This litigation was generated by the financial burden that NCLB put upon states, districts, schools, and educators. In *Pontiac v. Spellings* (*Pontiac*), perhaps the most high-profile NCLB lawsuit, the National Education Association (NEA) spearheaded litigation focusing on the funds provided by the federal government to implement NCLB. The NEA particularly argued that NCLB constituted an "unfunded mandate" and brought the lawsuit on behalf of urban and rural school districts across the country and ten state affiliates.[68] When the lawsuit was initiated (approximately two years into the implementation of NCLB), about one-fourth (21,350) of schools in the United States had failed to make AYP, and many of these schools included disproportionately high numbers of minority, low-income, and ELL students. Focusing primarily on cost studies conducted by states and school finance experts about the amount of funding needed to comply with accountability requirements and increase student proficiency, the NEA argued that the implementation of NCLB violated its unfunded mandates provision. Like the other lawsuits, *Pontiac* proved unsuccessful after bouncing between a federal district and appeals court for years and ultimately being decided by a highly divided appellate court hearing the case *en banc*.[69]

Several other lawsuits aimed at NCLB focused on a range of unrelated issues. Litigation highlighted implementation issues like the conflict of NCLB school choice provisions with judicially required desegregation plans, timely compliance of a state with the HQT requirements, and the procedure employed by ED to adopt regulations governing NCLB.[70] Courts largely found plaintiffs' arguments in these lawsuits unpersuasive for a range of technical legal reasons, including lack of standing, the unavailability of a section 1983 action, and the precise language in NCLB.[71] Still, the range of litigation spurred by the law is important to consider. Groups that have had traditionally similar interests in education have become involved in a variety of cases aimed at influencing NCLB in different ways. While some groups have remained focused on protecting the rights of students, other groups have become more concerned with the performance of the education system more generally and the policy instruments employed to enhance this performance. Indeed, although courts were not well positioned or willing to rule in favor of these groups, the NCLB litigation reflects a much changed landscape about how interested groups believed school reform should proceed.

FEDERAL EDUCATION POLICIES AFTER NO CHILD LEFT BEHIND

After NCLB was enacted, it quickly became the anchor for other federal laws aimed at spurring school reform throughout the 2000s. Perhaps most notably, the reauthorizations of IDEA and the ESRA were both grounded in the logic of NCLB. These two laws were broadly focused on different areas of education policy. As discussed in Chapter 4, the IDEA was originally enacted as the Education for All Handicapped Children Act in 1975 and has been reauthorized several times throughout its history. The 2004 reauthorization of the IDEA continued to focus on protecting the education of students with disabilities but was substantially modified to align with the standards and accountability requirements of NCLB. Also enacted in 2004, the ESRA was a completely new law that significantly modified the way in which ED funded education research. This law was also built to align with NCLB, particularly around developing an evidentiary basis for grounding education reform in scientific evidence and student outcome measures. Together, these laws reflect the strong effects of NCLB and its underlying principles on the federal education policy landscape.

2004 Reauthorization of the IDEA

Although the IDEA had been traditionally focused on protecting the civil rights of students with disabilities, the 2004 reauthorization of the IDEA reflected the broader trends in the transformation of the federal role that had animated NCLB. In comparison to many other federal education laws in the 2000s, the IDEA had already begun to change in line with the policy climate. With its 1997 reauthorization, Congress had required the test scores of students with disabilities to be included in state and local accountability systems. However, the law did not require the performance of mentally retarded students evaluated through alternate assessment practices to be included for accountability purposes.

The 2004 IDEA reauthorization increased the stakes of assessments for students with disabilities. The law required states to have in place performance goals for students with disabilities that matched those under the states' definitions of AYP, and schools were to be sanctioned if they failed to make AYP on the basis of their disabled students' performance.[72] Focusing on boosting schools' capacities to ensure that students with disabilities could be considered proficient, the IDEA also required every special education teacher to be highly qualified by the deadline set in NCLB.[73] As a result of such modifications to the IDEA and Title I, the practice quickly emerged of constructing individualized educational programs (IEPs) aimed at moving students toward proficiency on state standards.[74] Although the reauthorization required states to adopt alternative achievement standards for students with disabilities that were aligned with state content standards and alternate assessments aligned with the standards, these assessments were limited to students with the most significant cognitive disabilities.[75]

The focus in NCLB on implementing education reform strategies grounded in "scientifically based evidence" appeared in the 2004 IDEA reauthorization as well. The reauthorization allowed schools to use a process that assessed whether students responded to scientific, research-based interventions to determine whether they should be identified as having a learning disability. In response to these provisions, many schools implemented Response to Intervention (RtI) programs aimed at providing students with services before identification. RtI is generally a method of academic intervention for providing early, evidence-based assistance to students who are having difficulty learning. Under RtI programs, learning difficulties are addressed through early intervention, frequent progress measurement, and intensive "research-based" practices. If students do not respond to RtI programs, they are then identified as in need of special education.

The 2004 reauthorization included several other modifications as well. For example, it included pilot programs for multiyear individualized education programs and paperwork reduction and changed the statute of limitations for individuals to sue for violations of due process under the IDEA.[76] The law further included provisions solidifying students' rights to stay in their educational placement while parents challenged alleged violations of the law. However, the major modifications discussed previously strongly reflect the changing political climate and broader ideas emerging about education reform in the 2000s. Indeed, congressional testimony and debates during the reauthorization process also reflected this shift in climate. Although testimony and debates still referenced the importance of protecting the rights of students with disabilities, they did so to a lesser extent than in the past.[77] Particularly influential debates and testimony instead emphasized efficiency and the potential of school systems to provide stronger academic experiences for students with disabilities.

Although such changes in the IDEA began to make it more aligned with NCLB, critics have raised many concerns. Perhaps most prominently, critics have highlighted the disjuncture between the traditional purposes of the IDEA and the purposes of standards-based reform and accountability policies.[78] The IDEA has historically embraced the principle of individualization – that each child should be provided with an appropriate education given the child's unique characteristics. On the other hand, standards-based reform historically has been anchored in the notion that all students should learn the same skills and knowledge. So, although the 2004 IDEA reauthorization moved toward making federal education policy more coherent, several critics who adhered to a more traditional notion of educational rights for disabled students had strong concerns about the general direction in which federal education policy was moving.

The Education Sciences Reform Act

Like NCLB and the 2004 IDEA reauthorization, the ESRA reflected an increasing emphasis in federal education policy on grounding education reform decisions in scientific evidence. The ESRA was enacted in 2004 and authorized the creation of the Institute of Education Sciences (IES), the new research arm of ED.[79] While the ESRA generally articulated the administrative structure and functions of IES, the law specifically provided that IES may only fund educational research that comports with "scientifically based research" standards.

Such legislative priorities reflect a significant change from the ways in which the federal government has traditionally funded and regulated educational research.[80] While the federal government has collected, analyzed, and published education statistics for more than a century and has significantly increased its funding commitment to educational research since *Sputnik*'s launch in 1957, ED's funding priorities have never been so focused.[81] IES's predecessor, the Office of Educational Research and Improvement (OERI), was attacked for supporting fragmented, short-term, and overly politicized research, and funding for educational research has long been limited.[82] Congress enacted the ESRA largely in response to such concerns and particularly to develop high-quality research that could help schools meet the accountability requirements of NCLB – given the perceived failure of federal funding to boost educational quality and of educational research to provide clear directives to policy makers, the ESRA was aimed at tightening the relationship between federal funding and student performance.[83]

In order to achieve this goal, the ESRA established five divisions inside IES.[84] The National Center for Educational Research (NCER), the IES division most involved with research funding decisions, was required to support "scientifically valid research activities" and could only fund research conducted under "scientifically based research standards."[85] While this concept was defined slightly differently in the ESRA than "scientifically based research" was defined in NCLB, the focuses of these concepts were similar. Under the ESRA, "scientifically valid research" meant basic, applied, and field-initiated research in which the rationale, design, and interpretation are soundly developed in accordance with scientifically based research standards.[86] "Scientifically based research standards" were those that applied rigorous, systematic, and objective methodology to obtain reliable knowledge relevant to education programs, and to present findings that are supported by the methods employed.[87] This term included research employing systematic, empirical methods that drew on observation and experiment and made claims of causal relationships only in random assignment experiments or other designs that eliminate plausible competing explanations for the obtained results.[88] These standards were aimed at promoting the funding of research that was effective, cost efficient, and able to be scaled up for use in elementary and secondary classrooms.[89]

Many actions taken to implement the ESRA closely tracked the law's focus on producing research through randomized experiments to develop programs that could be deployed at scale to produce increases in student achievement. Guidelines and research priorities published by ED repeatedly prioritized educational research designs employing randomized controlled trials over other types of research designs and focusing on demonstrated increases in student performance.[90] IES funding priorities also stressed that researchers should employ "quasi-experiments," or research designs relying on large databases that allow researchers to correlate characteristics of students with each other and certain outcomes where randomized experiments are not possible.[91] Because of their power to control artificially (though incompletely) for different characteristics that can influence the relationship between programs and student outcomes, quasi-experiments allow researchers to make limited claims of causality.[92]

The wave of federal regulation under these standards quickly generated significant controversy among the educational research community. Some cast federal efforts to define and directly regulate educational research as a welcome remedy to what was perceived as irrelevant research and a poor evidentiary base for making education policy decisions. In accordance with the research priorities underlying the ESRA, skeptics of existing educational research argued that much existing educational research was methodologically suspect and low quality because it did not rely on randomized experiments or quasi-experiments, or prioritize examinations of the effects of educational programs on student achievement.[93] As many researchers have noted, conducting randomized experiments is one of the most powerful types of research because it allows researchers to control for various factors that can potentially influence observed outcomes. Randomized experiments accordingly enable researchers to make stronger claims of causality. Indeed, the health sciences have heavily employed research designs using randomized experiments to provide extremely valuable information for making decisions about health policy and practice.[94] Some researchers therefore argued that the research priorities of IES would lead to the identification and development of educational interventions based on evidence that "work" at scale and are effective at improving student achievement.[95]

On the other hand, many researchers framed such efforts as the inappropriate insertion of government into the research process. To this end, these researchers generally argued that the definition of educational research in the ESRA and the funding priorities of IES were too narrow. As some of these critics argued, "The law codifies one position in a complex, ongoing debate about the quality and rigor of educational research. While we do not question the elegance, power, and utility of experimental designs, they cannot answer all important questions the field faces; other genres of research are both necessary and relevant to maintain the vitality of educational research."[96] Grounded in such logic, the National Research Council (a part of the National Academy of Sciences) refused to recommend particular methods for conducting educational research and broadly argued that strong research poses significant questions that can be investigated empirically, links research to relevant theory, uses methods that permit direct investigation of the question, provides a coherent and explicit chain of reasoning, replicates and generalizes across studies, and discloses research to encourage professional scrutiny and critique.[97] As the educational researcher Stephen Raudenbush argued, a randomized trial is relevant only when one is investigating a causal question, and many important questions for education policy are not causal.[98] There are also many situations in which randomized experiments simply are not feasible because of issues such as the existing distribution of students across schools and school politics of giving treatments to one group of students but not another.

Given the research on policy implementation, many educational researchers have further argued that education is a field that can be heavily influenced by nuanced differences in context at the state, district, school, classroom, and individual levels. Because there are several powerful influences that impede, constrain, support, and promote student learning, and that teachers are often powerless to manipulate, effectively scaling-up educational interventions that may work in one particular setting is extremely difficult.[99] If one accepts that accounting for such differences in context is important for conducting strong research and developing effective education policy, several different types of research methodologies must be used. While randomized experiments and quasi-experimental research focusing on increases in student achievement are essential for understanding whether programs and practices can produce their intended effects, they are not sufficient. Nonexperimental qualitative studies (such as ethnographies) are also essential for analyzing how microlevel differences in context may impact what transpires in classrooms. This type of research is also essential for understanding why randomized experiments indicate that certain programs or interventions work in particular settings but not others.

In short, both the 2004 IDEA reauthorization and ESRA reflect major shifts in the federal education policy landscape in the years immediately following the passage of NCLB. The 2004 IDEA reauthorization required that students with disabilities be evaluated in relation to state standards and their performance be incorporated in AYP determinations. The ESRA focused on funding research tied to demonstrable increases of student performance at scale. Both laws also reflected the emphasis in NCLB of relying on scientific research to guide decision making. While these policies appear to have been reasoned responses to the lack of a solid evidentiary base for making effective education policy decisions, several concerns have remained about the potential of these policies to remedy the problems historically facing large-scale education reform. These problems have been grouped primarily around the tension of using centralized policy instruments to guide educational decisions that stretch across a range of different institutions and individuals, including states, districts, schools, classrooms, and students. It is precisely this tension that would continue to prove problematic for the final major federal education reform enacted to date in the 2000s – the American Recovery and Reinvestment Act.

THE AMERICAN RECOVERY AND REINVESTMENT ACT

As states, districts, and schools were implementing NCLB and related federal education laws through the first decade of the 2000s, they were also experiencing a severe economic crisis. Triggered especially by the 2008 collapse of the financial services industry at the end of President George W. Bush's time in office, the U.S. economy had gone into a tailspin, and school systems faced the prospect of severe budget cuts that had the potential to result in mass firings of teachers. The former senator Barack Obama (D-IL) assumed the presidential office in 2009 in the midst of this crisis. As one of his first major acts as President, Barack Obama signed into law the ARRA in 2009 to stimulate and stabilize the U.S. economy.[100] While the ARRA was aimed at helping a range of institutions weather the financial crisis, it included a particular focus on stabilizing school systems. Of its $787.2 billion total, the ARRA devoted approximately one-eighth, or $98.2 billion, to education.[101] Of this $98.2 billion, $80.2 billion was devoted to K-12 public education. While the ARRA was aimed at keeping school systems afloat in difficult financial times, it was also aimed at fixing existing education policy problems and sparking future education reform efforts.[102] In addition to its focus on saving jobs in education, the ARRA was designed to spur policy reform in areas considered by the Obama administration to be high priority. To this end, the ARRA contained several provisions focused on spurring the development of a handful of core reforms at the state level, including the improvement of standards and assessments, more robust charter school policies, school "turnaround" strategies, data systems linking student and teacher performance, and teacher incentive policies based on such data.

Design of the ARRA

The provisions of the ARRA aimed at education covered a wide range of programs and reform areas. The law devoted much of its education funding to existing federal education policies, such as NCLB and the IDEA. These funds were generally distributed by the federal government to states, and then distributed by states to districts under preexisting statutory formulas. Much of this funding was channeled into strategies such as increasing the amount of money available for the education of low-income students, increasing the capacities of schools that were continually failing to make AYP to improve, and generally ensuring that students with disabilities were provided with a "free appropriate public education" under the IDEA.[103]

The ARRA notably directed funds to other programs that reflected the educational priorities of President Obama. It channeled funds to teacher incentive project grants that were aimed at developing and implementing performance-based teacher and principal compensation systems in high-need schools. These compensation systems were required to incorporate information about gains in student achievement. The ARRA also provided funds for developing and implementing statewide data systems that stretch from when students enter school through college, include indicators for college readiness and postsecondary remedial coursework, and link student level data to individual teacher data.[104]

The ARRA further included the State Fiscal Stabilization Fund (SFSF), which was aimed at stabilizing state and local government budgets to minimize and avoid reductions in education and other essential public services.[105] Funded at $53.6 billion, the SFSF was the largest education appropriation in the ARRA.[106] The SFSF was composed of three funding streams. The first stream, which included most of the SFSF funds and generally allocated funds to schools by preexisting statutory formulas, was aimed at helping states avoid spending cuts in education and retain school personnel.[107] To receive these funds, governors submitted applications to ED that included several assurances. These assurances required states to commit to four types of education reform: (1) achieving equality in the distribution of highly qualified teachers between high- and low-poverty schools, (2) establishing a longitudinal data system of the type described previously, (3) enhancing the quality of standards and assessments, and (4) supporting struggling schools.[108] Although states were directly responsible for applying for SFSF funds, state governors had little control over these funds – states were required to allocate this funding by formula and distribute the funds to school districts, which then had significant flexibility in how they could use these funds.[109] However, given the financial turmoil they were experiencing, most states used their funds to avoid personnel cuts.[110]

The SFSF also included the high-profile "Race to the Top Fund" (RTT), a $4.35 billion fund targeted at spurring innovation in education.[111] Under this fund, the U.S. secretary of education determined which states received grants on the basis of the information provided in state applications for SFSF funds and other criteria that the secretary deemed appropriate, such as applications submitted specifically for RTT funding.[112] As discussed later, ED highlighted the importance of attention to the four reform areas included in SFSF applications and stressed that states should support charter schools to receive RTT funding. The potential to receive RTT funding was the major incentive for states and districts to engage in education reforms emphasized in the ARRA. Finally, the SFSF included some other smaller funding streams, such as a comparatively small "innovation fund" that provided money to school districts or partnerships of nonprofit organizations, districts, and school consortia that had demonstrably increased student achievement.[113] In short, the education provisions of the ARRA were aimed at helping states avoid significant budget cuts and spurring particular types of education reform. While school districts received most of the ARRA funds and were given a significant amount of flexibility to use these funds, the requirements of the SFSF and RTT in particular provided financial incentives to reinforce particular reform priorities.

Implementation of the ARRA

Soon after the ARRA was enacted, ED developed guidance to provide detailed information to states and districts about how the education provisions of the ARRA should be implemented. While much of this guidance focused on very specific and technical aspects of how states and districts could use ARRA funds for particular programs, such as Title I of the ESEA and the IDEA, the guidance also focused on the reform areas highlighted by the ARRA.[114] The SFSF guidance particularly reiterated that states could only receive SFSF funds in exchange for their assurances in their applications to advance education reform in the areas mentioned previously.[115] Moreover, the guidance indicated that state applications must include baseline data demonstrating their current status in each of the reform areas. States were particularly required to report on the number and percentage of teachers and principals scoring at each performance level on local districts' evaluation instruments and indicate whether their evaluation tools took student performance into account.

The final regulations for the RTT reinforced this approach. The regulations required states to have committed to the four priority areas of the SFSF to be eligible for an RTT award.[116] Notably, more than one-quarter of the possible score that states' RTT grant applications could attain (138 of 500 points) was earned in the Great Teachers and Leaders section of the applications. This section required states to demonstrate how they would recruit, train, and retain effective teachers and principals and particularly emphasized the importance of tying decisions about educator performance to student achievement data. Moreover, in the Data Systems to Support Instruction section (which could earn applications 47 of a possible 500 points), states were required to develop statewide data systems that include a unique, statewide student identifier and a unique teacher identifier allowing teachers to be matched to students.

In addition to releasing guidance and regulations, the Obama administration engaged in less formal means of communication to use the ARRA to promote education reform. U.S. Secretary of Education Arne Duncan made several statements focusing on the types of education policies states must have had in place to be competitive for an RTT award. Secretary Duncan warned the twenty-six states that imposed caps on the numbers of charter schools and the ten states that did not permit charter schools at all that they would be less likely to receive money under the RTT.[117] Secretary Duncan also publicly singled out states, such as Illinois, Indiana, and Maine, as being unacceptably hostile to charter schools.[118] Similarly reflecting education reform priorities in the ARRA, Secretary Duncan indicated his disapproval of states that had laws barring the use of student achievement data in teacher evaluation decisions.[119] He particularly criticized California, New York, and Wisconsin as states that maintained an unacceptable "firewall" between student and teacher data. Secretary Duncan further singled out states failing to maintain high-quality standards and pushed them to sign on to a movement among states to develop and adopt the Common Core Standards – a set of shared content standards developed on a volunteer basis by several states and coordinated by the National Governors Association and Council for Chief State School Officers.[120]

Given formal legal requirements and more informal communications, states engaged in a range of responses. States channeled almost all their ARRA funds to fill budget holes and save jobs.[121] Yet, a significant pushback against the educational strategy of the ARRA emerged in several states. For example, Governor Sarah Palin (R-AK) stated that Alaska would not accept ARRA money for education because doing so would permanently swell the state budget.[122] Texas similarly refused to apply for RTT funding and more broadly follow the lead of the Obama administration in reform areas such as standards.[123] Echoing such concerns, Republican leaders in Congress argued that the reform provisions of the ARRA could result in an undesirable expansion of federal power.[124] And despite federal pressure to enact policies supportive of charter schools, such pressure failed to generate change in several states.[125]

However, the combination of legal and regulatory requirements, financial incentives, and political pressure sparked substantial policy reform in several states. For example, Illinois, Indiana, Louisiana, and Tennessee lifted or raised their charter school caps.[126] In anticipation of drafting an RTT application, Governor Bill Ritter (D-CO) set aside $10 million for efforts such as expanding Colorado's data system and encouraging districts to experiment with alternative-compensation systems for teachers.[127] In the face of continuing political pressure and public criticism from Secretary Duncan, California ultimately eliminated its statutory prohibition against linking student and teacher data.[128] Indeed, the Obama administration made strong use of the "bully pulpit" in combination with the RTT to promote education reform.

As of 2010, it was very difficult to evaluate the effects of the ARRA and RTT in spurring actual reform in states, districts, schools, and classrooms. However, a significant amount of RTT money had been awarded. All the RTT applications from the fourteen states that won RTT awards shared a set of common strategies.[129] Each of these states committed to using student achievement data as a major part of teacher evaluation, supporting the development of alternative pathways to certification, and making personnel decisions with the use of teacher evaluation data. Each of these states also proposed modifications to their data systems that involved linking individual teacher and student performance data as part of a strategy to incentivize stronger teacher performance. Each of these states committed to adopting the Common Core Standards as well.

Still, there were salient differences in the reforms proposed by the states, particularly in how governance was structured. The ARRA and criteria for scoring applications barely addressed acceptable governance arrangements that would need to be instituted with RTT funding; the RTT largely functioned as a bare financial incentive mechanism to promote certain types of substantive reforms without dictating the governmental structure in which such reforms must be implemented. While some states centralized authority at the state level to make most of the major decisions about teacher evaluation, other states decentralized such authority by situating authority at the district level.

For example, after the announcement of the RTT competition, New York passed legislation to establish new teacher evaluation systems, more than double the number of charter schools allowed in the state, allow districts to contract out the management of their lowest-performing schools to third party educational management organizations, and adopt the Common Core Standards.[130] The state also made growth in student performance a significant part of a teacher's evaluation. Much of the decision-making authority under this reform resided at the state level. This reform required 40 percent of a teacher's evaluation to be derived from student growth measurements. Eventually, 25 percent of this 40 percent would be derived from student growth under a state-approved value-added assessment, while the remaining 15 percent would be derived from student growth on a locally selected assessment. The remaining 60 percent of a teacher's evaluation score would be derived from local measures developed through collective bargaining. New York was planning on using this evaluation system to inform a range of personnel decisions, including those governing tenure, dismissal, and compensation. The teacher evaluation system also had implications for promotion decisions – teachers who were evaluated as "effective" or "highly effective" would be given opportunities for increased responsibility and increased performance expectations.

Rhode Island, another state that won an RTT grant, proposed many of the same types of reforms as New York.[131] In preparation for its RTT application, Rhode Island designed a data system that could match student performance data to individual teachers. Rhode Island also adopted the Common Core Standards, raised its charter school cap, and began developing regulations for alternative teacher certification programs that required less coursework than existing programs. The teacher evaluation system adopted by Rhode Island similarly focused on evaluating teachers in relation to the demonstrable performance of their students – under the state's system, at least 51 percent of these evaluations were to be derived from a measurement of student growth, while the remaining portion was to be based on a range of factors, including the quality of instruction, demonstration of professional responsibilities, and content knowledge.

However, the governance structures framing the Rhode Island reforms significantly differed from those in New York. Rhode Island's RTT application stated:

> Rather than micromanaging the "how" of reform, the state: 1) sets clear expectations (standards and policies) for the outcomes…; 2) assists and builds the capacity of LEAs [districts] to achieve those goals; 3) provides them with the tools to do so; and 4) monitors their progress and holds them accountable.[132]

Where New York districts were primarily responsible for implementing the state's evaluation system, Rhode Island districts had the authority to develop their own evaluation systems so long as they adhered to the general state requirements. Rhode Island's concomitant efforts to tie teacher compensation to teaching effectiveness also reflected this approach toward governance. For example, the state planned on using its RTT funds to sponsor grant competitions for districts to develop performance-based compensation models. So, despite the similarities between the substantive reforms adopted by states such as New York and Rhode Island under the RTT, states were still given the flexibility to choose how much local discretion to employ.

Research on Reform Approaches Used in the ARRA

Like many other education reform strategies integrated into policy, the approaches employed by the ARRA were based on sometimes limited and ultimately mixed evidence. As discussed in Chapter 6, the debate surrounding charter schools has been highly public and politicized. But despite the publicity charter schools have received, the research base does not clearly indicate that charter schools can serve as a "magic bullet" to improve students' learning opportunities dramatically. There are strong charter schools and weak charter schools, innovative charter schools and charter schools focused on more traditional forms of organization and learning. But given the political feasibility of charter schools, they became a dominant reform strategy in the ARRA. In contrast, the focus on improving standards and assessments appears to be based on a more robust theory of action. As discussed in Chapter 5, standards and assessments became core elements of U.S. education policies, and the ARRA was aimed at remedying salient problems with them, such as the inconsistent and sometimes low quality across states. While addressing such problems is likely insufficient by itself to leverage significant change at the school level, it does appear to be a useful building block.

The school turnaround strategies in the ARRA have a particularly weak evidentiary base. Driven especially by the data about inequities in schooling, policy makers, educators, and other parties interested in education reform have called for dramatic actions to "turn around" poorly performing schools.[133] A turnaround school would ideally increase student performance by fundamentally changing basic features of its organization in a very short period, such as a few years.[134] However, there is very little evidence of the efficacy or effectiveness of this reform strategy in education. There is very limited educational research directly related to replacing school leadership or staff, and the extant evidence largely emerges from the limited experience with school turnarounds under NCLB.[135] So, there is little evidence that turnaround strategies generally result in significantly better academic outcomes.[136]

While there have been examples of turnarounds in noneducational organizations, such as churches, hospitals, universities, governmental entities, for-profit firms, and not-for-profit entities, these examples indicate that turnaround efforts may be much more likely to fail than succeed and can be very difficult on both organizations and the individuals in them.[137] And while there have been examples of turnarounds that dramatically increased school performance over a short period, simply replacing school leaders or staff appears insufficient to turn around a school; leaders and staff must engage in specific practices, which are thus far poorly understood, for a school turnaround to have a real chance of success.[138] Indeed, tailoring turnarounds to factors such as the governance, environmental, and organizational contexts of schools appears critical for implementing successful school turnarounds.[139] So, while school turnarounds appear to have been successful in isolated cases, the evidence underlying those for schools is sparse, and significantly more is needed to improve school performance at scale than simply replacing school staff and leaders.

The Educator Workforce and Linking Student and Teacher Data

The evidence on strategies aimed at boosting the quality and effectiveness of the educator workforce in the ARRA are especially important to consider because they built on the HQT requirements of NCLB and quickly became a focal point of federal and state strategies aimed at boosting the performance of the education system. The federal focus on teacher quality and effectiveness in NCLB and the ARRA broadly reflects federal expansion into a policy domain traditionally controlled by the states. All states have long required teachers to hold licenses.[140] But given that states have made licensure decisions independently, the nature and quality of licensing standards and assessments have varied widely.[141] States similarly have maintained the authority to approve teacher education, and training programs have varied in whether programs must meet national accreditation standards or be approved by the state.[142] States have also set teacher compensation policies, which have generally required teachers' salaries to follow state or local salary schedules on the basis of experience, credentials, and college credits earned.[143] While some states have attempted to modify these policies through strategies such as career ladders and merit pay, more recent efforts have varied significantly and included elements such as signing bonuses, housing supplements, higher pay in shortage areas such as mathematics, higher pay for teachers in hard-to-staff or low-performing schools, and elaborate knowledge- and skill-based incentives.[144] By requiring states to commit to the establishment of longitudinal data systems that stretch from when students enter school through college and that link student level data to individual teachers, the ARRA ultimately laid the foundation for restructuring such policies around holding teachers accountable for the performance of their students.

Although the research base on such strategies to improve the performance of the teacher workforce is not extensive, there is some evidence bearing upon the effectiveness of this strategy. A growing consensus has emerged that the quality of teachers significantly influences student learning and achievement.[145] Teacher quality appears especially important for boosting the performance of poor and minority students.[146] Still, the research base on how teacher quality influences student performance is generally limited, sometimes conflicting, and ultimately inconclusive. For example, teacher quality can be defined in relation to a range of characteristics, including subject matter knowledge, qualifications and experience, and the ability to create a classroom environment motivating to students.[147] Yet, there is little consistent evidence about the teacher qualities that facilitate student learning at high levels.[148] Although policies to reform the teacher workforce, such as merit pay strategies, theoretically can improve teacher quality, there is therefore very limited empirical evidence for this claim. More generally, there is little persuasive research on the effects of any alternative-compensation scheme on student learning and achievement.[149]

Given such limited information about strategies to reform the teacher workforce and the consensus about the importance of teachers for student learning and performance, data systems linking teachers and students would seem to make much sense. If carefully designed and implemented, these systems could offer more evidence about the qualities of effective teachers. However, several concerns persist. The data systems required by federal law could potentially focus on overly narrow indicators of student and teacher quality – while student performance data and teacher certification status are arguably revealing, they do not reflect what teachers actually do in the classroom.[150] These sorts of indicators also do not account for the variation that may be necessary to teach effectively in different local contexts.[151] Exacerbating such problems, few states have extensively used data to drive educational decision making, implementers of the data systems (such as administrators in schools and districts) may not have the technical capacities to do so, and there has been almost no culture of data-driven decision making in education.[152]

So, the focus of the ARRA on building more robust data systems in relation to the teacher workforce appears to emphasize a key area of reform that is directly related to what transpires in schools and classrooms. The focus on gathering robust data about students and teachers to guide decisions further appears to be a much more measured approach than simply instituting quick-fix organizational reform policies, such as those focusing on turnaround strategies. However, there is little indication that the data systems required by the ARRA can provide the range of evidence needed to make more effective decisions about how to reform teacher workforce policies. Moreover, there is little indication that such data systems, as they currently stand, can serve as a solid foundation for reform strategies focused on measuring teacher performance for the purpose of holding teachers individually accountable.

CONCLUSION

The first decade of the twenty-first century was a time of continuing change for the concept of equality in education law and policy. As discussed in Chapter 5, school finance reform cases continued to be litigated, and the core issues in these cases moved closer to the school and classroom levels. As discussed in Chapter 6, charter schools also rapidly expanded in states, and the Supreme Court almost completely ended desegregation litigation. However, the most significant change for education law during this time was arguably the evolution of the federal role and the fundamental ways in which states modified their policies to comply with new federal requirements.

While NCLB and the ARRA were the most high-profile and far-reaching federal laws passed during this time, other new laws like the ESRA and 2004 IDEA reauthorization subtly changed the landscape of educational equality as well. Together, all these laws reflected a deepening focus on adequacy – ensuring that all students attain at least a minimum level of education – especially in relation to proficiency as defined by state standards. Indeed, standards became even more ingrained in education law and policy and the culture of education policy more generally in the 2000s. While NCLB was the major federal driver of this focus on standards, the ARRA, ESRA, and 2004 IDEA reauthorization also included a focus on improving standards or aligning programs and research with standards and student performance data.

Responding to concerns about the historical ineffectiveness of federal education policy and quickly changing education politics centered on the appropriateness of the federal role, new federal laws also included a pronounced emphasis on holding schools accountable for their performance. Although there were some measures in NCLB aimed at increasing schools' capacities to improve, these measures were minimal in comparison to the strong requirements of the law's accountability mechanisms. Building on NCLB, the ARRA focused intensely on laying the groundwork for holding teachers accountable for their performance. As such, federal education law and policy during the 2000s reflected a continuing emphasis on the educational goals of international competitiveness and efficiency, and the utility of business management principles for attaining these goals. While a more traditional vision of equality still animated federal education law and policy to a certain degree, as reflected by the NCLB requirements to disaggregate data by racial and ethnic subgroup (and the law's very name), this vision of equality was fading. Even the IDEA had begun to incorporate the principles of standards and accountability. Highlighting this trend, a significant amount of education litigation, which had traditionally focused on protecting the rights of underserved students, shifted to enforcing NCLB and ensuring that it operated effectively.

While such developments built directly on changes in federal education law during the 1990s, they also required continuing shifts in educational governance. As noted previously, the federal role not only changed but also expanded. It did so particularly around the federal policy instruments of standards and accountability, which were essentially centralized requirements for states regarding the ways in which they needed to structure their own education systems. While the NCLB requirements about standards and accountability were technically voluntary (as states only had to comply with these requirements in exchange for continuing receipt of Title I funds), they essentially operated as mandates; it would have been very difficult for states to refuse Title I funding, given their historical receipt of them and severe budget shortfalls. These requirements also addressed the relationship between students and teachers at the classroom level to a greater extent than ever before. Standards directly specified what students should know and be able to do. Although arguably poorly designed, the HQT requirements of NCLB were the most significant federal involvement in teacher quality in U.S. history at the time. Still, reflecting the influence of traditional governance structures and politics, the standards and accountability requirements involved some flexibility as well – states were given the autonomy to craft their own standards, adopt their own assessments, and define what constituted AYP within certain boundaries.

The federal government notably employed several other strategies to restructure the educational federalism. In order to promote reforms that could be enacted at scale, Congress created centralized definitions of "scientifically based research" to govern the quality of education programs implemented by states and research funded under federal law. Drawing on very different types of policy instruments, Congress used NCLB sanctions to integrate decentralizing approaches into state education systems, such as public school choice and supplemental education services. In part responding to the highly charged politics (and perhaps litigation) growing from the centralized requirements of new federal laws, the Obama administration employed policy instruments that could be more clearly labeled as voluntary through the RTT and bully pulpit. Still, with the ARRA's focus on improving state standards, measuring teacher performance, and promoting particular organizational approaches such as school turnarounds and charter schools, the ARRA delved even more deeply into school organization than NCLB. Indeed, these various strategies employed by Congress significantly influenced the operation of states' education policies. In light of robust federal enforcement of NCLB, all states enacted systems of standards and accountability that shared several key features. To compete for RTT grants, several states also changed their requirements governing standards, charter schools, and teacher evaluation.

Still, evaluations of the effectiveness of these laws remained mixed at best, and much remained unknown by 2010. Many of these strategies, such as school turnarounds, have lacked a solid evidentiary base. While more is known about some strategies, such as charter schools, there is very little indication that such strategies are efficacious – as Chapter 6 discusses, charter schools reflect the political middle ground to a much greater extent than an evidence-based approach to significantly improving school performance at scale. Without more school capacity to increase student performance, unreachable goals and strong accountability measures have also combined to have narrowing effects on curriculum and negative effects on school climate. NCLB had relatively few provisions aimed at increasing school capacities to improve school performance, and these provisions were poorly enforced. Requirements governing sanctions like school choice and supplemental educational services were incompletely implemented as well, and very few parents took advantage of the programs when actually offered. Despite significant increases in federal education funding, there were still insufficient funds to implement the administrative infrastructure for NCLB and create high-functioning testing systems. The political backlash to NCLB and wave of litigation that followed it highlight these problems as significant pressure points in federal policy.

Moreover, the implementation of these laws has been widely variable across different locations. In large part because of the flexibility accorded to states under NCLB, standards and assessments were of uneven and sometimes low quality. States' definitions of AYP were similarly variable. While RTT winners focused on the same broad types of substantive reforms, the actual structure of these reforms varied widely. And while the expansion of the federal role had a centralizing effect on education policy, there was a significant degree of flexibility for states and localities integrated into the federal approach. Given the traditional principles and politics of federalist governance, this flexibility should not be surprising. On one hand, the flexibility accorded to states appears very useful. As a significant amount of education policy research has emphasized, reforms are rarely effective if they are not tailored to local conditions. But, on the other hand, states and localities were not accorded flexibility in the areas that make federal action effective. Much of the flexibility allowed by NCLB has yielded inconsistent and sometimes low quality standards, assessments, and accountability systems. Similarly, the flexibility of the RTT failed to reflect solid research on the types of discretion needed to implement effective educator workforce development systems. Indeed, the flexibility incorporated into federal education law appears determined much more by political compromise than strategy built on a hard look at the available evidence.

The structure of the scientifically based research requirements of NCLB and the ESRA exacerbated these problems. The scientifically based research requirements were ultimately aimed at addressing school capacity problems by ensuring that the reforms instituted were based on attention to evidence. However, these requirements failed to account for the complex and heavily contextualized nature of education in any nuanced way, and that is one of the primary problems that education law and policy have historically faced. As a result, these requirements decreased the sort of flexibility that was needed for more effective reform. Indeed, this disconnect between the type of flexibility needed and the type actually cemented into law underscores how historical governance structures and politics power a significant amount of law and policy focused on educational equality and adequacy.

In short, driven by attention to efficiency and international competitiveness in a political environment that had quickly become more open to an expanded federal role, traditional concerns for equality were minimized in education law and policy. In its place, education law and policy grew around a construction of adequacy that applied to all students and served as an anchor for an increasingly centralized policy system that required results without sufficient attention to how these results could actually be attained. This system did not focus on building the capacity of school systems to improve, ignored the knowledge gap in education and much evidence that was actually available, and poorly integrated flexibility at state and local levels. With the exception of the growing focus on teaching, learning, and evidence in the form of data, this system has this given little indication that it has the potential to significantly boost the quality of the lowest-performing schools or schools more generally.

8

Conclusion

Educational equality has long been a driving force in U.S. law and policy and has become engrained as a fundamental and widely held social value. Since the Supreme Court decided *Brown v. Board of Education*, reformers have framed educational equality as central to ongoing law and policy reform efforts and broader social movements affecting a wide range of policy fields. As such, various actors have tied education to lofty social goals, such as the maintenance of a democracy and an internationally competitive economy, and laws and policies aimed at instituting large-scale educational changes have proceeded across several major U.S. governmental institutions.

Given the centrality of the concept of educational equality in the United States, continual waves of education reform have swept through the American education system since *Brown*, including desegregation, school finance reform, the education of English language learners (ELLs) and students with disabilities, standards-based reform and accountability, school choice, and teacher evaluation. Yet, the vast attention given to education reform has yielded mixed results at best, and many of the problems that education law and policy have aimed at remedying since *Brown* persist. Indeed, educational equality, its underlying goals, and its governance structures have proven to be moving targets as different education reforms have involved not only different practices and procedures but also different visions of pressing educational problems. Examining these shifting visions and ways of concretely operationalizing them can help us explain how our education system has arrived at its current state. Perhaps more importantly, such an examination can help us figure out how best to move forward. This concluding chapter accordingly synthesizes the examinations conducted throughout this book and provides principles and concrete recommendations for reforming education law and policy.

THE TRANSFORMATION OF EQUALITY

The concept of equality in education law and policy has transformed dramatically since 1954. Although equality has appeared in many different forms in education law and policy since *Brown*, constructions of equality have moved along at least three major trajectories: from the protection of rights of harmed groups and individuals to the reform of entire school systems, from a focus on educational inputs to school and student performance, from an emphasis on sameness between individuals and groups to an adequate education for all students. While there is an almost limitless range of factors one could highlight to explain the transformation of educational equality in law and policy, educational goals and governance constitute useful touchstones for examining how educational equality has changed. Conceptualizing the transformation of equality in relation to interweaving changes in educational goals and governance over time is particularly useful for considering how current law and policy can and should be modified.

When the concept of educational equality took center stage in *Brown*, it was largely structured around ensuring that African American students have access to the same schools that white students do. Especially given the ambiguous language of the equal protection clause, the concept of equality proved to be very malleable. As desegregation litigation progressed, equality was defined in several different but overlapping ways across governmental decisions, including in relation to the *Green* factors, precise mathematical ratios signifying integration, the absence of de jure segregation, and the concrete practice of busing. As federal district courts and the Supreme Court gained more experience with desegregation and the range of issues that emerged upon the implementation of court decisions, judicial constructions of equality quickly sharpened.

These various constructions of equality were anchored in particular political and social goals. In *Brown* and the wave of desegregation litigation and legislation that emerged after the era of massive resistance, education reform was largely grounded in the idea that education must be equal in ways that can support a robust democracy and social mobility. Educational access for African Americans appeared central to achieving these goals. Still, the goals already contained an inherent tension. While democracy is a public good that relates to social ends, social mobility is a private good that relates to an individual's social and economic position and how it can be improved. This tension would later be exposed by subsequent reform efforts grounded in other constructions of educational equality. Given that *Brown* required deep shifts in education policy around the United States, the decision also reflected a vision of what government fundamentally can and should do to effect social change. In *Brown*, the Supreme Court positioned education as one of the most important functions of government. Moreover, the case signaled the beginning of public law litigation, which centered on the use of the courts to advance large-scale social goals. As such, the federal courts became the primary governmental institution involved with reform efforts centered on educational equality in the early stages of desegregation.

The courts faced significant challenges in this role. For example, given the permissive mandate to desegregate schools "with all deliberate speed," district courts were not institutionally able or willing to enforce desegregation in a hostile political climate during the era of massive resistance, and little desegregation actually occurred. However, the courts were very successful in other respects. They drew on their strengths when they laid down canonical legal principles by publicly working through ideas that held much weight in the social consciousness. The courts also acted as trailblazers in a political climate did not favor change for underserved minority groups. When the courts acted in concert with the legislative and executive branches in the mid-1960s, the courts were at their strongest. They continued to work through important philosophical and moral concepts and push reform forward while drawing on precise standards worked out by other bodies with more expertise and enforcement capacities. As a result, schools in the South rapidly desegregated between the late 1960s and early 1970s in one of the most successful periods of education reform in U.S. history.

Given the perceived success of the movement to advance the social and political goals underlying the desegregation movement, reformers looked to the principles of desegregation to advance other civil rights movements. These efforts, in combination with the seemingly limitless potential of the concept of educational equality to expand, fueled the rapid emergence of educational equality in several other areas of law and policy in the 1960s and 1970s. School finance litigation initially focused on equality in terms of sameness of funding for low-income students. The ESEA focused on equalizing funding for low-income students through federal legislation. Court-driven and legislative reforms established formal procedures for protecting the rights of disabled students, particularly in light of their individual characteristics. Reforms aimed at ELL students treated them as more of a homogeneous group that sometimes required different treatment than their non-ELL peers through native language instruction. As such, the concept of educational equality emerged as a driving force in various areas of law and policy but proved quite flexible.

Although these law and policy efforts shared broadly similar goals, the various constructions of equality were strongly influenced by differences in governance arrangements and the specific issues to which they responded. For example, given the vagueness of relevant language in state constitutions, state courts interpreted the concept of educational equality primarily in terms of funding but also in several additional ways, such as the various goods or services bought with funds. In contrast, Title I of the Elementary and Secondary Education Act (ESEA) reflected an early attempt by the federal legislative and executive branches to equalize educational opportunities through statute and agency action. Under early iterations of Title I, educational equality was structured almost exclusively in terms of funding – especially given the lack of experience that the federal government had with education until the 1960s, funding was relatively easy to quantify and subject to centralized regulation. Moreover, funding made much sense as a tool for federal reform because widespread funding allowed Congress to navigate the difficult political landscape facing the original passage and early implementation of the ESEA.

Despite this expansion of educational equality, large-scale education laws and policies continued to face a range of problems. Certain problems surfaced through the implementation process. For example, there was initially limited state and local capacity to comply with the distribution requirements of the ESEA, and Title I funding was improperly allocated partly as a result. Reforms also faced political pushback, such as the refusal of state legislatures to respond fully to court orders to reform school funding systems in school finance litigation. The governance structures of reforms drove other problems. Although Title I and school finance reform were ultimately aimed at equalizing students' educational opportunities at scale, both reforms focused on the centralized regulation of funding instead of tackling educational elements that are closer to the core of what happens in schools and classrooms. As such, there was little indication that the quality of education for students receiving Title I funds was improving even with an increased emphasis on financial compliance in the 1970s and 1980s. Similarly, there has been little indication that even successfully litigated school finance cases have consistently resulted in better or more equal educational opportunities for students.

New sets of problems began to emerge in desegregation litigation as well. In the context of political pushback against desegregation strategies like busing and a changing political composition of Supreme Court membership, courts in the 1970s started to become skeptical about the efficacy of the largely top-down, court-centered governance arrangements of desegregation. As courts continued to gain experience with desegregation, they began to express their reluctance to engage in system-level change as it became clear that each reform only required a more fundamental reform in order to be truly effective. Although justices of the Supreme Court originally believed that school desegregation would take only a couple of decades, the implementation of desegregation decrees revealed how difficult desegregation really was – such reform increasingly seemed to require deep changes in the schooling process and attention to even more diffuse social issues, such as demographic changes and the factors impacting where people live. This was precisely the sort of thinking driving the growing public hostility to the Great Society programs and the politics of the Supreme Court justices appointed by President Nixon in the 1970s. The idea of local control – a notion that essentially acted as a counterpoint to centralized governance authority – accordingly emerged in the Supreme Court as a limit to the continuing expansion of the concept of educational equality in both desegregation and school finance settings in cases like *Milliken v. Bradley* and *San Antonio Independent School District v. Rodriguez*. Given this constellation of political, administrative, and legal problems, deep cracks in law and policy efforts centered on educational equality began to emerge just as these efforts were quickly expanding.

The education law and policy reforms that followed developed in response to such problems and the new sets of politics that coalesced during the early 1980s. The election of Ronald Reagan to the U.S. presidency marked an increasing emphasis on the power of individuals and the free market to achieve social and economic ends. These politics foregrounded the importance of individual rights and the ability of individuals, if given sufficient freedom, to drive innovation and improve their social and economic stations. Such a shift laid the groundwork for education to be considered more of a private good aimed at facilitating social mobility. Moreover, sparked by a significant economic downturn and the beginning of globalization, U.S. politics increasingly focused on the goal of international economic competitiveness. While this goal had certainly been present (and focused at least as much on military competitiveness) throughout the cold war, it strongly reemerged under the Reagan administration. In the wake of *A Nation at Risk*, the business community accordingly began to play a primary role in education reform, and education law and policy began to concentrate to a much greater extent on driving up student performance to increase the economic productivity of states and the United States as a whole. Grounded in this logic, educational equality in law and policy started to transform into a concept focused on adequacy of education for all students, the restructuring of school systems, and an emphasis on student performance.

State governors and legislatures were at the forefront of this new movement in education law and policy. Building on efforts in the late 1970s such as the high-stakes testing movement, states enacted reforms under the banner of educational excellence after *A Nation at Risk*. Beginning in the mid-1980s and through the 1990s, states began to institute standards-based reforms. This type of reform aimed at ensuring that all students learn particular sets of skills and knowledge and required fundamental changes in the operation of schools by aligning elements of schooling such as curriculum, teacher training, testing, and professional development with standards. In this way, law and policy reforms directly responded to the problems raised by focusing reforms primarily on issues far from the classroom, such as the inequality of funds and other goods that could easily be regulated.

As states were assuming a greater role in education law and policy, other major governance shifts were occurring at the same time. Many state standards-based reform systems involved the institution of accountability structures for school or student performance, a policy instrument reorganizing the relationships between schools and state governments. Grounded in the notion that education is a national imperative, the federal role also intensified with events such as the Charlottesville Education Summit and the passage of the Goals 2000: Educate America Act and Improving America's Schools Act. These laws positioned the federal government as a major player driving the development of standards-based reform and accountability systems in states. Courts in school finance cases similarly shifted their focus to educational adequacy and began looking to standards to help respond to institutional weaknesses that they had explicitly identified, such as their lack of educational expertise. Indeed, in part mirroring the role of the courts in the 1960s in desegregation, the courts in some of these cases acted as a destabilizing institution that broadly managed reform and relied on other institutions to craft more concrete standards.

Despite such shifts in governance and fundamental goals, familiar problems persisted. Laws and policies continued to face significant political challenges. Although the emphasis on adequacy in school finance litigation mitigated political pushback to judicial orders, legislatures still failed consistently to craft strong reforms in response. Moreover, given the politics and traditions of federalism and resistance to more traditional notions of educational equality, opportunity-to-learn standards were removed from Goals 2000 and faded from the political discourse. The limited capacities and expertise of many governmental decision makers drove other problems that surfaced upon the implementation of law and policy. Even with a burgeoning focus in school finance litigation on channeling money into specific reform strategies, there was mixed evidence at best that these decisions increased or equalized students' educational opportunities. Implementing valid testing practices at scale also proved challenging because of the lack of technical and financial capacities at state and federal levels. The increasing emphasis on changing what happens in schools and classrooms also required significant shifts not just in educators' skill and will but also in their understandings of reform. As reforms such as those based on standards flowed through a multilayered governance system, huge variability in educators' practices emerged. So, although school finance reform and standards-based reform in the 1990s responded to some of the major problems that had historically plagued reforms, students' educational opportunities remained resistant to significant change through law and policy.

Despite this broad move to governance centered on state and federal legislatures and agencies, and aimed more directly at addressing what happens in schools and classrooms, some law and policy reforms became grounded in the notion of local control at the same time. On one hand, the notion of local control continued to serve as a central justification for courts to back away from more traditional notions of equality. Driven by three cases decided by the Supreme Court in the 1990s, local control served as a primary legal reason for federal courts to withdraw from desegregation cases around the country. As a partial result, the levels of segregation in many schools returned to those at the time when *Brown v. Board of Education* was decided. Yet, anchored in the neoliberal logic that gained significant traction during the 1980s, school choice reforms emphasizing the value of local control widely spread during the 1990s. This movement, which largely proceeded through tuition voucher programs and especially charter school policies, was partly predicated on the idea that local control supports equality instead of limits it. Although the school choice movement treated education as a "black box," it was ultimately aimed at improving school performance by giving individuals and local organizations the room to innovate, compete, and adapt to local conditions. As such, school choice focused on restructuring school systems at the level of governance as did many other large-scale education reforms at the end of the twentieth century and beginning of the twenty-first century.

Despite such commonalities with other concurrent education law and policy movements, the school choice movement was based on a fundamentally different ideology. In contrast to many of the other education reform movements of the time, school choice treated education as much more of a private good. At its core, school choice aimed at empowering individuals to select schools that make the most sense for them. Indeed, although the Supreme Court's decision in *Parents Involved in Community Schools v. Seattle School District No. 1* does not seem to square with the logic of local control at first glance, this decision also focused on treating education as more of a private good. This emphasis on the individual underscores the inherent tension in educational equality as articulated in *Brown*: while school choice entails the potential for significant curricular differentiation and does not directly support the common education required for a democratic education, it has garnered support as a way for individual students to escape the public education system and get the education they would not otherwise receive. Despite this theory of action, school choice reforms have also fallen short of their goals as they have demonstrated little capacity to improve schools consistently at scale.

The passage of No Child Left Behind (NCLB) in early 2002 built directly on the law and policy changes of the 1980s and 1990s. Given the continuing focus on enhancing the educational performance of the United States as a whole, the role of the federal government in education continued to expand. Reflecting the increased influence of business organizations and think tanks on school reform, the policy instrument of accountability also began to play a more central role in structuring relationships between educational institutions and organizations. As such, educational equality in law and policy largely became a matter of proficiency against state standards and school success in ensuring that all subgroups make adequate yearly progress (AYP). The federal American Recovery and Reinvestment Act (ARRA) continued to push reform in this direction. Although the Race to the Top Fund (RTT) relied on incentive mechanisms to leverage reform, it built on the highly qualified teacher requirements of NCLB to induce states to institute teacher evaluation systems grounded in state standards and student performance, in addition to other particular strategies such as charter school and school turnarounds. The Education Sciences Reform Act (ESRA) was further aimed at building the knowledge base for improving student performance at scale. Indeed, these reforms reflected a federal push toward adequacy, fundamental reform of school systems, and educational outputs.

Despite a growing consensus about the legitimacy of an expanded federal role in education, federal action continued to be subject to political and legal limitations. The charter of ED and the political climate required many key educational decisions (such as the content of standards and AYP decisions under NCLB) to be left to the states even as the federal government constructed a framework for reform. As a partial result, the quality of state standards and AYP requirements differed dramatically. Such political pushback to the expansion of the federal role also continued to surface in the development of the ARRA. In response to the flexibility built into the RTT, different states developed teacher evaluation systems that shared many broad characteristics (such as the use of student performance data) but differed with regard to other characteristics (such as the amount of local control over evaluation practices). While such differences theoretically allowed states to tailor their teacher evaluation systems to their local context, these differences also allowed states to engage in very inconsistent and sometimes low-quality evaluation practices.

To some extent, these laws and policies have yielded some positive results. Given the centrality of standards, reforms have become more attuned to what should happen in schools and classrooms, and data on student and teacher performance could prove invaluable in equalizing and improving students' learning opportunities. The ESRA was aimed at further developing a needed knowledge base for school reform, and the ARRA was partly aimed at improving the performance of teachers, who are clearly central for improving schools. Yet, like all other large-scale education reforms focused on equality, these reforms have faced a range of problems. Without more capacity at the local level to increase student performance, unreachable goals and strong accountability measures have combined to have negative effects on school climate and narrowing effects on curriculum. Several NCLB sanctions have been poorly enforced and incompletely implemented. While the ESRA was aimed at ensuring that education reforms are based on attention to evidence, the law failed to account for the heavily contextualized nature of education in a nuanced way. Many of the reforms promoted by the ARRA lack a solid evidentiary base, and the focus on student outputs in teacher evaluation systems appears overly narrow. Although these reforms involved some responses to major problems historically facing education by broadly focusing on teaching, learning, and data, they accordingly reflect the political middle ground much more than an evidence-based approach to improving schools at scale.

When taking a bird's-eye view of major law and policy efforts centered on educational equality since *Brown*, it quickly becomes clear that reform is not simple. Education reform does not happen in a vacuum in which law and policy can be developed solely on the basis of a reasoned examination of evidence and quickly implemented with fidelity across a large area. Laws and policies centered on educational equality are driven forward by a large range of factors, notably involving the complex interweaving of social and political goals and governance over time as reforms are implemented in concrete, real-world settings. As a result, few education laws and policies focused on equality can be deemed "effective" at scale for more than a short time at best, and students' educational opportunities have remained persistently unequal. Yet, there have been some critical successes and elements of various reforms that have proven particularly promising. This book turns now to the lessons that can be learned from an examination of both the problems and successes of education law and policy since *Brown*.

MOVING FORWARD

Given the transformation of equality since *Brown* and the problems and successes that education laws and policies have faced, what approach should be taken moving forward? Grounded in the examination of education laws and policies conducted throughout this book, this section articulates four overlapping principles for reform: (1) build stronger political consensus around educational goals, (2) strategically restructure educational governance, (3) engage with schools and classrooms, and (4) use strong evidence while accounting for local context. Then, this section presents concrete reform recommendations to illustrate how these principles can be fruitfully applied.

Principle One: Build Stronger Political Consensus around Educational Goals

Policy makers and the general public should reach a stronger political consensus on the goals of education and the construction of equality that flows from them. While many scholars have argued for the importance of gaining such a consensus, our politics of education remain conceptually fragmented in several ways. Reforms have been grounded in goals such as supporting a robust democracy, social mobility, and international economic competitiveness. Given these various goals, reforms have differed in relation to the extent to which notions of private good or public good should be foregrounded in our understanding of educational equality. In part because of such variation, law and policy reforms have focused on several different types of educational equality, ranging from equalizing educational opportunities for underserved groups to ensuring that all students receive an adequate or even high-quality education.

As some education researchers have argued, it is precisely the lack of agreement about education goals that has constituted one of the most significant barriers to lasting education reform.[1] Indeed, sustained political support and engagement of governmental institutions in a shared direction have proven key for the successful implementation of reforms focused on educational equality. The engagement of the federal courts, legislature, and executive branch during the 1960s produced one of the most effective periods of education reform. Similarly, the engagement of various governmental branches, grassroots groups, and business groups produced quick education reform in Kentucky in the late 1980s around school funding and standards. By opening a more direct conversation among policy makers, the public, and educators about goals for our education system, we would also be able to ensure that reform efforts rest on a more stable and coherent foundation, which would allow for a more strategically designed approach to education reform.

To be sure, it is highly unlikely that a single goal or construction of equality will or even can fully prevail over the others. None of the broad social goals that have historically driven efforts focused on educational equality have ever operated fully in isolation or disappeared. Various social and political goals for education have risen and declined concurrently, reflecting the complex landscape of political and social ideas that are held across governmental bodies, reformers, and the public. However, there is little reason to believe that all these goals are mutually exclusive, as reflected by the various interests that converged under the banners of standards-based reform and school choice. Carefully framed reforms may therefore be able to generate greater political consensus. In particular, an education system truly focused on ensuring that all students demonstrate a strong understanding of high-quality knowledge and skills while ensuring that they receive equal educational opportunities could potentially generate such consensus. Although educational goals conceived in such a way would reflect the notion that education is much more of a public good than a private good, it would incorporate theoretical tenets that span across these constructions. Indeed, especially given the renewed focus on the lowest-performing schools in recent federal law, a reinvigorated notion of opportunity to learn coupled with strong learning goals for all students could provide an important anchor for political conversations about education. Such a construction would connect tightly with major aspects of the modern political discourse, serve pressing policy needs, and safeguard the needs of our most vulnerable populations.

Principle Two: Strategically Restructure Educational Governance

Education reform should be based on an analysis of how governance can be structured strategically to accomplish goals or sets of goals. Given such goals, governmental institutions should be accorded the amount and type of decision-making authority that aligns with their strengths and weaknesses. For example, legislatures and executive bodies (such as federal and state education agencies) should maintain a significant amount of governance authority over modern reforms because they are comparatively well positioned for making decisions that depend on an array of complex information. However, because these institutions are heavily influenced by the vagaries of the political process, the courts should be used strategically as well. The courts are particularly useful for driving changes in education policy when other institutions fail to address policy problems because of political inertia and for giving legitimacy to efforts to address social problems that have affected underserved groups. Although the courts generally do not decide against a large political consensus for extended period, they are also very useful for focusing public attention in certain directions and maintaining an ongoing "conversation" about pressing policy issues. As discussed later, substantial thought should also be given to how much authority should be placed at the local level, including among teachers and principals.

While no governance reform would ensure that law and policy decisions are always made by the actors or institutions best suited to make them, such reform would at least put our education system in a position to win as many of these "matchups" as possible. The details of particular education laws and policies focused on equality are clearly critical. However, governance functions almost as an operating system on which laws and policies run. In crafting any reform strategy focused on educational equality, the first task should be devoting concerted attention to developing governance arrangements that are tightly aligned with educational goals. Strategically designed governance arrangements will in turn lead to more effective law and policy decisions as they arise.

Principle Three: Engage with Schools and Classrooms

Reform focused on educational equality must directly engage with transforming the inner workings of schools and classrooms. As discussed throughout this book, many reforms have dealt with elements of education that exist far from the learning that actually happens in schools. For example, reforms such as school finance litigation and Title I have historically focused on educational elements like funding that are clearly important for structuring students' educational opportunities and comparatively easy to regulate. However, such reforms by themselves have proven clearly insufficient to equalize or increase students' educational opportunities. In order to equalize and increase the educational opportunities that students receive significantly, reforms must more directly engage with what actually transpires in schools and classrooms and thereby increase schools' capacities to improve.

Since the 1990s, education reform efforts have moved increasingly in this direction. Although their quality has differed, state standards have specified what students should know and be able to do, and testing and accountability structures have focused on school and student performance in relation to academic content and skills. And although charter schools are based on the idea that school structure and activities are best made locally and should not be specified from above, the charter movement has focused on restructuring the fundamental operations of schools. The school turnaround strategies highlighted in NCLB and the ARRA are specific approaches to restructuring the basic operations of schools. Each of these reform strategies involves particular challenges, notably including the difficulty of ensuring that educators have the skill, will, and understanding to improve students' educational opportunities. Indeed, tackling elements that are close to the core of what happens in schools and classrooms is arguably even more difficult than implementing a reform such as desegregation that has faced strong political, legal, administrative, and financial barriers.

Still, without directly aiming at improving what happens in schools and classrooms, there is little chance that laws and policies aimed at leveraging educational equality will reach their goals. Many types of reforms that were widespread in 2010 are clearly insufficient by themselves. Widespread testing and accountability, school choice, and turnaround strategies have not proven sufficient to leverage improvement in students' educational opportunities at scale and have in fact exacerbated some preexisting problems. Yet, the recent strategies aimed more directly at schools and classrooms reflect a basic movement that should be extended and improved in future reform efforts to effect greater educational equality.

Principle Four: Use Strong Evidence While Accounting for Local Context

Education laws and policies should be grounded in strong evidence of their effectiveness and efficacy. At the same time, laws and policies should account for variation in local context and ensure that the will and capacity at the local level to implement reform are in place. There are certainly several promising education reforms that have been implemented in the past. For example, certain preschool programs have proven effective at influencing not only students' academic performance but also their opportunities throughout their lives. Governmental institutions, such as courts in school finance litigation, have accordingly identified preschool as a particularly promising reform for states to fund. Given the success of such programs and the glaring need for educational improvement across the country, it makes much sense that many would point to such programs as models that could boost the entire quality of our entire education system if implemented more broadly. However, because of the complex state of evidence and myriad pitfalls inherent in the implementation process, there does not appear to be any simple or mechanical way to replicate these programs effectively. Such programs often require large amounts of funding, rely on substantial political backing, have very high-quality staffing, and are difficult to sustain over long periods given the characteristics of particular locations.

Such an interplay between centralized educational reform and local context points to a fundamental tension to which this book has repeatedly turned: large-scale education law and policy reforms are by nature aimed at governing across broad areas. Yet, the actual terrain – the states, districts, schools, and even classrooms – is far from uniform. Centralized governance structures are needed to mitigate educational differences that stem from inequalities in other policy fields, such as health and housing, in addition to addressing broader historical inequalities. Moreover, centralized governance is sometimes necessary to overcome political resistance and inertia, and ensuring that educational programs and practices are based on evidence instead of bare political preference. Indeed, data from well-constructed testing practices should play a central role in building such an evidentiary base and providing ongoing information about the effectiveness of educational strategies from the federal to classroom levels as these strategies are being implemented. But the idea in education law and policy that local control is valuable should also be preserved. Local control is not only a cultural, political, and legal value, but an important element of effective policy as well. Without the ability to adapt education reform to local context and leverage local engagement, education reforms simply do not work.

Given this tension, effective education laws and policies require the negotiation of a difficult balance between regulating implementers to ensure that their practices are driven by solid evidence and giving them freedom to adjust to local conditions. The approach taken to developing reform focused on educational equality should therefore be grounded in the idea of "bounded autonomy." Because reforms aimed at educational equality should move closer to schools and classrooms, efforts to further the educational research base should generally be aimed at developing broad, evidence-based principles that can be actively applied by educators to the contextual interactions and ever-changing environments that influence the implementation of educational programs. As a result of both the data produced by the educational research community and governmental regulation of such research, the evidentiary base and accompanying methodological tools for articulating such principles are currently limited. However, a commitment by both the policy making and research communities to developing such a research base is critical for designing and implementing more effective educational reforms.

Flowing from this notion about the relationship between evidence and local context, education reform should also be based on significant attention to the capacities of local actors and maintenance of local engagement and support. One of the most significant problems facing reforms focused on educational equality has been the lack of attention to ensuring that key implementers (such as teachers) have the various capacities needed to improve the instruction that students receive. Ensuring that implementers have such capacities is critical as reform cuts closer to elements of education that are not easy to regulate directly. For example, while some state standards have entailed novel visions of teaching and learning, the institution of standards alone has proven insufficient to leverage deep changes in teachers' instructional practices. Similarly, while the accountability mechanisms of NCLB have focused teachers on content in tests and involved substantial accountability for schools, many schools have found it impossible to meet the AYP requirements of NCLB. Without ensuring that local engagement and capacities are in place, local implementers – one of the key links in the entire education law and policy process – will not make consistently effective decisions about how to improve educational opportunities in light of the available evidence for the variety of situations they encounter.

Putting Principles into Practice: The Case of Teacher Workforce Reform

Because the principles discussed previously are broad, there are several ways to craft law and policy reforms around them. This section applies these principles to detail how law and policy governing the teacher workforce should be reformed. This type of reform is especially important because it is aimed at enhancing the capacities of local law and policy implementers, which is crucial for effectively implementing education reform across a variety of contexts. This type of reform is also aimed at enhancing teachers' instructional practices, which is one of the core educational functions of schools and is at least somewhat aligned with the current political climate focused on teacher quality and evaluation. Perhaps most importantly, we already have consensus that teachers are one of the most important elements, if not the most important, for structuring students' educational opportunities.

Education reform focused on improving the teacher workforce ideally begins in Congress. First, Congress should modify the ESRA to focus the Institute of Education Sciences (IES) to a greater extent on the development of evidence-based principles for effective instructional practices. Because variation in light of local context is both desirable and necessary, it is very difficult, if not impossible, to define these practices precisely here and in federal law more broadly. Flowing from the notion that reforms aimed at improving teacher quality and effectiveness should act more as a blueprint than a set of rules for instructional practices, research focused on enhancing these practices should not precisely dictate their content. Although much modern governmental regulation depends on regimes requiring implementers to engage in specified "best practices," such regulation appears to be inappropriate – while these regimes nominally allow for some flexibility in implementation, they generally include sets of practices that must be applied fairly rigidly and promote uniformity among implementers in practice.[2] Instead, evidence-based principles should serve as broad guidelines for teachers and local administrators who would need to make active decisions about how such principles should be applied in their local contexts. To ensure coherence with other education reforms, these principles should further be linked to the Common Core Standards, which have been adopted by a large majority of states and directly involve what happens in schools and classrooms.

Congress in turn should modify federal law to provide a framework for states for the monitoring and management of the teacher workforce. As the flagship law historically focused on educational equality and more recently on large-scale school improvement, the ESEA stands out as the primary candidate for incorporating a framework built around instructional principles. A modified ESEA should incentivize states to develop systems for the monitoring and management of the teacher workforce that are built around such principles, much as it incentivized states to develop standards-based reform systems in the 1990s and 2000s. The bully pulpit and financial incentive tactics recently employed by the Obama administration to implement the RTT could prove particularly effective. While Congress ultimately could not modify the ESEA to require states' adoption of specific principles because of the traditions of federalism and the charter of ED, the evidence-based principles developed by IES should serve as models for states. In this way, a modified ESEA could continue to employ accountability mechanisms as a core policy instrument but would structure this tool in a way that better accounts for the strengths of the federal government to promote and frame reform, while avoiding the pitfalls of precisely specifying particular actions upon implementation. Moreover, such an approach would build on the political foundation established in NCLB and the ARRA and focus on extending and improving promising developments in these policies.

While states would require some flexibility in how they structure teacher workforce systems around such principles, there are a few substantive tenets that also should be incorporated into ESEA sections focused on teacher workforce development. As literature on both the teacher workforce and other types of large workforces indicates, effective monitoring and management do not simply involve targeting a small handful of "high-leverage" practices and ensuring that they are performed well. Instead, monitoring and management should emphasize the coherent, congruent, and strategic use of different combinations of practices over time because these workforces exist in ever-changing contexts.[3] As such, a wide range of functions related to the teacher workforce should be addressed in comprehensive legislation and regulation, including developing the supply of potential teachers, credentialing, promoting quality of initial preparation, recruiting and hiring, promotion, on-the-job training and development, retaining, terminating, and compensating.[4] Indeed, evidence-based instructional principles should constitute the core of such a monitoring and management system. Given the need to apply the evidence-based principles in light of local context, local administrators (such as principals and school district officials) should monitor teachers' instructional practices and manage teachers accordingly. States in turn should ensure that school districts are rigorously employing such a monitoring and management system.

There are of course a range of potential pitfalls to avoid in enacting and implementing such a teacher workforce improvement policy. Under the Obama administration, Congress has been extremely politicized and has accordingly faced political gridlock in enacting many reform packages. Political pushback in states to comprehensive reform could also emerge, and there could be a lack of local engagement. Because states would need to be given flexibility, they could fail to adopt high-quality or evidence-based principles for instructional practices or could continue to enact evaluation and management systems focused narrowly on teacher performance. The courts should be used strategically to address these sorts of problems. In line with their institutional strengths, they should particularly ensure that the process for addressing such problems is not overly politicized and that key stakeholders remain active throughout the process.

Given the withdrawal of the federal courts from the issue of equal educational opportunities, a court-focused approach should be founded on the basic law underlying school finance litigation. As an initial step, litigants should bring a lawsuit in state court under the education clause of a state's constitution focused on the failure of a state to provide students with adequate educational opportunities. Indeed, although the idea of students' opportunity to learn was not politically sustainable in legislation in the 1990s, courts have essentially kept this idea alive in the context of school finance reform. Litigants should particularly focus on a state's continuing failure to ensure that all students are provided with "adequate" teachers on the basis of a well-reasoned examination of evidence and failure of schools to help all students meet standards. In light of their increasing willingness to integrate scientific evidence into their decision-making processes in school finance litigation and understanding that education systems must be restructured, courts should then focus litigation on reforming educational systems to produce better decisions.

The stage of litigation focused on reforming educational systems should draw on a range of institutions and actors. Reflecting the ways in which some courts in school finance litigation have looked to state standards to define adequacy and provide a substantive anchor for other educational remedies, courts should look to the principles for instructional practices adopted by states and potentially developed by the federal government. Grounded in the logic employed by courts examining governance arrangements in cases like *Williams v. State*, courts should then ensure that states craft teacher workforce systems grounded in such principles. Moreover, courts should initiate negotiations among the parties and stakeholders (such as teachers, parents, schools, districts, and state government) to ensure that there are local input and engagement around the development of such a system. Once these other institutions and actors have become involved with the litigation process, courts should periodically check to ensure that states have constructed and are implementing evidence-based teacher workforce systems, and to supervise midcourse corrections with input from stakeholders and local implementers. In this way, courts would ensure that states focus on the process of developing and implementing teacher workforce systems in an evenhanded manner while requiring action not far out of step with the current political climate. Moreover, by looking to implementers who are closer to local conditions and drawing on other governmental institutions, courts can simultaneously avoid decisions outside their institutional competencies and wield their institutional power to break political deadlock effectively.

Of course, there are several other potential problems that this strategy does not address. For example, the federal government would bear the burden of developing effective instructional practices in a nonpoliticized fashion, and it is far from clear whether it can do so at this point. To the extent that these principles are defined in a highly politicized way, state courts should rule that they may not be used by states to anchor teacher workforce systems. Such critiques of federal action could put significant pressure on the federal government to define these practices in a more evenhanded way. Moreover, even with the voluntary nature of federal instructional principles, the charter of ED may need to be changed to allow the federal government to engage more deeply with instruction. The political climate may prevent such a change, especially with its current emphasis on decentralization of educational authority.

Even if teacher workforce reform proceeds robustly, several other types of reforms would be needed to equalize and increase students' educational opportunities. For example, curricula would need to be modified at scale to align with reforms in instructional practices. Aligned systems for the development of the school leader workforce would need to be created. Assessment and accountability practices for gauging student understanding and influencing school performance would have to be dramatically modified. Indeed, it would take a complete and fundamental overhaul of the educational system actually to accomplish this sort of change in any coherent fashion, and the political will to do so has unfortunately been lacking in the past. Still, such a system would move us much closer to accomplishing many of the lofty goals for schools that we have long held.

CONCLUSION

Since the midpoint of the twentieth century, reform centered on educational equality has been a primary focus of U.S. law and policy. Such reform has demanded the attention of all our governmental branches at federal and state levels and the public more broadly. As such, the notion of educational equality has been tied to our most fundamental social goals and our understandings of what government can and should do. As our understandings of government and social context have shifted over time, so too has our notion of what an equal education is. It is in part because of educational equality's malleability that the concept has proven so durable as a driving force in law and policy. Still, law and policy reforms focused on educational equality have faced a range of significant challenges, including those grounded in political difference, lack of individual and organizational capacities to improve students' learning opportunities, lack of knowledge about what reforms are most effective and efficacious, and the basic challenge of implementing large-scale law and policy in a domain in which local context is so important.

When broadly examining the path of educational equality in the United States, one could find many reasons to doubt the potential of law and policy to effect greater educational equality. Although the concept itself has continued to animate major law and policy initiatives, students' educational opportunities – arguably the bottom line for reform efforts – have proven remarkably difficult to equalize or increase at scale. Yet, there is much that we can improve. While there is likely no perfect strategy for education reform that can be easily integrated into law and policy and implemented across the United States, a close examination reveals certain principles that could prove very useful for impacting students' learning opportunities. Boiled down to its core, education reform has proven most effective when governmental institutions strategically work in concert with each other toward shared goals. Coupled with an increased sensitivity to scientific evidence and its limitations, what actually happens in schools and classrooms, and the related dilemma of implementing education reform across a range of administrative levels and locations, such an approach could yield immense benefits for students.

This type of reform is not easy. Law and policy cannot be used as they all too often have been simply to pile education reform on top of education reform with the unfounded hope that new means better. Instead, we must use law and policy to reform what happens in schools fundamentally and strategically; that requires thoughtful attention not just to particular reform strategies, but to our basic governance arrangements and why we have repeatedly instituted reform in the first place. If we can engage in such a process, we will have taken the first step toward providing stronger and more equitable educational opportunities for all students across the country.

Notes

1 INTRODUCTION

1 *Brown v. Board of Education*, 347 U.S. 483 (1954). For an overview of major civil rights decisions and legislation following *Brown v. Board of Education*, see Chapters 3 and 4.
2 Elementary and Secondary Education Act, 20 U.S.C. § 6301 et seq. (1965). This law is one of the most sweeping pieces of federal legislation in U.S. history and has channeled billions of dollars of federal funds into state educational programs. The passage of this law is discussed in greater detail in Chapter 3, and its various reauthorizations are discussed throughout this book.
3 No Child Left Behind Act of 2001, 20 U.S.C. § 6301 et seq. (2002); American Recovery and Reinvestment Act of 2009, P. L. 111–5 (2009).
4 Mark A. Chesler, Joseph Sanders, and Debra S. Kalmuss, *Social Science in Court: Mobilizing Experts in the School Desegregation Cases* (Madison: University of Wisconsin Press, 1988).
5 Michael Heise, "Litigated Learning and the Limits of Law," *Vanderbilt Law Review* 57 (2004): 2417–61.
6 Maris A. Vinovskis, *From a Nation at Risk to No Child Left Behind: National Education Goals and the Creation of Federal Education Policy* (New York: Teachers College Press, 2008).
7 Gary Orfield, "Conservatives and the Rush toward Resegregation," in *Law and School Reform*, ed. Jay P. Heubert (New Haven, CT: Yale University Press, 1999).
8 Susan H. Fuhrman, Margaret E. Goertz, and Elliot H. Weinbaum, "Educational Governance in the United States: Where Are We? How Did We Get Here? Why Should We Care?" in *The State of Education Policy Research*, ed. Susan H. Fuhrman, David K. Cohen, and Fritz Mosher (Mahway, NJ: Lawrence Erlbaum, 2007).
9 Richard F. Elmore, "Unwarranted Intrusion: Isn't It Ironic That Republicans Sponsored the Single Largest – and Potentially the Single Most Damaging – Expansion of Federal Power of the Nation's Education System in History?" *Education Next* 2, no. 1 (2002): 31–5.

10 Julie F. Mead, "Devilish Details: Exploring Features of Charter School Statutes That Blur the Public/Private Distinction," *Harvard Journal on Legislation* 40, no. 2 (2003): 349–94.

11 *Why Do We Educate? Voices from the Conversation*, ed. Mark. A Smylie (Malden, MA: Wiley-Blackwell, 2008).

12 Carl Kaestle, *Pillars of the Republic* (New York: Hill & Wang, 1983).

13 David F. Labaree, "Public Goods, Private Goods: The American Struggle over Educational Goals," *American Educational Research Journal* 34, no. 1 (1997): 39–81.

14 Peter B. Dow, *Schoolhouse Politics: Lessons from the Sputnik Era* (Cambridge, MA: Harvard University Press, 1991).

15 Margaret Spellings, "Building on Results: A Blueprint for Strengthening the *No Child Left Behind Act*" (Washington, DC: U.S. Department of Education, 2007).

16 *Brown v. Board of Education*, 347 U.S. 483, 493 (1954).

17 Bruce A. Ackerman, *We the People*. Vol. 1. *Foundations* (Cambridge, MA: Harvard University Press, 1993).

18 David Tyack and Larry Cuban, *Tinkering toward Utopia: A Century of Public School Reform* (Cambridge, MA: Harvard University Press, 1997).

19 James Forman, "Do Charter Schools Threaten Public Education? Emerging Evidence from Fifteen Years of a Quasi-market for Schooling," *University of Illinois Law Review* 2007 (2007): 839–80; Michael Heise, "Equal Educational Opportunity by the Numbers: The Warren Court's Empirical Legacy," *Washington and Lee Law Review* 59, no. 4 (2002): 1309–42; Rachel Moran, "*Brown*'s Legacy: The Evolution of Educational Equity," *University of Pittsburgh Law Review* 66, no. 1 (2004): 155–79; James Ryan, "Schools, Race, and Money," *Yale Law Journal* 109, no. 2 (1999): 249–316; Benjamin Superfine, "Court-driven Reform and Equal Educational Opportunity: Centralization, Decentralization, and the Shifting Judicial Role," *Review of Educational Research* 80, no. 1 (2010): 108–37.

20 The legal analyses employed in this book primarily involved thorough searches for relevant legal cases, statutes, regulations, and other binding legal sources. Once these sources were identified and collected, the legal analysis involved a detailed consideration of the various legal rules and principles embedded in these sources, how they interact with each other, and how they apply in concrete, real-world situations.

21 David Tyack and Aaron Benavot, "Courts and Public Schools: Educational Litigation in Historical Perspective," *Law and Society Review* 19, no. 3 (1985): 339–80.

22 *Brown v. Board of Education*, 347 U.S. 483, 493 (1954).

23 For perhaps the most famous work on the limitations of law and policy to spur educational change in the area of desegregation, see Gerald N. Rosenberg, *The Hollow Hope: Can Courts Bring About Social Change?* (Chicago: University of Chicago Press, 1991). Researchers have made similar arguments in other areas of education law and policy, and particularly in the area of school finance reform. See, for example, John Dayton, "Examining the Efficacy of Judicial Involvement in Public School Funding Reform," *Journal of Education Finance* 22, no. 1 (1996): 1–27.

24 Amy Gutmann, *Democratic Education* (Princeton, NJ: Princeton University Press, 1999).

25 David Tyack and Larry Cuban, *Tinkering toward Utopia: A Century of Public School Reform.*

26 There are far too many studies in major fields of education reform, such as desegregation, school finance reform, school choice, and standards-based reform and accountability systems, to include here. However, strong overviews of studies on desegregation include David. J. Armor, *Forced Justice: School Desegregation and the Law* (New York: Oxford University Press, 1995); Gary Orfield, "Turning Back to Segregation," in *Dismantling Desegregation: The Quiet Reversal of* Brown v. Board of Education, ed. Gary Orfield and Susan E. Eaton (New York: New Press, 1996); Mark G. Yudof, "School Desegregation: Legal Realism, Reasoned Elaboration, and Social Science Research in the Supreme Court," *Law and Contemporary Problems* 42, no. 4 (1978): 57–110. Strong overviews of studies on school finance reform litigation include Peter Enrich, "Leaving Equality Behind: New Directions in School Finance Reform," *Vanderbilt Law Review* 48, no. 1 (1995): 101–94; Michael Heise, "Litigated Learning and the Limits of Law," *Vanderbilt Law Review* 57 (2004): 2417–61; Douglas R. Reed, *On Equal Terms: The Constitutional Politics of Educational Opportunity* (Princeton, NJ: Princeton University Press, 2001). Strong overviews of studies on school choice include Jeffrey R. Henig, *The Spin Cycle: How Research Is Used in Policy Debates* (New York: Russell Sage Foundation, 2008); Christopher A. Lubienski, Peter Weitzel, and Sarah T. Lubienski, "Is There a 'Consensus' on School Choice and Achievement? Advocacy Research and the Emerging Political Economy of Knowledge Production," *Educational Policy* 23, no. 1 (2009): 161–93. Strong overviews of studies on standards, testing, and accountability include Richard F. Elmore, "Accountability and Capacity," in *The New Accountability*, ed. Martin Carnoy, Richard F. Elmore, and Leslie Santee Siskin (New York: Routledge Farmer, 2003); Benjamin M. Superfine, *The Courts and Standards-Based Education Reform* (New York: Oxford University Press, 2008).

27 For example, see David K. Cohen and Susan L. Moffitt, *The Ordeal of Equality: Did Federal Regulation Fix the Schools?* (Cambridge, MA: Harvard University Press, 2009); Patrick McGuinn, *No Child Left Behind: The Transformation of Federal Education Policy, 1965–2005* (Lawrence: University of Kansas Press, 2006).

28 For example, see Robert L. Crain, *The Politics of School Desegregation* (Garden City, NY: Anchor Books, 1969); Labaree, "Public Goods, Private Goods"

29 Jay P. Heubert, "Introduction," in *Law and School Reform*, ed. Jay P. Heubert (New Haven, CT: Yale University Press, 1999).

30 The distinction between public and private goods in education, specifically in relation to educational goals, is analyzed in depth in Labaree, "Public Goods, Private Goods." For more on this distinction, see Chapter 2.

31 The "command-and-control" role of courts was first identified in Mark G. Yudof, "Implementation Theories and Desegregation Realities," *Alabama Law Review* 32 (1981): 441–64.

32 A policy regimes framework has been fruitfully employed in various areas of public policy, such as immigration. See Daniel J. Tichenor, *Diving Lines: The*

Politics of Immigration Control in America (Princeton, NJ: Princeton University Press, 2002). This theoretical perspective has also recently been used in education to explore the evolution of the federal role. See McGuinn, *No Child Left Behind: The Transformation of Federal Education Policy, 1965–2005*.

33 This book primarily looks to institutional choice theory as articulated in Neil Komesar, *Imperfect Alternatives: Choosing Institutions in Law, Economics, and Public Policy* (Chicago: University of Chicago Press, 1994).

34 Civil Rights Act of 1964, 42 U.S.C. § 2000 et seq. (1964).

35 Education for All Handicapped Children Act, 20 U.S.C. § 1400 et seq. (1975).

36 National Commission on Excellence in Education, *A Nation at Risk: The Imperative for Education Reform* (Washington, DC: U.S. Government Printing Office, 1983).

37 Goals 2000: Educate America Act, 20 U.S.C. § 5801 et seq. (1994); Improving America's Schools Act, 20 U.S.C. § 6301 et seq. (1994).

2 GOVERNMENT, EQUALITY, AND SCHOOL REFORM

1 Lorraine McDonnell, "A Political Science Perspective on Education Policy Analysis," in *Handbook of Education Policy Research*, ed. Gary Sykes, Barbara Schneider, and David N. Plank (New York: Routledge, 2009).

2 Jeffrey R. Henig, "Foreword," in *To Educate a Nation: Federal and National Strategies of School Reform*, ed. Carl F. Kaestle and Alyssa E. Lodewick (Lawrence: University Press of Kansas, 2007).

3 For example, see Elizabeth DeBray, *Politics, Ideology and Education: Federal Policy during the Clinton and Bush Administrations* (New York: Teachers College Press, 2006); Patrick McGuinn, *No Child Left Behind: The Transformation of Federal Education Policy, 1965–2005* (Lawrence: University of Kansas Press, 2006).

4 McDonnell, "A Political Science Perspective on Education Policy Analysis."

5 Lora Cohen-Vogel and Michael K. McLendon, "New Approaches to Understanding Federal Involvement in Education," in *Handbook of Education Policy Research*, ed. Gary Sykes, Barbara Schneider, and David N. Plank (New York: Routledge, 2009).

6 McGuinn, *No Child Left Behind: The Transformation of Federal Education Policy, 1965–2005*.

7 For example, John Kingdon presented the multiple streams model in which reform ideas suddenly emerge to enact sweeping change. John W. Kingdon, *Agendas, Alternatives, and Public Policies* (Boston: Little Brown, 1984). Baumgartner and Jones alternatively proposed the punctuated equilibrium model, in which sudden and transformative change occurs in a system that is otherwise stable. Frank L. Baumgartner and Bryan D. Jones, *Agendas and Instability in American Politics* (Chicago: University of Chicago Press, 1993).

8 McGuinn, *No Child Left Behind: The Transformation of Federal Education Policy, 1965–2005*.

9 Carter Wilson, "Policy Regimes and Policy Change," *Journal of Public Policy* 20, no. 3 (2000): 247–74.

10 Cohen-Vogel and McLendon, "New Approaches to Understanding Federal Involvement in Education."

11 Hanne B. Mahwhinney, "Theoretical Approaches to Understanding Interest Groups," *Educational Policy* 15, no. 1 (2001): 187–214.

12 Ibid.

13 Kay L. Schlozman and John T. Tierney, *Organized Interests and the American Democracy* (New York: Harper & Row, 1986).

14 Andrew S. McFarland, "Interest Groups and Theories of Power in America," *British Journal of Political Science* 17, no. 2 (1987): 129–47.

15 Paul Sabatier and Hank C. Jenkins-Smith, *Policy Change and Learning: An Advocacy Coalition Approach* (Boulder, CO: Westview Press, 1993).

16 Frank L. Baumgartner and Beth L. Leech, *Basic Instincts: The Importance of Groups in Politics and Political Science* (Princeton, NJ: Princeton University Press, 1998).

17 Mahwhinney, "Theoretical Approaches to Understanding Interest Groups."

18 Thomas Gais and Jack Walker, Jr., "Pathways to Influence in American Politics," in *Mobilizing Interest Groups in America,* ed. Jack Walker, Jr. (Ann Arbor: University of Michigan Press, 1991).

19 Baumgartner and Leech, *Basic Instincts: The Importance of Groups in Politics and Political Science.*

20 Diane Ravitch, "The Search for Order and the Rejection of Conformity: Standards in American Education," in *Learning from the Past: What History Teaches Us about School Reform,* ed. Diane Ravitch and Maris Vinovskis (Baltimore: Johns Hopkins University Press, 1995).

21 McDonnell, "A Political Science Perspective on Education Policy Analysis."

22 Ibid.

23 Deborah A. Stone, *Policy Paradox: The Art of Political Decision Making* (New York: W. W. Norton, 1997).

24 David F. Labaree, "Public Goods, Private Goods: The American Struggle over Educational Goals," *American Educational Research Journal* 34, no. 1 (1997): 38–81 at 41.

25 John Dewey concisely framed the arguments about whether schools should be vehicles to preserve or change society in John Dewey, "Education and Social Change," *Social Frontier* 1937, no. 3 (May 1937): 235–8.

26 Carl Kaestle, *Pillars of the Republic* (New York: Hill & Wang, 1983).

27 Amy Gutmann, *Democratic Education* (Princeton, NJ: Princeton University Press, 1999).

28 Labaree, "Public Goods, Private Goods: the American Struggle over Educational Goals."

29 Herbert M. Kliebard, *Schooled to Work: Vocationalism and the American Curriculum, 1876–1946* (New York: Teachers College Press, 1999).

30 Labaree, "Public Goods, Private Goods: the American Struggle over Educational Goals."

31 Jennifer L. Hochschild and Nathan B. Scvoronick, *The American Dream and the Public Schools* (New York: Oxford University Press, 2003).

32 Stone, *Policy Paradox: The Art of Political Decision Making.*

33 McDonnell, "A Political Science Perspective on Education Policy Analysis."

34 Kingdon, *Agendas, Alternatives, and Public Policies.*
35 Catherine Marshall, Douglas E. Mitchell, and Frederick Wirt, "Assumptive Worlds of Education Policy Makers," *Peabody Journal of Education* 62, no. 4 (1985): 90–115.
36 David A. Gamson, "From Progressivism to Federalism: The Pursuit of Equal Educational Opportunity," in *To Educate a Nation: Federal and National Strategies for School Reform*, ed. Carl Kaestle and Alyssa E. Lodewick (Lawrence: University Press of Kansas, 2007).
37 James G. March and Johan P. Olsen, "The New Institutionalism: Organizational Factors in Public Life," *American Political Science Review* 78, no. 3 (1984): 734–49.
38 David K. Cohen, "Policy and Organization: The Impact of State and Federal Education Policy on School Governance," *Harvard Educational Review* 52, no. 4 (1982): 474–99.
39 Paul Manna, *School's In: Federalism and the National Education Agenda* (Washington, DC: Georgetown University Press, 2006).
40 Edward L. Rubin, "The New Legal Process, The Synthesis of Discourse, and the Microanalysis of Institutions," *Harvard Law Review* 109 (1996): 1393–438.
41 Ronald Coase, "The Problem of Social Cost," *Journal of Law and Economics* 3, no. 1 (1960): 1–44; Neil Komesar, *Imperfect Alternatives: Choosing Institutions in Law, Economics, and Public Policy* (Chicago: University of Chicago Press, 1994).
42 Komesar, *Imperfect Alternatives: Choosing Institutions in Law, Economics, and Public Policy.*
43 Ibid.
44 Helen Hershkoff, "Positive Rights and State Constitutions: The Limits of Federal Rationality Review," *Harvard Law Review* no. 112 (1999): 1131–96.
45 David B. Spence and Frank Cross, "A Public Choice Case for the Administrative State," *Georgetown Law Journal* 97 (2000): 106–42.
46 Matthew C. Stephenson, "Legislative Allocation of Delegated Power: Uncertainty, Risk, and the Choice between Agencies and Courts," *Harvard Law Review* 119 (2006): 1035–70.
47 Richard Pierce, "Political Control versus Impermissible Bias in Agency Decision Making: Lessons from *Chevron* and *Mistretta*," *University of Chicago Law Review* 57 (1990): 481–519.
48 Cornell W. Clayton, "The Supreme Court and Political Jurisprudence: New and Old Institutionalisms," in *Supreme Court Decision-making: New Institutionalist Approaches*, ed. W. Cornell Clayton and Howard Gillman (Chicago: University of Chicago Press, 1999).
49 Michael A. Rebell and Robert L. Hughes, "Efficacy and Engagement: The Remedies Problem Posed by *Sheff v. O'Neill*," *Connecticut Law Review* 29, no. 3 (1997): 1115–86.
50 Malcom M. Feeley and Edward L. Rubin, *Judicial Policy Making and the Modern State: How the Courts Reformed America's Prisons* (Cambridge: Cambridge University Press, 1998); Komesar, *Imperfect Alternatives: Choosing Institutions in Law, Economics, and Public Policy.*

51 Michael A. Rebell and Arthur R. Block, *Educational Policy Making and the Courts: An Empirical Study of Judicial Activism* (Philadelphia: Temple University Press, 1982).

52 Alexander Bickel, *The Least Dangerous Branch: The Supreme Court at the Bar of Politics*, 2nd ed. (New Haven, CT: Yale University Press, 1986).

53 Mark A. Graber, "The Law Professor as Populist," *University of Richmond Law Review* 34 (2000): 373–413. Supreme Court decisions have often remained in line with legislative majorities at the national level as well. Robert A. Dahl, "Decision-Making in a Democracy: The Role of the Supreme Court as a National Policy-Maker," *Journal of Public Law* 6, no. 2 (1957): 279–95.

54 Robert C. Post, "Fashioning the Legal Constitution: Culture, Courts, and Law," *Harvard Law Review* 117 (2003): 4–112.

55 Bruce A. Ackerman, *We the People*. Vol. 1. *Foundations* (Cambridge, MA: Harvard University Press, 1991).

56 Richard Primus, "Public Consensus as Constitutional Authority," *George Washington Law Review* 78, no. 6 (2010): 1207–31.

57 Larry D. Kramer, "Popular Constitutionalism, Circa 2004," *California Law Review* 92 (2004): 959–1011. Reva B. Seigel, "Constitutional Culture, Social Movement Conflict, and Constitutional Change: The Case of the De Facto ERA," *California Law Review* 94 (2006): 1323–419.

58 Komesar, *Imperfect Alternatives: Choosing Institutions in Law, Economics, and Public Policy*.

59 Charles J. Ogletree, *All Deliberate Speed: Reflections on the First Half Century of Brown v. Board of Education* (New York: W. W. Norton, 2004).

60 Gerald N. Rosenberg, *The Hollow Hope: Can Courts Bring About Social Change?* (Chicago: University of Chicago Press, 1991).

61 Robert C. Post and Reva B. Seigel, "Protecting the Constitution from the People: Juricentric Restrictions on Section Five Power," *Indiana Law Journal* 78, no. 1 (2003): 1–46. Still, it is worth noting that the Rehnquist Court repeatedly highlighted that the Supreme Court is the ultimate arbiter of how the Constitution should be interpreted.

62 A special master is typically a lawyer, magistrate, or scientist appointed by a court to assist with difficult issues at trial, including understanding expert testimony about scientific claims. After the presentation of scientific evidence, special masters generally submit reports to the court, which in turn become evidence.

63 Michael Heise, "Equal Educational Opportunity by the Numbers: The Warren Court's Empirical Legacy," *Washington and Lee Law Review* 59 (2002): 1309–42; Kevin G. Welner and Haggai Kupermintz, "Rethinking Expert Testimony in Education Rights Litigation," *Educational Evaluation and Policy Analysis* 26, no. 2 (2004): 127–42.

64 Erwin Chemerinsky, "The Segregation and Resegregation of American Public Education: The Courts' Role," *North Carolina Law Review* 81 (2003): 1597–622.

65 Michael Kaufman, "Rhetorical Questions Concerning Justice and Equality in Educational Opportunities," *Loyola University of Chicago Law Journal* 36, no. 2 (2005): 495–511.

66 David N. Plank and William L. Boyd, "Antipolitics, Education, and Institutional Choice: The Flight from Democracy," *American Educational Research Journal* 31, no. 2 (1994): 263–81.

67 David N. Plank, "The Politics of Basic Education Reform in Brazil," *Comparative Education Review* 34, no. 4 (1990): 538–60.

68 Herbert Kaufman, "Emerging Conflicts in the Doctrines of Public Administration," *American Political Science Review* 50, no. 4 (1956): 1057–73.

69 John E. Chubb and Terry M. Moe, *Politics, Markets, and America's Schools* (Washington, DC: Brookings Institution Press, 1990).

70 William W. Buzbee, "Sprawl's Dynamics: A Comparative Institutional Analysis Critique," *Wake Forest Law Review* 35, no. 3 (2000): 509–37.

71 Komesar, *Imperfect Alternatives: Choosing Institutions in Law, Economics, and Public Policy:* 141–2.

72 Paul Sabatier and Daniel Manzmanian, "The Implementation of Public Policy: A Framework of Analysis," *Policy Studies Journal* 8, no. 4 (1980): 538–60.

73 Meredith L. Honig, "Complexity and Policy Implementation: Challenges and Observations for the Field," in *New Directions in Education Policy Implementation*, ed. Meredith L. Honig (Albany: State University of New York Press, 2005).

74 James P. Spillane, "Cognition and Policy Implementation: District Policymakers and the Reform of Mathematics Education," *Cognition and Instruction* 18, no. 2 (2000): 141–79.

75 Ibid.

76 Mary K. Stein and Cynthia E. Coburn, "Architectures for Learning: A Comparative Analysis of Two Urban School Districts," *American Journal of Education* 114, no. 4 (2008): 583–626.

77 Jennifer A. Mueller and Katherine H. Hoyde, "Theme and Variation in the Enactment of Reform: Case Studies," in *The Implementation Gap: Understanding Reform in High Schools*, ed. Jonathan A. Supovitz and Elliot H. Weinbaum (New York: Teachers College Press, 2008).

78 Ibid.

79 Robert J. Marzano, *What Works in Schools: Translating Research into Action* (Alexandria, VA: Association for Supervision and Curriculum Development, 2003).

80 Michael Lipsky, *Street-level Bureaucracy: Dilemmas of the Individual in Public Services* (New York: Russell Sage Foundation, 1980).

81 Lorraine M. McDonnell and Richard F. Elmore, "Getting the Job Done: Alternative Policy Instruments," *Educational Evaluation and Policy Analysis* 9, no. 2 (1987): 133–52.

82 Milbrey McLaughlin, "Implementation Research in Education: Lessons Learned, Lingering Questions, and New Opportunities," in *New Directions in Education Policy Implementation: Confronting Complexity*, ed. Meredith L. Honig (Albany: State University of New York Press, 2006).

83 Mark A Smylie and Andrea E. Evans, "Social Capital and the Problem of Implementation," in *New Directions in Education Policy Implementation: Confronting Complexity*, ed. Meredith L. Honig (Albany: State University of New York Press 2006).

84 Jean Anyon, *Radical Possibilities: Public Policy, Urban Education, and a New Social Movement* (New York: Routledge, 2005).
85 David Tyack and Larry Cuban, *Tinkering Toward Utopia: A Century of Public School Reform* (Cambridge, MA: Harvard University Press, 1995).
86 Honig, "Complexity and Policy Implementation: Challenges and Observations for the Field."
87 McLaughlin, "Implementation Research in Education: Lessons Learned, Lingering Questions and New Opportunities."
88 While early research on policy implementation did not formally articulate the range of factors contributing to the complexity of implementation, several factors were recognized as important, including the evolutionary nature of policy. Giandomenico Majone and Aaron B. Wildavsky, "Implementation as Evolution," in *Implementation: How Great Expectations in Washington Are Dashed in Oakland*, ed. Jeffrey L. Pressman and Aaron B. Wildavsky (Berkeley: University of California Press, 1979).

3   *BROWN* AND THE FOUNDATIONS OF EDUCATIONAL EQUALITY

1 Abram Chayes, "The Role of the Judge in Public Law Litigation," *Harvard Law Review* 89 (1976): 1281–316.
2 Jack M. Balkin, "*Brown* as Icon," in *What* Brown v. *Board of Education Should Have Said: The Nation's Top Legal Experts Rewrite America's Landmark Civil Rights Decision*, ed. Jack M. Balkin (New York: New York University Press, 2002).
3 Martha Minow, *In Brown's Wake* (New York: Oxford University Press, 2010).
4 U.S. Constitution, Amendment XIV.
5 *Plessy v. Ferguson*, 163 U.S. 537 (1896).
6 David. J. Armor, *Forced Justice: School Desegregation and the Law* (New York: Oxford University Press, 1995).
7 Michael Klarman, *From Jim Crow to Civil Rights: The Supreme Court and the Struggle for Racial Equality* (New York: NY: Oxford University Press, 2004).
8 Ibid.
9 *McLaurin v. Oklahoma State Regents*, 339 U.S. 637 (1950); *Sweatt v. Painter*, 339 U.S. 629 (1950).
10 Lino A. Graglia, *Disaster by Decree: The Supreme Court Decisions on Race and the Schools* (Ithaca, NY: Cornell University Press, 1976).
11 *McLaurin v. Oklahoma State Regents*, 339 U.S. 637 (1950); *Briggs v. Elliott*, 342 U.S. 350 (1952); *Davis v. County School Board of Prince Edward County*, 103 F. Supp. 337 (E.D. Va. 1952); *Gebhart v. Belton*, 91 A.2d 137 (Del. 1952); *Bolling v. Sharpe*, 347 U.S. 497 (1954).
12 Robert J. Cottrol, Raymond T. Diamond, and Leland B. Ware, Brown v. Board of Education: *Caste, Culture, and the Constitution* (Topeka: University Press of Kansas, 2003).
13 *Amicus curiae* briefs, or "friend of the court" briefs, are often filed in Supreme Court cases by interested parties that are not directly impacted by the litigation. These briefs can offer advisory opinions from the perspectives of interested parties.

14 *Brown v. Board of Education*, 347 U.S. 483, 493 (1954).

15 Ibid., 495.

16 Ibid., 493.

17 Ibid., 494.

18 Angelo N. Ancheta, "Civil Rights, Education Research, and the Courts," *Educational Researcher* 35, no. 1 (2006): 26–9.

19 Michael Heise, "Equal Educational Opportunity by the Numbers: The Warren Court's Empirical Legacy," *Washington and Lee Law Review* 59 (2002): 1309–42.

20 Herbert Wechsler, "Toward Neutral Principles of Constitutional Law," *Harvard Law Review* 73 (1959): 1–35, in Michael Heise, "Footnote 11, and Multidisciplinarity," *Cornell Law Review* 90 (2005): 320;

21 John P Jackson,. Jr., "The Triumph of the Segregationists? A Historiographical Inquiry into Psychology and the *Brown* Litigation," *History of Psychology* 3, no. 3 (2000): 239–61; Kevin G. Welner and Haggai Kupermintz, "Rethinking Expert Testimony in Education Rights Litigation," *Educational Evaluation and Policy Analysis* 26, no. 2 (2004): 127–42;.

22 James Ryan, "The Limited Influence of Social Science Evidence in Modern Desegregation Cases," *North Carolina Law Review* 81 (2003): 1659–702.

23 *Brown v. Board of Education*, 347 U.S. 483, 495 (1954)

24 It is worth noting that the Fifth Amendment of the Constitution does not contain an equal protection clause. Still, the Court held that the principles of equal protection applied through the Fifth Amendment. *Bolling v. Sharpe*, 347 U.S. 497 (1954).

25 Minow, *In Brown's Wake*.

26 *Brown v. Board of Education*, 349 U.S. 294 (1955).

27 Ibid., 301.

28 Ibid., 300.

29 For example, see Klarman, *From Jim Crow to Civil Rights: The Supreme Court and the Struggle for Racial Equality*.

30 Graglia, *Disaster by Decree: The Supreme Court Decisions on Race and the Schools*.

31 Klarman, *From Jim Crow to Civil Rights: The Supreme Court and the Struggle for Racial Equality*.

32 U.S. Congress, 102 *Congressional Record* 4, 4515–16 (1956).

33 Klarman, *From Jim Crow to Civil Rights: The Supreme Court and the Struggle for Racial Equality*.

34 James W. Guthrie and Mathew G. Springer, "Returning to Square One: From *Plessy* to *Brown* and Back to *Plessy*," *Peabody Journal of Education* 79, no. 2 (2004): 2–32.

35 For a thorough discussion of the strategies southern states employed to respond to *Brown v. Board of Education*, see Mark Whitman, *The Irony of School Desegregation Law: 1955–1995: Essays and Documents* (Princeton, NJ: Markus Weiner, 1998).

36 Klarman, *From Jim Crow to Civil Rights: The Supreme Court and the Struggle for Racial Equality*. While several scholars have detailed the southern political response to *Brown*, Klarman does a particularly thorough job.

37 Ibid.

38 *Briggs v. Elliott*, 132 F. Supp. 776, 777 (E.D.S.C. 1955).

39 Ibid.

40 Graglia, *Disaster by Decree: The Supreme Court Decisions on Race and the Schools.*

41 *Cooper v. Aaron*, 359 U.S. 1 (1958).

42 *Goss v. Board of Education*, 373 U.S. 683 (1963).

43 *Griffin v. County School Board of Prince Edward County*, 377 U.S. 218 (1964).

44 Minow, *In Brown's Wake.*

45 Klarman, *From Jim Crow to Civil Rights: The Supreme Court and the Struggle for Racial Equality.* Klarman specifically argued that desegregation litigation was much less responsible for desegregation than the politics of the civil rights movement. Klarman has been strongly criticized for this argument. For example, see David J. Garrow, "'Happy' Birthday, *Brown v. Board of Education? Brown*'s Fiftieth Anniversary and the New Critics of Supreme Court Muscularity," *Virginia Law Review* 90, no. 2 (2004): 693–729. However, this book argues that litigation and social movements (in addition to several other factors) spurred the desegregation that occurred.

46 For example, the Land Ordinance of 1785 and Northwest Ordinance of 1787 required states to reserve land for public schools.

47 Maris Vinovskis, "School Reforms and Equal Education Opportunities for Children: The Changing Federal Role in Education," in *Stimulating Equity: The Impact of the Federal Stimulus Act on Educational Equity* (New York: Campaign for Educational Equity, 2010).

48 Serviceman's Readjustment Act, 38 U.S.C. § 3701 et seq. (1944); National School Lunch Act, 42 U.S.C. § 1751 et seq. (1946).

49 National Defense Education Act, 20 U.S.C. § 401 et seq. (1958).

50 Peter B. Dow, *Schoolhouse Politics: Lessons from the Sputnik Era* (Cambridge, MA: Harvard University Press, 1991).

51 John F. Jennings, "Title I: Its Legislative History and Its Promise," in *Compensatory Education at the Crossroads*, ed. Geoffrey D. Borman, Samuel C. Stringfield, and Robert E. Slavin (Mahwah, NJ: Lawrence Erlbaum Associates, 2001).

52 Civil Rights Act of 1964, 42 U.S.C. § 2000 et seq. (1964); Economic Opportunity Act, 42 U.S.C. § 2701 et seq. (1964); Elementary and Secondary Education Act, 20 U.S.C. § 6301 et seq. (1965); Voting Rights Act, 42 U.S.C. § 1973 et seq. (1965).

53 For a detailed examination of the early history of Project Head Start, see Maris Vinovskis, *The Birth of Head Start: Preschool Education Policies in the Kennedy and Johnson Administrations* (Chicago: University of Chicago Press, 2005).

54 Patrick McGuinn, *No Child Left Behind: The Transformation of Federal Education Policy, 1965–2005* (Lawrence: University of Kansas Press, 2006).

55 Civil Rights Act of 1964, 42 U.S.C. § 2407(b) (1964).

56 Civil Rights Act of 1964, 42 U.S.C. § 2401(a) (1964).

57 John G. Stewart, "The Civil Rights Act of 1964: Strategy," in *The Civil Rights Act of 1964: The Passage of The Law That Ended Racial Segregation*, ed. Robert D. Loevy (Albany: State University of New York Press, 1997).

58 Civil Rights Act of 1964, 42 U.S.C. § 2601 (1964).
59 As discussed in Chapter 4, there was no cabinet-level department for education until 1979. In the 1960s, the U.S. Department of Health, Education, and Welfare oversaw federal education programs.
60 Graglia, *Disaster by Decree: The Supreme Court Decisions on Race and the Schools*.
61 Charles C. Bolton, *The Hardest Deal of All: The Battle over School Integration in Mississippi, 1870–1980* (Jackson: University Press of Mississippi, 2005).
62 Ibid.
63 Graglia, *Disaster by Decree: The Supreme Court Decisions on Race and the Schools*.
64 *United States v. Jefferson County Board of Education*, 372 F.2d 836 (5th Cir. 1966).
65 *U.S. v. Jefferson County Board of Education*, 389 U.S. 840 (1967).
66 David K. Cohen and Susan L. Moffit, *The Ordeal of Equality: Did Federal Regulation Fix the Schools?* (Cambridge, MA: Harvard University Press, 2009).
67 McGuinn, *No Child Left Behind: The Transformation of Federal Education Policy, 1965–2005*.
68 Julia Hanna, "The Elementary and Secondary Education Act: 40 Years Later," *Ed. Magazine*, June 1, 2005. http://www.gse.harvard.edu/news/ed/ (accessed May 14, 2012).
69 Lee W. Anderson, *Congress and the Classroom: From the Cold War to No Child Left Behind* (University Park: Pennsylvania State University Press, 2007).
70 Jerome T. Murphy, "Title I of the ESEA: The Politics of Implementing Federal Education Reform," *Harvard Educational Review* 40, no. 4 (1971): 35–63.
71 Cohen and Moffit, *The Ordeal of Equality: Did Federal Regulation Fix the Schools?*
72 McGuinn, *No Child Left Behind: The Transformation of Federal Education Policy, 1965–2005*.
73 *Green v. County School Board*, 391 U.S. 430 (1968).
74 California Constitution, Art. IX. § 140 (1902); Virginia Code § 22–221 (1950).
75 *Green v. County School Board of New Kent County*, 382 F.2d 339 (4th Cir. 1967).
76 *Green v. County School Board of New Kent County*, 391 U.S. 430, 437–8 (1968).
77 Ibid., 438.
78 Ibid., 435.
79 *Raney v. Board of Education*, 391 U.S. 443 (1968).
80 James Bolner and Robert Shanley, *Busing: The Political and Judicial Process* (New York: Praeger, 1974).
81 *U.S. v. Montgomery County Board of Education*, 395 U.S. 225 (1969).
82 *Alexander v. Holmes County Board of Education*, 396 U.S. 19 (1969).
83 Ibid., 19.
84 Graglia, *Disaster by Decree: The Supreme Court Decisions on Race and the Schools*.

85 Gary Orfield, "Schools More Separate: Consequences of a Decade of Resegregation" (Los Angeles: Civil Rights Project, 2001).

86 Klarman, *From Jim Crow to Civil Rights: The Supreme Court and the Struggle for Racial Equality.*

87 Ibid.

88 Bolner and Shanley, *Busing: The Political and Judicial Process.*

89 Ibid., 136.

90 *Swann v. Charlotte-Mecklenburg Board of Education,* 402 U.S. 1 (1971).

91 Ibid.

92 *Swann v. Charlotte-Mecklenburg Board of Education,* 431 F.2d 138, 142 (4th Cir. 1970).

93 *Swann v. Charlotte-Mecklenburg Board of Education,* 402 U.S. 1, 14 (1971).

94 Ibid., 25.

95 Ibid., 28.

96 Ibid., 29.

97 Select Committee on Equal Educational Opportunity of the United States Senate, *Hearings before the Select Committee on Equal Educational Opportunity of the United States Senate,* 1st Session, June 15, 1971. The evidence from this hearing is particularly highlighted by Graglia, *Disaster by Decree: The Supreme Court Decisions on Race and the Schools.*

98 Graglia, *Disaster by Decree: The Supreme Court Decisions on Race and the Schools.*

99 Ibid.

100 Ibid.

101 J. A. Lukas, *Common Ground: A Turbulent Decade in the Lives of Three American Families* (New York: Vintage Books, 1985).

102 *Keyes v. School District No. 1,* 413 U.S. 189 (1973).

103 James J. Fishman and Lawrence Strauss, "Endless Journey: Integration and the Provision of Equal Educational Opportunity in Denver's Public Schools: A Study of *Keyes v. School District No. 1,*" in *Justice and School Systems: The Role of the Courts in Education Litigation,* ed. Barbara Flickr (Philadelphia: Temple University Press, 1990).

104 Armor, *Forced Justice: School Desegregation and the Law.*

105 The Resolutions adopted by the Denver School Board to desegregate Park Hill Schools were Resolutions 1520, 1524, and 1531.

106 *Keyes v. School District No. 1,* 413 U.S. 189, 192 (1973).

107 *Keyes v. School District No. 1,* 313 F. Supp. 61 (D. Colo. 1970).

108 Ibid., 73.

109 *Keyes v. School District No. 1,* 445 F.2d 990 (10th Cir. 1971).

110 *Keyes v. School District No. 1,* 413 U.S. 189, 202 (1973).

111 Ibid., 208.

112 Ibid., 209.

113 Armor, *Forced Justice: School Desegregation and the Law.*

114 Howard I. Kalodner, "Overview of Judicial Activism in Education Litigation," in *Justice and School Systems: The Role of the Courts in Education Litigation,* ed. Barbara Flickr (Philadelphia: Temple University Press, 1990).

4   THE MATURATION OF EDUCATIONAL EQUALITY

1 See Chapter 3 for a detailed discussion of *Keyes v. School District No. 1*, 413 U.S. 189 (1973).
2 Robert J. Cottrol, Raymond T. Diamond, and Leland B. Ware, Brown v. Board of Education: *Caste, Culture, and the Constitution* (Topeka: University Press of Kansas, 2003).
3 *Milliken v. Bradley*, 418 U.S. 717 (1974).
4 The demographics of Detroit and Detroit Public Schools during the 1960s and 1970s were provided in Lino A. Graglia, *Disaster by Decree: The Supreme Court Decisions on Race and the Schools* (Ithaca, NY: Cornell University Press, 1976).
5 *Milliken v. Bradey*, 484 F.2d 215, 245 (6th Cir. 1973).
6 *Milliken v. Bradley*, 418 U.S. 717, 742 (1974).
7 Ibid., 743.
8 *Milliken v. Bradley II*, 433 U.S. 267 (1977).
9 Susan E. Eaton, Joseph Feldman, and Edward Kirby, "The Limits of *Milliken II*'s Monetary Compensation to Segregated Schools," in *Dismantling Desegregation: The Quiet Reversal of* Brown v. Board of Education, ed. Gary Orfield and Susan E. Eaton (New York: New Press, 1997).
10 Ibid., 145.
11 *Washington v. Davis*, 426 U.S. 229 (1976).
12 Ibid., 239.
13 Gary Orfield, "The Growth of Segregation," in *Dismantling Desegregation: The Quiet Reversal of* Brown v. Board of Education, ed. Gary Orfield and Susan E. Eaton (New York: New Press, 1997).
14 *Riddick v. School Board of the City of Norfolk, Virginia*, 784 F.2d 521 (4th Cir. 1986).
15 The description of San Francisco's experience with school desegregation is based on Stuart Biegel, "Court-mandated Education Reform: The San Francisco Experience and the Shaping of Educational Policy after *Seattle-Lousiville* and *Ho v. SFUSD*," *Stanford Journal of Civil Rights and Civil Liberties* 4, no. 2 (2008): 159–214.
16 Ibid.
17 Joanne L. Huston, "Inclusion: A Proposed Remedial Approach Ignores Legal and Educational Issues," *Journal of Law & Education* 27 (1998): 249–56.
18 Biegel, "Court-mandated Education Reform: The San Francisco Experience and the Shaping of Educational Policy after *Seattle-Lousiville* and *Ho v. SFUSD*."
19 Michael A. Rebell and Robert L. Hughes, "Efficacy and Engagement: The Remedies Problem Posed by *Sheff v. O'Neill*," *Connecticut Law Review* 29, no. 3 (1997): 1115–86.
20 Peter Enrich, "Leaving Equality Behind: New Directions in School Finance Reform," *Vanderbilt Law Review* 48, no. 1 (1995): 101–94. Much of the information about the barriers to the success of first and second waves of school finance litigation is directly drawn from this article, which provides a comprehensive overview of the early history of this litigation.
21 *Serrano v. Priest*, 487 P.2d 1241 (Cal. 1971).

22 *Robinson v. Cahill*, 303 A.2d 273 (N.J. 1973).

23 William Thro, "To Render Them Safe: The Analysis of State Constitutional Provisions in School Finance Litigation," *Virginia Law Review* 75 (1989): 1639–78.

24 *U.S. v. Carolene Products*, 304 U.S. 144 (1938).

25 *San Antonio Independent School District v. Rodriguez*, 337 F. Supp. 280 (W.D. Tex. 1971).

26 *San Antonio Independent School District v. Rodriguez*, 411 U.S. 1 (1971).

27 Ibid., 25.

28 Ibid., 24.

29 Ibid., 35–6.

30 Ibid., 36.

31 Robert F. Williams, "Equality Guarantees in State Constitutional Law," *Texas Law Review* 63 (1985): 1195–223.

32 Enrich, "Leaving Equality Behind: New Directions in School Finance Reform." Every state constitution with the arguable exception of Mississippi's contains an education clause.

33 Ibid.

34 Ibid.

35 For example, see *Danson v. Casey*, 399 A.2d 360 (Pa. 1979); *Abbott v. Burke*, 575 A.2d 359 (N.J. 1990).

36 For example, see *McDaniel v. Thomas*, 285 S.E.2d 156 (Ga. 1981).

37 For example, see *Olsen v. State*, 55 P.2d 139 (Or. 1976); *Levittown Union Free School District v. Nyquist*, 439 N.E.2d 359 (N.Y. 1982).

38 National Education Access Network, "Legal Developments" (New York: National Education Access Network, 2011).

39 Michael A. Rebell, "Educational Adequacy, Democracy, and the Courts," in *Achieving High Educational Standards for All*, ed. Timothy Ready, Christopher F. Edley, and Catherine E. Snow (Washington, DC: National Academies Press, 2002). The discussion about successful second wave cases and their results is largely drawn from this source.

40 William S. Koski, "Of Fuzzy Standards and Institutional Constraints: A Re-Examination of the Jurisprudential History of Educational Finance Reform Litigation," *Santa Clara Law Review* 43, no. 4 (2003): 1185–298.

41 California's Proposition 13 was formally titled "People's Initiative to Limit Property Taxation" (1978).

42 While the school finance litigation in New Jersey originally appeared as *Robinson v. Cahill*, 303 A.2d 273 (N.J. 1973), the litigation transformed into *Abbott v. Burke*, 495 A.2d 376 (N.J. 1985). This case is discussed on more detail in Chapter 5.

43 General Accounting Office, "School Finance: State Efforts to Equalize Funding between Wealthy and Poor School Districts" (Washington, DC: Government Printing Office, 1998).

44 David K. Cohen, Steven W. Raudenbush, and Deborah L. Ball, "Resources, Instruction, and Research," *Educational Evaluation and Policy Analysis* 25, no. 2 (2003): 119–42.

45 Chapter 5 addresses the shift in equality at the end of the 1980s in detail.

46 Thomas Hehir and Susan Gamm, "Special Education: From Legalism to Collaboration," in *Law and School Reform*, ed. Jay P. Heubert (New Haven, CT: Yale University Press, 1999).

47 *Buck v. Bell*, 274 U.S. 200 (1927).

48 Ibid., 207.

49 *Pennsylvania Association for Retarded Citizens v. Commonwealth of Pennsylvania*, 334 F. Supp. 1257 (E.D. Pa. 1971).

50 *Mills v. Board of Education*, 347 U.S. 483 (1972).

51 Tiina Itkonen, *The Role of Special Education Interest Groups in National Policy* (Amherst, NY: Cambria Press, 2009).

52 Rehabilitation Act, 29 U.S.C. § 794 et seq. (1973).

53 Ibid.

54 34 C.F.R. § 104 (1976).

55 Education for All Handicapped Children Act, 20 U.S.C. § 1400 et seq. (1975).

56 Itkonen, *The Role of Special Education Interest Groups in National Policy*. Congress also enacted the Occupational Safety and Health Act, 29 U.S.C. § 651 et seq. (1970) in addition to the Rehabilitation Act.

57 The EAHCA was passed by the House of Representatives in a 404–7 vote and by the Senate in an 87–7 vote.

58 Education for All Handicapped Children Act, 20 U.S.C. § 1401 (1975).

59 Elizabeth Palley, "The Role of the Courts in the Development and Implementation of the IDEA," *Social Service Review* 77, no. 4 (2003): 605–18.

60 Itkonen, *The Role of Special Education Interest Groups in National Policy*.

61 Ibid.

62 *Hendrick Hudson School District v. Rowley*, 458 U.S. 176 (1982).

63 For examples of cases that interpreted *Rowley* as providing more benefit than simply moving from grade to grade, see *Hall v. Vance*, 774 F.2d 629 (4th Cir. 1985); *Polk v. Central Susquehanna Intermediate Unit 161*, 853 F.2d 171 (3d. Cir. 1988). For examples of cases that interpreted *Rowley* as providing only a minimum benefit, see *J.D. v. Pawlet School District*, 224 F.3d 60 (2d. Cir. 2000); *Zumwalt School District v. Clynes*, 119 F.3d 607 (8th Cir. 1997). For more detail on how the courts have interpreted the right to an appropriate education, see Andrea F. Blau, "The IDEIA and the Right to an 'Appropriate' Education," *BYU Education and the Law Journal* 15, no. 1 (2007): 1–22.

64 *Roncker v. Walters*, 700 F.2d 1058 (1983).

65 Ibid., 1065.

66 *Sacramento City School District v. Rachel H.*, 14 F.3d 1398 (9th Cir. 1994).

67 *Daniel R. R. v. State Board of Education*, 874 F.2d 1036 (5th Cir. 1989).

68 *Oberti v. Board of Education*, 995 F.2d 1204 (3d. Cir. 1993).

69 *Hartmann v. Loudoun County Board of Education*, 118 F.3d 996 (4th Cir. 1997).

70 Itkonen, *The Role of Special Education Interest Groups in National Policy*.

71 *Jose P. v. Ambach*, 669 F.2d 865 (5th Cir. 1982).

72 The discussion of *Jose P. v. Ambach* is largely derived from Samuel R. Bagenstos, "The Judiciary's Now-Limited Role in Special Education," in *From Schoolhouse to Courthouse: The Judiciary's Role in American Education*, ed. Joshua M. Dunn and Martin R. West (Washington, DC: Brookings Institution Press, 2009).

73 Ibid.
74 David Mayrowetz and John F. Lapham, "'But We're in a Court of Law. We're Not in a Legislature.' The Promise and Pitfalls of Educational Policy Reform through the Judicial Branch," *Educational Policy* 22, no. 3 (2008): 379–421.
75 Itkonen, *The Role of Special Education Interest Groups in National Policy.*
76 Hehir and Gamm, "Special Education: From Legalism to Collaboration."
77 Ibid.
78 Federal Education Budget Project, "Individuals with Disabilities Education Act – Cost Impact on Local School Districts" (Washington, DC: New America Foundation, 2011).
79 *Meyer v. Nebraska*, 262 U.S. 390 (1923); *Farrington v. Tokushige*, 273 U.S. 284 (1927).
80 David Nieto, "A Brief History of Bilingual Education in the United States," *Perspectives on Urban Education* 6, no. 1 (2009): 61–72.
81 Bilingual Education Act, 20 U.S.C. § 3281 et seq. (1968).
82 Gareth Davies, "The Great Society after Johnson: The Case of Bilingual Education," *The Journal of American History* 88, no. 4 (2002): 1405–29.
83 Ibid.
84 J. S. Pottinger, "Developing Programs for English Language Learners: HEW Memorandum" (Washington, DC: Department of Health Office of Civil Rights, Education, and Welfare, 1970).
85 Ibid.
86 Ibid.
87 *Lau v. Nichols*, 414 U.S. 563 (1974).
88 Ibid.
89 California Education Code § 71 (1974).
90 *Lau v. Nichols*, 414 U.S. 563, 564 (1974).
91 Equal Educational Opportunities Act, 20 U.S.C. § 1703(f) (1974).
92 Department of Health Office for Civil Rights, Education, and Welfare, "Task-Force Findings Specifying Remedies Available for Eliminating Past Educational Practices under *Lau v. Nichols*" (Washington, DC: Education Department of Health, and Welfare, 1975).
93 Nieto, "A Brief History of Bilingual Education in the United States."
94 *Castaneda v. Pickard*, 648 F.2d 989 (5th Cir. 1981).
95 Marcelo Suarez-Orozco, Peter Roos, and Caroloa Suarez-Orozco, "Cultural, Educational, and Legal Perspectives on Immigration: Implications for School Reform," in *Law and School Reform*, ed. Jay P. Heubert (New Haven, CT: Yale University Press, 1999).
96 Ibid.
97 Michael Fix and Jeffrey S. Passel, "U.S. Immigration – Trends and Implications for Schools," in *NCLB Implementation Institute* (New Orleans: National Association for Bilingual Education, 2003).
98 Nieto, "A Brief History of Bilingual Education in the United States."
99 There is a substantial amount of research on the history of laws prohibiting illegal immigrants from taking advantage of public education and banning bilingual education. For example, see Kevin R. Johnson and George A. Martinez, "Discrimination by Proxy: Proposition 227 and the Ban on Bilingual Education," *U.C. Davis Law Review* 33, no. 4 (2000): 1227–76.

100 *Plyler v. Doe*, 457 U.S. 202 (1982).

101 *Plyler v. Doe*, 457 U.S. 202, 202 (1982).

102 Jerome T. Murphy, "Title I of the ESEA: The Politics of Implementing Federal Education Reform," *Harvard Educational Review* 41, no. 1 (1971): 35–63.

103 Paul E. Peterson, Barry George Rabe, and Kenneth K. Wong, "The Maturation of Redistributive Programs," in *Education Policy Implementation*, ed. Allan Odden (Albany: State University of New York Press, 1991).

104 Murphy, "Title I of the ESEA: The Politics of Implementing Federal Education Reform."

105 Ruby Martin and Phyllis McClure, "Title I of ESEA: Is It Helping Poor Children?" (Washington, DC: NAACP Legal Defense and Educational Fund, 1969).

106 David K. Cohen and Susan L. Moffit, *The Ordeal of Equality: Did Federal Regulation Fix the Schools?* (Cambridge, MA: Harvard University Press, 2009).

107 James Coleman et al., "Equality of Educational Opportunity Study" (Washington, DC: U.S. Government Printing Office, 1966).

108 Elementary and Secondary Education Act, 20 U.S.C. § 6321(a) (1974).

109 Elementary and Secondary Education Act, 20 U.S.C. § 6321(c) (1974).

110 Elementary and Secondary Education Act, 20 U.S.C. § 6321(b) (1974).

111 Cohen and Moffit, *The Ordeal of Equality: Did Federal Regulation Fix the Schools?*

112 John F. Jennings, "Title I: Its Legislative History and Its Promise," in *Compensatory Education at the Crossroads*, ed. Geoffrey D. Borman, Samuel C. Stringfield, and Robert E. Slavin (Mahwah, NJ: Lawrence Erlbaum Associates, 2001).

113 Gene V. Glass and Mary L. Smith, "'Pull Out' in Compensatory Education" (Washington, DC: Department of Health, Education, and Welfare, 1977).

114 Lorraine McDonnell and Milbrey McLaughlin, "Education Policy and the Role of the States" (Santa Monica, CA: RAND, 1982).

115 Cohen and Moffit, *The Ordeal of Equality: Did Federal Regulation Fix the Schools?*

116 McDonnell and McLaughlin, "Education Policy and the Role of the States."

117 Ellen C. Lagemann, *Elusive Science: The Troubling History of Education Research* (Chicago: University of Chicago Press, 2000).

118 Maris A. Vinovskis, "Do Federal Compensatory Education Programs Really Work? A Brief Historical Analysis of Title I and Head Start," *American Educational Research Journal* 107, no. 3 (1999): 187–209.

119 Cohen and Moffit, *The Ordeal of Equality: Did Federal Regulation Fix the Schools?*

120 Ibid.

121 Patrick McGuinn, *No Child Left Behind: The Transformation of Federal Education Policy, 1965–2005* (Lawrence: University of Kansas Press, 2006).

122 Department of Education Organization Act, 20 U.S.C. § 3401 et seq. (1979). For a thorough discussion of the politics underlying the creation of the U.S. Department of Education, see Lee W. Anderson, *Congress and the*

Classroom: From the Cold War to No Child Left Behind (University Park: Pennsylvania State University Press, 2007).

123 Department of Education Organization Act, 20 U.S.C. § 3401 et seq. (1979).

124 Notably, there was some opposition among congressional liberals to the creation of the U.S. Department of Education (ED) on the grounds that ED diminished local control over education and that it would decrease the federal commitment to civil rights enforcement. Given diminished conservative opposition, the politics underlying the passage of ED reflect a breakdown of the traditional political division over the federal role in education. Anderson, *Congress and the Classroom: From the Cold War to No Child Left Behind.*

125 McGuinn, *No Child Left Behind: The Transformation of Federal Education Policy, 1965–2005.*

126 For a detailed discussion of research on the relationship between money and learning opportunities, see Chapter 5.

5 THE TURN TO ADEQUACY, OUTCOMES, AND SYSTEMIC CHANGE

1 William L. Boyd, "How to Reform Schools without Half Trying: Secrets of the Reagan Administration," *Educational Administration Quarterly* 24, no. 3 (1988): 299–309.

2 William L. Boyd, "The Power of Paradigms: Reconceptualizing Educational Policy and Management," *Educational Administration Quarterly* 28, no. 4 (1992): 504–28.

3 Maurice R. Berube, *American Presidents and Education* (Westport, CT: Greenwood Press, 1991).

4 James W. Guthrie and Mathew G. Springer, "*A Nation at Risk* Revisited: Did 'Wrong' Reasoning Result in 'Right' Results? At What Cost?" *Peabody Journal of Education* 79, no. 1 (2004): 7–35.

5 Maris A. Vinovskis, *From a Nation at Risk to No Child Left Behind: National Education Goals and the Creation of Federal Education Policy* (New York: Teachers College Press, 2008).

6 Boyd, "How to Reform Schools without Half Trying: Secrets of the Reagan Administration."

7 Bernard Weinraub, "The Reagan Legacy," *New York Times*, June 22, 1986. http://www.lexis.com (accessed May 15, 2012).

8 Central components of the Omnibus Budget Reconciliation Act can be found at 42 U.S.C. § 9822 et seq. (1981).

9 Education Consolidation and Improvement Act of 1981, 20 U.S.C. § 3581 et seq. (1981).

10 Michael Kirst, "Beyond Mutual Adaptation" (Washington, DC: National Institute of Education, 1986).

11 Michael W. Kirst, "Who's in Charge? Federal, State, and Local Control," in *Learning from the Past: What History Teaches Us about School Reform*, ed. Diane Ravitch and Maris Vinovskis (Baltimore: Johns Hopkins University Press, 1995).

12 Technical Amendments to the ECIA, 20 U.S.C. § 3581 et seq. (1983).

13 National Commission on Excellence in Education, *A Nation at Risk: The Imperative for Educational Reform* (Washington, DC: U.S. Government Printing Office, 1983).

14 National Commission on Excellence in Education, *A Nation at Risk: The Imperative for Educational Reform*, 5.

15 For perhaps the most prominent attack on the findings of *A Nation at Risk*, see David C. Berliner and Bruce J. Biddle, *The Manufactured Crisis: Myths, Fraud, and the Attack on American Public Schools* (New York: Basic Books, 1996).

16 Guthrie and Springer, "*A Nation at Risk* Revisited: Did 'Wrong' Reasoning Result in 'Right' Results? At What Cost?"

17 Ibid.

18 Ibid. President Reagan was initially very surprised at the contents of *A Nation at Risk*. When the report was first presented to the president, Reagan praised the National Commission on Educational Excellence for endorsing school vouchers, prayer in public schools, and the abolition of ED – none of which was actually included in the report.

19 Boyd, "How to Reform Schools without Half Trying: Secrets of the Reagan Administration."

20 Patrick McGuinn, *No Child Left Behind: The Transformation of Federal Education Policy, 1965–2005* (Lawrence: University of Kansas Press, 2006).

21 Lee W. Anderson, *Congress and the Classroom: From the Cold War to No Child Left Behind* (University Park: Pennsylvania State University Press, 2007).

22 Ibid., 94.

23 Lorraine McDonnell, "No Child Left Behind and the Federal Role in Education: Evolution or Revolution?" *Peabody Journal of Education* 80, no. 2 (2005): 19–38.

24 Anderson, *Congress and the Classroom: From the Cold War to No Child Left Behind*.

25 Richard F. Elmore, "Contested Terrain: The Next Generation of Educational Reform" (Sacremento: Association of California School Administrators, 1988).

26 Diane Ravitch, "The Search for Order and the Rejection of Conformity: Standards in American Education," in *Learning from the Past: What History Teaches Us about School Reform*, ed. Diane Ravitch and Maris Vinovskis (Baltimore: Johns Hopkins University Press, 1995).

27 Martin R. West and Paul E. Peterson, "The Politics and Practice of Accountability," in *No Child Left Behind: The Politics and Practice of School Accountability*, ed. Paul E. Peterson and Martin R. West (Washington, DC: Brookings Institution Press, 2003).

28 High-stakes testing practices generally hinge students' ability to move to a higher grade, be placed in a particular track, or receive a diploma on the basis of a standardized test. While the popularity of such testing practices has waxed and waned since the 1980s, twenty-two states were implementing high school exit exams in 2006. Center on Education Policy, "State High School Exit Exams: A Challenging Year" (Washington, DC: Center on Education Policy, 2006).

29 High-stakes testing practices have generally been challenged in court under regulations implementing the Civil Rights Act of 1964. For an overview of the case law surrounding high-stakes testing practices, see National Research Council, *High Stakes: Testing for Tracking, Promotion, and Graduation*, ed. Jay P. Heubert and Robert M. Hauser (Washington, DC: National Academy Press, 1999). However, under *Alexander v. Sandoval*, 532 U.S. 275 (2001), litigants can no longer bring claims in federal court under these regulations. Instead, a complaint must be filed with ED.

30 Kirst, "Beyond Mutual Adaptation."

31 McDonnell, "No Child Left Behind and the Federal Role in Education: Evolution or Revolution?"

32 Michael Kirst, "Accountability: Implications for State and Local Policymakers" (Washington, DC: Office of Educational Research and Improvement, U.S Department of Education, 1990).

33 Kirst, "Who's in Charge? Federal, State, and Local Control."

34 Margaret E. Goertz, "State Educational Standards" (Princeton: NJ: Educational Testing Service, 1986).

35 A. H. Passow, "Whither (or Wither?) School Reform?" *Educational Administration Quarterly* 24, no. 3 (1988): 246–56.

36 Richard F. Elmore and Milbrey McLaughlin, "Steady Work: Policy, Practice, and the Reform of American Education" (Santa Monica, CA: RAND Corporation, 1988).

37 Richard F. Elmore and Associates, *Restructuring Schools: The Generation of Education Reform* (San Francisco: Jossey-Bass, 1990).

38 Bruce S. Cooper, "School Reform in the 1980s: The New Right's Legacy," *Educational Administration Quarterly* 24, no. 3 (1988); Education Consolidation and Improvement Act of 1981, 20 U.S.C. § 3581 et seq. (1981).

39 Education Consolidation and Improvement Act of 1981, 20 U.S.C. § 3581 et seq. (1981).

40 Richard F. Elmore, "The Problem of Quality in Chapter 1" (Washington, DC: U.S. Department of Education, 1987).

41 Ibid. A typical recipient of Chapter 1 services was exposed to approximately ¾ hour of reading and mathematics 4 times a week, with about 10 students and 2 adults in a separate classroom. So, Chapter 1 instruction constituted about 12 to 15 percent of a student's time in school. For a discussion of the origins of pullout classes, see Chapter 4.

42 Michael Kirst, "State Policy in an Era of Transition," *Education and Urban Society* 16, no. 2 (1984): 225–37.

43 Michael Kirst, "Recent State Education Reform in the United States: Looking Backward and Forward," *Educational Administration Quarterly* 24, no. 3 (1988): 319–28.

44 Michael Kirst, "Recent Research on Intergovernmental Relations in Education Policy," *Educational Researcher* 24, no. 9 (1995): 18–22.

45 David Tyack and Larry Cuban, *Tinkering toward Utopia: A Century of Public School Reform* (Cambridge, MA: Harvard University Press, 1995).

46 Elmore, "Contested Terrain: The Next Generation of Educational Reform."

47 Diane Ravitch, "The Search for Order and the Rejection of Conformity: Standards in American Education," in *Learning from the Past: What History Teaches Us about School Reform*, ed. Diane Ravitch and Maris Vinovskis (Baltimore: Johns Hopkins University Press, 1995).

48 National Governors Association, "Time for Results" (Washington, DC: National Governors Association, 1986), 3.

49 Ibid., 3–4.

50 The eight states that originally agreed to administer the NAEP were Arkansas, Florida, Louisiana, North Carolina, South Carolina, Tennessee, Virginia, and West Virginia. Diane Ravitch, "The Search for Order and the Rejection of Conformity: Standards in American Education,"

51 Hawkins-Stafford Amendments of 1988, 20 U.S.C. § 2701 et seq. (1988).

52 Mary Ann Millsap et al., *The* Chapter 1 *Implementation Study: Interim Report* (Washington, DC: U.S. Government Printing Office, 1992).

53 National Council of Teachers of Mathematics, "Curriculum and Evaluation Standards for School Mathematics" (Reston, VA: National Council of Teachers of Mathematics, 1989), 2.

54 Lynn Olsen and Julie A. Miller, "The 'Education President' at Midterm: Mismatch between Rhetoric, Reality," *Education Week*, June 9, 1991. http://www.lexis.com (accessed May 15, 2012). The quote is specifically referenced by Maris A. Vinovskis, "The Road to Charlottesville: The 1989 Education Summit" (Washington, DC: National Education Goals Panel, 1999).

55 Vinovskis, "The Road to Charlottesville: The 1989 Education Summit."

56 John F. Jennings, "Title I: Its Legislative History and Its Promise," in *Compensatory Education at the Crossroads*, ed. Geoffrey D. Borman, Samuel C. Stringfield, and Robert E. Slavin (Mahwah, NJ: Lawrence Erlbaum Associates, 2001).

57 National Governors Association, "National Education Goals" (Washington, DC: National Governors Association, 1990), 3–6.

58 John F. Jennings, *Why National Standards and Tests? Politics and the Quest for Better Schools* (Thousand Oaks, CA: Sage Publications, 1998).

59 George H. W. Bush et al., "A Jeffersonian Compact," *New York Times*, October 1, 1989. http://www.lexis.com. (accessed May 15, 2012).

60 *America 2000: Excellence in Education Act*, H.R. 2460, 102nd Congress (1991).

61 George H. W. Bush, "Remarks by the President at Presentation of National Office Strategy" (Washington, DC: Office of the White House Press Secretary, 1990).

62 George H. W. Bush, "The Bush Strategy for Excellence in Education," *Phi Delta Kappan* 70, no. 2 (1988): 112–26.

63 Ibid.

64 For example, see U.S. Congress, *Congressional Record* (May 8, 1991). http://www.gpoaccess.gov/bills/index.html (accessed May 15, 2012).

65 Strengthening Education for American Families Act, S.2., 102nd Congress (1992).

66 Julie A. Miller, "Lawmakers, Administration Negotiate on Reform Bill," *Education Week*, September 30, 1992. http://www.lexis.com. (accessed May 15, 2012).

67 David K. Cohen, "Policy and Organization: The Impact of State and Federal Education Policy on School Governance," *Harvard Educational Review* 52, no. 4 (1982): 474–99.

68 Maris A. Vinovskis, "An Analysis of the Concept and Uses of Systemic Educational Reform," *American Educational Research Journal* 33, no. 1 (1996): 53–85.

69 The effective schools movement was a strand of education research generally asserting that reforms must work together to produce changes in school culture, which would significantly contribute to the effective functioning of schools. Stewart C. Purkey and Marshall S. Smith, "School Reform: The District Policy Implications of the Effective Schools Literature," *Elementary School Journal* 85, no. 3 (1985): 353–89.

70 Jennifer A. O'Day and Marshall S. Smith, "Systemic Reform and Educational Opportunity," in *Designing Coherent Education Policy: Improving the System*, ed. Susan Fuhrman (San Francisco: Jossey-Bass, 1993), 251.

71 Ibid.

72 Diane Massell, Michael Kirst, and Margaret Hoppe, "Persistence and Change: Standards-based Systemic Reform in Nine States" (Philadelphia: Consortium for Policy Research in Education, 1997).

73 Ibid.

74 Christopher B. Swanson and David Lee Stevenson, "Standards-based Reform in Practice: Evidence on State Policy and Classroom Instruction from the NAEP State Assessments," *Educational Evaluation and Policy Analysis* 24, no. 1 (2002): 1–27.

75 McGuinn, *No Child Left Behind: The Transformation of Federal Education Policy, 1965–2005.*

76 Achieve, Inc. "Staying on Course: Standards-based Reform in America's Schools: Progress and Prospects" (Washington, DC: Achieve, Inc., 2002).

77 Goals 2000: Educate America Act, 20 U.S.C. § 5801 et seq. (1994).

78 Improving America's Schools Act, 20 U.S.C. § 6301 et seq. (1994).

79 Jonathan Riskind, "State Board Turns Away Protesters; Superintendent Says Meeting Room Too Tiny for Crowd," *Columbus Dispatch*, October 12, 1994. http://www.lexis.com. (accessed May 15, 2012).

80 Katharine Seeyle, "G.O.P. Set to Lead Congress on Path Sharply to Right," *New York Times*, January 3, 1995. http://www.lexis.com. (accessed May 15, 2012). The bills introduced by members of Congress to repeal or alter Goals 2000 include H.R. 997 (1995), H.R. 1045 (1995), H.R. 1558 (1995), H.R., 3313 (1996), S. 323 (1995), S. 469 (1995), and S. 1301 (1995).

81 Mark Pitsch, "Conservatives Vie to Use Momentum to Push Reform Agenda," *Education Week*, February 1, 1995. http://www.lexis.com. (accessed May 15, 2012).

82 Benjamin M. Superfine, "The Politics of Accountability: The Rise and Fall of Goals: 2000," *American Journal of Education* 112, no. 1 (2005): 449–81.

83 General Accounting Office, "Goals 2000: Flexible Funding Supports State and Local Education Reform" (Washington, DC: General Accounting Office, 1998).

84 U.S. Department of Education, "High Standards for All Students: A Report from the National Assessment of Title I on Progress and Challenges since

the 1994 Reauthorization" (Washington, DC: Government Printing Office, 2001).

85 Reading Excellence Act, 20 U.S.C. § 6601 et seq. (1997).

86 Vinovskis, *From a Nation at Risk to No Child Left Behind: National Education Goals and the Creation of Federal Education Policy.*

87 U.S. Department of Education, "Promising Results, Continuing Challenges: The Final Report of the National Assessment of Title I" (Washington, DC: Government Printing Office, 1999).

88 Margaret E. Goertz, Mark C. Duffy, and Kerstin C. Le Floch, "Assessment and Accountability Systems in the 50 States: 1999–2000" (Philadelphia: Consortium for Policy Research in Education, 2001).

89 Chester E. Finn and Michael J. Petrilli, "The State of State Standards 2000" (Washington, DC: Fordham Foundation, 2000); Scott Joftus and Ilene Berman, "Great Expectations: Defining and Assessing Rigor in State Standards for Mathematics and English Language Arts" (Washington, DC: Council for Basic Education, 1998).

90 Ravitch, "The Search for Order and the Rejection of Conformity: Standards in American Education."

91 Diane Ravitch, *The Language Police: How Pressure Groups Restrict What Students Learn* (New York: Alfred A. Knopf, 2003).

92 Richard F. Elmore, "Accountability and Capacity," in *The New Accountability*, ed. Martin Carnoy, Richard F. Elmore, and Leslie S. Siskin (New York: Routledge Farmer, 2003).

93 Heather C. Hill, "Professional Development Standards and Practices in Elementary School Mathematics," *Elementary School Journal* 104, no. 3 (2004): 215–31.

94 American Federation of Teachers, "Making Standards Matter" (Washington, DC: American Federation of Teachers, 2001).

95 Eric A. Hanushek and Margaret E. Raymond, "Lessons about the Design of State Accountability Systems," in *No Child Left Behind? The Politics and Practice of School Accountability*, ed. Paul E. Peterson and Martin R. West (Washington, DC: Brookings Institution Press, 2003); Andrew C. Porter, "Measuring the Content of Instruction: Uses in Research and Practice," *Educational Researcher* 31, no. 7 (2002): 3–14.

96 Jamal Abedi, "The No Child Left Behind Act and English Language Learners: Assessment and Accountability Issues," *Educational Researcher* 33, no. 1 (2004): 4–14; National Research Council, *Education One and All: Students with Disabilities and Standards-based Reform*, ed. Lorraine McDonnell, Milbrey McLaughlin, and Patricia Morrison (Washington, DC: National Academy Press, 1997).

97 James P. Spillane and Nancy E. Jennings, "Aligned Instructional Policy and Ambitious Pedagogy: Exploring Instructional Reform from the Classroom Perspective," *Teachers College Record* 98, no. 5 (1997): 449–81.

98 Charles G. Abelmann and Richard F. Elmore, "When Accountability Knocks, Will Anyone Answer?" (Philadelphia: Consortium for Policy Research in Education, 1999).

99 Linda Skrla, James Joseph Scheurich, and Joseph F. Jr. Johnson, "Equity-driven Achievement-focused School Districts" (Austin: Charles A. Dana Center, University of Texas at Austin, 2000).

100 Lora F. Monfils et al., "Teaching to the Test," in *The Ambiguity of Teaching to the Test*, ed. William A. Firestone, Roberta Y. Schorr, and Lora F. Monfils (Mahwah, NJ: Lawrence Erlbaum, 2004).

101 U.S. Department of Education, "High Standards for All Students: A Report from the National Assessment of Title I on Progress and Challenges since the 1994 Reauthorization."

102 Susan H. Fuhrman, "Introduction," in *From the Capitol to the Classroom: Standards-based Reform in the States*, ed. Susan H. Fuhrman (Chicago: National Society for the Study of Education, 2001).

103 Martin Carnoy and Susanna Loeb, "Does External Accountability Affect Student Outcomes? A Cross-State Analysis," *Educational Evaluation and Policy Analysis* 24, no. 4 (2002): 305–31.

104 Walt Haney, "The Myth of the Texas Miracle in Education," *Education Policy Analysis Archives* 8, no. 41 (2000). http://www.epaa.asu.edu (accessed May 15, 2012).

105 Anthony S. Bryk, "No Child Left Behind, Chicago-Style," in *No Child Left Behind? The Politics and Practice of School Accountability*, ed. Paul E. Peterson and Martin R. West (Washington, DC: Brookings Institution Press, 2003).

106 Brian A. Jacob, "A Closer Look at Achievement Gains under High-Stakes Testing in Chicago," in *No Child Left Behind? The Politics and Practice of School Accountability*, ed. Paul E. Peterson and Martin R. West (Washington, DC: Brookings Institution Press, 2003).

107 *San Antonio Independent School District v. Rodriguez*, 411 U.S. 1 (1973). For a detailed discussion of this case, see Chapter 4.

108 William S. Koski, "Of Fuzzy Standards and Institutional Constraints: A Re-Examination of the Jurisprudential History of Educational Finance Reform Litigation," *Santa Clara Law Review* 43, no. 4 (2003): 1185–298.

109 *Robinson v. Cahill*, 303 A.2d 273 (N.J. 1973).

110 *Northshore School District No. 417 v. Kinnear*, 530 P.2d 178 (Wash. 1974); *Pauley v. Kelley*, 255 S.E.2d 859 (W.Va. 1979).

111 Michael Heise, "State Constitutions, School Finance Litigation, and the 'Third Wave': From Equity to Adequacy," *Temple Law Review* 68, no. 3 (1995): 1151–76.

112 *Rose v. Council for Better Education*, 790 S.W.2d 186 (Ky. 1989).

113 Molly Hunter, "All Eyes Forward: Public Engagement and Educational Reform in Kentucky," *Journal of Law and Education* 28 (1999): 485–516.

114 Ibid.

115 Kentucky State Constitution § 183.

116 *Rose v. Council for Better Education*, 790 S.W.2d 186, 212 (Ky. 1989).

117 Kentucky Education Reform Act, Ky. Rev. Ann § 156.005 et seq. (1991).

118 Hunter, "All Eyes Forward: Public Engagement and Educational Reform in Kentucky."

119 *McDuffy v. Secretary of Education*, 615 N.E.2d 516 (Mass. 1993); *Claremont School District v. Governor*, 703 A.2d 1353 (N.H. 1997).

120 William S. Koski and Rob Reich, "When 'Adequate' Isn't: The Retreat from Equity in Educational Law and Policy and Why It Matters," *Emory Law Journal* 56, no. 3 (2006): 545–617.

121 Regina R. Umpstead, "Determining Adequacy: How Courts Are Redefining State Responsibility for Educational Finance, Goals, and Accountability," *BYU Education & Law Journal* (2007): 281–316.

122 Ibid.

123 Peter Enrich, "Leaving Equality Behind: New Directions in School Finance Reform," *Vanderbilt Law Review* 48, no. 1 (1995): 101–94.

124 Rachel Moran, "Sorting and Reforming: High-stakes Testing in the Public Schools," *Akron Law Review* 34, no. 1 (2000): 107–35.

125 Every state constitution (with the arguable exception of Mississippi's) contains an education clause. For a more detailed discussion of state education clauses, see Chapter 4.

126 For example, see *Abbott v. Burke*, 748 A.2d 82 (N.J. 2002); *Claremont School District v. Governor*, 794 A.2d 744 (N.H. 2002).

127 Jay P. Greene and Julie R. Trivitt, "Can Judges Improve Academic Achievement?" *Peabody Journal of Education* 83, no. 2 (2008): 224–37.

128 For arguments that money does not matter, see Eric A. Hanushek, "The Impact of Differential Expenditures on School Performance," *Educational Researcher* 18, no. 4 (1989): 45–65; Eric A. Hanushek, "Money Might Matter Somewhere: A Response to Hedges, Laine, and Greenwald," *Educational Researcher* 23, no. 4 (1994): 5–8. For arguments that money does matter, see Larry V. Hedges, Richard D. Laine, and Rob Greenwald, "Does Money Matter? A Meta-Analysis of Studies of the Effects of Differential School Inputs on Students Outcomes," *Educational Researcher* 23, no. 3 (1994): 5–14; Larry V. Hedges, Richard D. Laine, and Rob Greenwald "Money Does Matter Somewhere: A Reply to Hanushek," *Educational Researcher* 23, no. 4 (1994): 9–10.

129 Deborah A. Stone, *Policy Paradox: The Art of Political Decision Making* (New York: W. W. Norton, 1997). In this work, Stone uses the term "security" analogously to adequacy and discusses how this term can be defined in several different ways. For more on the ambiguity of concepts like adequacy and equality, see Chapter Two.

130 *Leandro v. State*, 488 S.E.2d 249 (N.C. 1997).

131 Courts have cited the political question doctrine in several school finance cases. In these cases, courts have generally found that the notion of adequacy is too vague and therefore does not involve judicially manageable standards. Under this logic, other governmental branches are better suited for the task of ruling. For example, see *Coalition for Adequacy and Fairness in School Funding, Inc. v. Chiles*, 680 So.2d 400 (Fla. 1996); *Committee for Educational Rights v. Edgar*, 672 N.E.2d 1178 (Ill. 1996); *Danson v. Casey*, 399 A.2d 360 (Pa. 1979).

132 Molly S. McUsic, "The Law's Role in the Distribution of Education: The Promises and Pitfalls of School Finance Litigation," in *Law and School Reform*, ed. Jay P. Heubert (New Haven, CT: Yale University Press, 1999).

133 *Leandro v. State*, 488 S.E.2d 249 (N.C., 1997).

134 *Leandro v. State*, 488 S.E.2d 249, 259–60 (N.C., 1997).

135 *Hoke County Board of Education v. State*, 95 CVS 1158 (N.C. Super. Ct., Oct. 12, 2000) 109, 111 (*Hoke I*).

136 *Hoke County Board of Education v. State of North Carolina*, 599 S.E.2d 365 (N.C., 2004). Upon being interviewed, both Judge Manning and Chief Justice Mitchell of the North Carolina Supreme Court indicated that standards and test results made it significantly easier to rule in the school finance litigation. Tico A. Almeida, "Refocusing School Finance Litigation on At-Risk Children: *Leandro v. State of North Carolina*," *Yale Law and Policy Review* 22 (2004): 525–69.

137 Campaign for Fiscal Equity, Inc., "Costing Out Chart" (New York: Campaign for Fiscal Equity, 2006).

138 Koski, "When 'Adequate' Isn't: The Retreat from Equity in Educational Law and Policy and Why It Matters"; Michael A. Rebell, "Professional Rigor, Public Engagement and Judicial Review: A Proposal for Enhancing the Validity of Education Adequacy Studies," *Teachers College Record* 109, no. 6 (2007): 1303–73.

139 For example, in the *Campaign for Fiscal Equity* litigation in New York, three separate cost studies were conducted that recommended $1.9 billion to $5.3 billion additional annual funding. *Campaign for Fiscal Equity, Inc. v. State of New York*, 801 N.E.2d 326 (N.Y. 2003).

140 Patricia F. First, "The Meaning of Educational Adequacy: The Confusion of DeRolph," *Journal of Law and Education* 32, no. 2 (2003): 185–215.

141 Northwest Evaluation Association, "The State of State Standards: Research Investigating Proficiency Levels in Fourteen States" (Northwest Evaluation Association, 2004).

142 Deborah A. Verstegen, "Has Adequacy Been Achieved? A Study of Finances and Costs a Decade after Court-Ordered Reform," *Journal of Education Finance* 32, no. 3 (2007): 304–27.

143 For example, see William Duncombe, "Responding to the Charge of Alchemy: Strategies for Evaluating the Reliability of Costing-Out Research," *Journal of Education Finance* 32, no. 2 (2006): 137–69; Greene and Trivitt, "Can Judges Improve Academic Achievement?."

144 McUsic, "The Law's Role in the Distribution of Education: The Promises and Pitfalls of School Finance Litigation."

145 Benjamin M. Superfine, "Using the Courts to Influence the Implementation of No Child Left Behind," *Cardozo Law Review* 28, no. 2 (2006): 779–846.

146 Aaron J. Saiger, "Legislating Accountability: Standards, Sanctions, and School District Reform," *William and Mary Law Review* 46, no. 3 (2005): 1655–732.

147 Michael Heise, "Equal Educational Opportunity by the Numbers: The Warren Court's Empirical Legacy," *Washington and Lee Law Review* 59, no. 4 (2002): 1309–42.

148 *Campaign for Fiscal Equity, Inc. v. State of New York*, 719 N.Y.S.2d 475 (N.Y. 2001).

149 *Campaign for Fiscal Equity, Inc. v. State of New York*, 801 N.E.2d 326 (N.Y., 2003).

150 Ibid.
151 No Child Left Behind Act of 2001, 20 U.S.C. § 6301 et seq. (2002). This law is discussed at length in Chapter 7.
152 Courts have ordered the implementation of standards-based accountability systems in *Hancock v. Driscoll*, 2003 WL 8777984 (Mass. Super. 2004); *Claremont School District v. Governor*, 635 A.2d 1375 (N.H. 1993).
153 Complaint, *Williams v. State*, No. 312236 (Ca. Sup. Ct., filed May 17, 2000).
154 Order, *Williams v. State*, No. 312236 (Ca. Sup. Ct., Nov. 14, 2000).
155 The bills in California were S.B. 550 (2004); A.B. 2727 (2004).
156 ACLU Foundation of Southern California and Public Advocates, Inc., "*Williams v. California*: The Statewide Impact of Two Years of Implementation" (Los Angeles, CA: ACLU 2007).
157 Courts have ordered the implementation of class size reduction programs in at least two states. See *Abbott v. Burke*, 710 A.2d 450 (N.J. 1998); *Campbell County Sch. Dist. v. State*, 907 P.2d 1238 (Wyo. 1998). Courts have ordered the implementation of whole school reform programs in at least one case. *Abbott v. Burke*, 710 A.2d. 450 (N.J. 1998). Courts have ordered free preschool for children in at least five cases. *Abbott v. Burke*, 907 A.2d. 450 (N.J. 1998); *Abbeville County School District v. State,* No. 31-0169, (S.C. Ct. Comm. Pl. Dec. 29 2005); *Hancock v. Driscoll*, 822 N.E.2d 1134 (Mass. 2005); *Hoke County Board of Education v. State*, 2000 WL 1639686 (N.C. Super. Oct. 12, 2000); *Lake View School District No. 25 v. Huckabee*, 257 S.W.3d 879 (Ark. 2005).
158 *Abbott v. Burke*, 710 A.2d 450 (N.J. 1998); *Hoke County. Board of Education,* 2000 WL 1639686 (N.C. Super. Oct. 12, 2000).
159 For example, in the trial court in North Carolina, the plaintiffs called 26 witnesses and introduced other testimony by deposition, and the defendants called 17 witnesses. By the time the trial had concluded, the parties had submitted 670 documentary exhibits totaling thousands of pages. *Hoke County Board of Education*, 2000 WL 1639686 (N.C. Super. Oct. 12, 2000).
160 James Ryan, "A Constitutional Right to Preschool?" *California Law Review* 94 (2006): 49–99.
161 Douglas R. Reed, *On Equal Terms: The Constitutional Politics of Educational Opportunity* (Princeton, NJ: Princeton University Press, 2001).
162 Benjamin M. Superfine and Roger Goddard, "The Expanding Role of the Courts in Education Policy: The Preschool Remedy and an Adequate Education," *Teachers College Record* 111, no. 7 (2009): 1796–833.
163 *Hoke County Board of Education v. State*, 599 S.E.2d 365, 394–95 (N.C. 2004).
164 Ryan, "A Constitutional Right to Preschool?"
165 Steven W. Raudenbush, "Learning from Attempts to Improve Schooling: The Contribution of Methodological Diversity," *Educational Researcher* 34, no. 5 (2005): 25–31.
166 Janet Currie, "Early Childhood Intervention Programs: What Do We Know?" (Los Angeles: UCLA, 2000).
167 Diana Pullin, "Ensuring an Adequate Education: Opportunity to Learn, Law, and Social Science," *Boston Third World Law Journal* 27, no. 1 (2007): 83–130.

168 Patrice Iatrola and Norm Fruchter, "An Alternative Method for Measuring Cost-Effectiveness: A Case Study of New York City's Annenberg Challenge Grant," *Journal of Education Finance* 32, no. 3 (2006): 276–96.

169 For example, see James W. Guthrie, "Next Needed Steps in the Evolution of American Education Finance and Policy," *Peabody Journal of Education* 83, no. 2 (2008): 259–84; Helen F. Ladd, "High-Poverty Schools and the Distribution of Teachers and Principals," *North Carolina Law Review* 85, no. 5 (2007): 1345–79.

6 DEVELOPMENTS IN LOCAL CONTROL

1 Jennifer T. Wall, "The Establishment of Charter Schools: A Guide to Legal Issues for Legislatures," *BYU Education and Law Journal* 1998 (1998): 60–102.

2 James Forman, "The Rise and Fall of School Vouchers: A Story of Religion, Race, and Politics," *UCLA Law Review* 54, no. 3 (2007): 547–604.

3 *Zelman v. Simmons-Harris*, 536 U.S. 639 (2002).

4 See Chapter 7 for a detailed analysis of the Obama administration's treatment of charter schools in the 2000s.

5 Much of the history of school choice before the 1990s is from Jeffrey R. Henig, *The Spin Cycle: How Research Is Used in Policy Debates* (New York: Russell Sage Foundation, 2008).

6 For a detailed history of the role of grassroots groups and business in shaping Chicago school reform in the 1980s and 1990s, see Dorothy Shipps, "The Invisible Hand: Big Business and Chicago School Reform," *Teachers College Record* 99, no. 1 (1997): 73–116.

7 The discussion of the organizations supporting school choice is drawn from Kevin G. Welner, "Free-market Think Tanks and the Marketing of Education Policy," *Dissent* Spring (2011): 39–43.

8 Staige D. Blackford and Margaret Long, "Six Years of Southern Free Choice," *New South* 19, no. 4 (1964): 1–19.

9 Jim Carl, *Freedom of Choice: Vouchers in American Education* (Santa Barbara, CA: Praeger, 2007).

10 Kevin G. Welner, *NeoVouchers: The Emergence of Tuition Tax Credits for Private Schooling* (New York: Rowman & Littlefield, 2008).

11 Carl, *Freedom of Choice: Vouchers in American Education.*

12 Danny K. Weil, *School Vouchers and Privatization: A Reference Handbook* (Santa Barbara, CA: ABC-CLIO, 2002).

13 Ibid.

14 Carl, *Freedom of Choice: Vouchers in American Education.*

15 Ibid.

16 Weil, *School Vouchers and Privatization: A Reference Handbook.*

17 For example, the House of Representatives considered the Help Empower Low-Income Parents Act, H.R. 2746, 105th Congress (1997), and the Senate considered the A+ Education Savings Account Bill, H.R. 2746, 105th Congress (1997).

18 *Simmons-Harris v. Goff*, 711 N. E. 2d 203 (Ohio 1999).

19 U.S. Constitution, Amendment I.

20 *Zelman v. Simmons-Harris*, 732 F. Supp. 2d 834 (N.D. Ohio 1999); *Zelman v. Simmons-Harris*, 234 F.3d 945 (6th Cir, 2000).
21 *Zelman v. Simmons-Harris*, 536 U.S. 639 (2002).
22 Ibid., 649.
23 Ibid., 652.
24 Ibid., 682.
25 Martha Minow, "Public and Private Partnerships: Accounting for the New Religion," *Harvard Law Review* 116 (2003): 1229–70.
26 Ibid.
27 Roderick Paige, "A Win for America's Children," *Washington Post*, June 28, 2002. http://www.lexis.com (accessed May 15, 2012).
28 Chad d'Entremont and Luis A. Huerta, "Irreconcilable Differences? Education Vouchers and the Suburban Response," *Educational Policy* 21, no. 1 (2007): 40–72. Notably, Vermont and Maine have had in place laws permitting rural students to attend nonreligious private schools since the 1800s.
29 Ibid.
30 Ibid.
31 Kavan Peterson, "School Vouchers Slow to Spread," *Stateline*, May 5, 2005. http://www.lexis.com (accessed May 15, 2012).
32 d'Entremont and Huerta, "Irreconcilable Differences? Education Vouchers and the Suburban Response."
33 Clint Bolick, "Voting Down Vouchers," *Education Next* 8, no. 2 (2008): 46–51.
34 Frank R. Kemerer, "The U.S. Supreme Court's Decision in Cleveland: Where to from Here?" (New York: Teachers College Press, 2002).
35 *Cain v. Horne*, 202 P.3d 1178 (Ariz. 2009).
36 Preston C. Green and Peter L. Moran, "The State Constitutionality of Voucher Programs: Religion Is Not the Sole Determinant," *BYU Education and the Law Journal* 2010 (2010): 275–306.
37 *Bush v. Holmes*, 919 So.2d 392 (Fla. 2006).
38 Jamie S. Dycus, "Lost Opportunity: *Bush v. Holmes* and the Application of State Constitutional Uniformity Clauses to School Voucher Schemes," *Journal of Law & Education* 35 (2006): 415–59. The Wisconsin Supreme Court found the Milwaukee voucher program constitutional in *Davis v. Grover*, 480 NW.2d 460 (Wis. 1992).
39 Green and Moran, "The State Constitutionality of Voucher Programs: Religion Is Not the Sole Determinant."
40 *Owens v. Colorado Congress of Parents*, 93 P.3d 933 (Colo. 2004).
41 Welner, *NeoVouchers: The Emergence of Tuition Tax Credits for Private Schooling*.
42 An excellent discussion of the effects of vouchers appears in Welner, *NeoVouchers: The Emergence of Tuition Tax Credits for Private Schooling*. This discussion references the most important research on the effects of vouchers, including General Accounting Office, "School Vouchers: Publicly Funded Programs in Cleveland and Milwaukee" (Washington, DC: General Accounting Office, 2001); W. G. Howell et al., *The Education Gap: Vouchers and Urban Schools* (Washington, DC: Brookings Institution Press, 2002); Patrick Wolf

et al., "Evaluation of the DC Opportunity Scholarship Program" (Washington, DC: U.S. Department of Education, 2008).

43 Jeffrey R. Henig, "School Choice Outcomes," in *School Choice and Social Controversy: Politics, Policy, and Law*, ed. Stephen D. Sugarman and Frank R. Kemerer (Washington, DC: Brookings Institution Press, 1999).

44 Patrick J. McEwan, "The Potential Impact of Vouchers," *Peabody Journal of Education* 79, no. 1 (2004): 57–80; Welner, *NeoVouchers: The Emergence of Tuition Tax Credits for Private Schooling*.

45 National Conference of State Legislatures, "Publicly Funded School Voucher Programs" (Washington, DC: National Conference of State Legislatures, 2011).

46 Natalie Lacireno-Paquet, "Charter School Enrollments in Context: An Exploration of Organization and Policy Influences," *Peabody Journal of Education* 81, no. 1 (2006): 79–102.

47 Wall, "The Establishment of Charter Schools: A Guide to Legal Issues for Legislatures."

48 Jeffrey R. Henig, *Rethinking School Choice: Limits of the Market Metaphor* (Princeton, NJ: Princeton University Press, 1994).

49 Ibid.

50 Jeffrey R. Henig, *The Spin Cycle: How Research Is Used in Policy Debates*.

51 For one of the most famous discussions of the benefits of school choice based on competition, see John E. Chubb and Terry M. Moe, *Politics, Markets, and America's Schools* (Washington, DC: Brookings Institution, 1990).

52 Julie F. Mead, "Devilish Details: Exploring Features of Charter School Statutes That Blur the Public/Private Distinction," *Harvard Journal on Legislation* 40, no. 2 (2003): 349–94; Christopher A. Lubienski, "Redefining 'Public' Education: Charter Schools, Common Schools, and the Rhetoric of Reform," *Teachers College Record* 103, no. 4 (2001): 634–66.

53 Henig, *The Spin Cycle: How Research Is Used in Policy Debates*.

54 Improving America's Schools Act, 20 U.S.C. § 6301 et seq. (1994). The Public Charter Schools Program was integrated into the Elementary and Secondary Education Act in 1994 as Title X, Part C. The early appropriations for the Public Charter Schools Program in 1994 can be found in U.S. Department of Education, "The Public Charter Schools Program and the Charter School Movement – Evaluation of the Public Charter School Program: Year One Evaluation Report" (Washington, DC: U.S. Department of Education, 2000).

55 Charter School Expansion Act, 20 U.S.C. § 8061 et seq. (1998).

56 Center on Education Reform, "Facts" (Washington, DC: Center on Education Reform, 2011).

57 For example, see Diane Ravitch, *The Death and Life of the Great American School System: How Testing and Choice Are Undermining Education* (New York: Basic Books, 2010).

58 Henig, *The Spin Cycle: How Research Is Used in Policy Debates*.

59 Ibid., 90.

60 *Council of Organizations and Others v. Michigan*, 566 N.W.2d 208 (Mich. 1997); *In re Grant of the Charter School Application of Englewood on the*

Palisades Charter School, 727 A.2d 15 (N.J. Super. 1999); *Wilson v. State Board of Education*, 89 Cal. Rptr. 2d 745 (Cal. App. 1999).

61 Aaron J. Saiger, "School Choice and States' Duty to Support 'Public' Schools," *Boston College Law Review* 48, no. 3 (2007): 909–69.

62 *Ohio ex rel Ohio Congress of Parents & Teachers v. State Board of Education*, 857 N.E.2d 1148 (Ohio 2006).

63 *Villanueva v. Carere*, 85 F.3d 481 (10th Cir. 1996).

64 Megan Callahan, Susan Krebs, and Erik Bondurant, "Charter School Liability," in *Current Issues in Educational Policy and the Law*, ed. Kevin G. Welner and Wendy C. Chi (Charlotte, NC: Information Age, 2008).

65 Julie F. Mead and Preston C. Green, "Keeping Promises: An Examination of Charter Schools' Vulnerability to Claims for Educational Liability," *BYU Education and Law Journal* 2001 (2001): 35–64.

66 Kevin S. Huffman, "Charter Schools, Equal Protection Litigation, and the New School Reform Movement," *NYU Law Review* 73 (1998): 1290–328.

67 A comprehensive discussion of research on charter schools that guided the discussion in this chapter is found in Henig, *The Spin Cycle: How Research Is Used in Policy Debates*.

68 Martin Carnoy et al., *The Charter School Dust-Up: Examining the Evidence on Enrollment and Achievement* (New York: Teachers College Press, 2005).

69 For example, see National Charter School Research Project, "Working Smarter: How Charter School Leaders Can Get the Help They Need" (Seattle: Center on Reinventing Public Education, 2009).

70 Henry Braun, Frank Jenkings, and Wendy Grigg, "A Closer Look at Charter Schools Using Hierarchical Linear Modeling" (Washington, DC: U.S. Department of Education, National Center for Education Statistics, 2006). It is worth noting that at least one high-quality study has found that students in charter schools outperform students in traditional schools. Caroline M. Hoxby, Sonali Murarka, and Jenny Kang, "How New York City's Charter Schools Affect Achievement" (Stanford, CA: New York City Charter Schools Evaluation Project, 2009).

71 Jack Buckley and Mark Schneider, "Are Charter School Parents More Satisfied with Schools? Evidence from Washington, D.C.," *Peabody Journal of Education* 81, no. 7 (2006): 57–78.

72 Braun, Jenkings, and Wendy Grigg, "A Closer Look at Charter Schools Using Hierarchical Linear Modeling."

73 Jane Hannaway and Nicola Woodruffe, "Policy Instruments in Education," *Review of Research in Education*, 27, no. 1 (2003): 1–24.

74 Ibid.

75 Henig, *The Spin Cycle: How Research is Used in Policy Debates*. For a discussion of the use of technology to facilitate distance learning in charter schools, see Kevin P. Brady, Regina R. Umpstead, and Suzanne Eckes, "Uncharted Territory: The Current Legal Landscape of Public Cyber Charter Schools," *BYU Education and the Law Journal* 2010 (2010): 191–225.

76 For an argument that charter schools have positive competitive effects, see Caroline M. Hoxby, "Rising Tide: New Evidence on Competition and the

Public Schools," *Education Next* 1, no. 4 (2001): 69–74. For an argument that charter schools have negative competitive effects, see Ron Zimmer and Richard Buddin, "Making Sense of Charter Schools" (Santa Monica, CA: RAND, 2006).

77 Center for Research on Education Outcomes, "Multiple Choice: Charter School Performance in 16 States" (Stanford, CA: Stanford University, 2009).

78 *Board of Education v. Dowell*, 498 U.S. 237 (1991).

79 Ibid.

80 Ibid., 249–50.

81 *Freeman v. Pitts*, 503 U.S. 467 (1992).

82 For a detailed discussion of the "*Green*" factors, see Chapter 3.

83 *Freeman v. Pitts*, 887 F.2d 1438 (11th Cir. 1989).

84 *Freeman v. Pitts*, 503 U.S. 467, 495 (1992).

85 Ibid., 489.

86 Ibid., 492.

87 *Missouri v. Jenkins*, 525 U.S. 70 (1995).

88 *Missouri v. Jenkins*, 11 F. 3d 755 (11th Cir. 1993).

89 Danielle Holley-Walker, "After Unitary Status: Examining Voluntary Integration Strategies for Southern School Districts," *North Carolina Law Review* 88, no. 3 (2009): 877–910. For a detailed look at school districts that had their desegregation decrees lifted in the 1990s and beyond, and the increase of segregation specifically in these districts, see Gary Orfield and Chungmei Lee, "*Brown* at 50: King's Dream or *Plessy*'s Nightmare?" (Cambridge, MA: Civil Rights Project, Harvard University, 2004).

90 Erica Frankenberg and Chungmei Lee, "Race in American Public Schools: Rapidly Resegregating School Districts" (Cambridge, MA: Civil Rights Project: Harvard University, 2002).

91 Orfield and Lee, "*Brown* at 50: King's Dream or *Plessy*'s Nightmare?"

92 Gary Orfield and Jaekyung Lee, "Racial Transformation and the Changing Nature of Segregation" (Cambridge, MA: Civil Rights Project, Harvard University, 2006).

93 Ibid.

94 Frankenberg and Lee, "Race in American Public Schools: Rapidly Resegregating School Districts."

95 National Academy of Education, "Race-Conscious Policies for Assigning Students to Schools: Social Science Research and the Supreme Court Cases," ed. Robert L. Linn and Kevin G. Welner (Washington, DC: National Academy of Education, 2007).

96 *Parents Involved in Community Schools v. Seattle School District No. 1*, 551 U.S. 701 (2007).

97 Holley-Walker, "After Unitary Status: Examining Voluntary Integration Strategies for Southern School Districts."

98 *Parents Involved in Community Schools v. Seattle School District No. 1*, 551 U.S. 701 (2007).

99 See Chapter Four for a discussion of how courts conduct Equal Protection analyses.

100 *Grutter v. Bollinger*, 539 U.S. 306 (2003).
101 *Parents Involved in Community Schools v. Seattle School District No. 1*, 551 U.S. 701, 724 (2007).
102 Ibid., 727.
103 Ibid., 760.
104 Michael Heise, "Judicial Decision-Making, Social Science Evidence, and Equal Educational Opportunity: Uneasy Relations and Uncertain Futures," *Seattle University Law Review* 31, no. 4 (2008): 863–90.
105 Holley-Walker, "After Unitary Status: Examining Voluntary Integration Strategies for Southern School Districts," 924.
106 Christopher Lubienski, "Redefining 'Public' Education: Charter Schools, Common Schools, and the Rhetoric of Reform," *Teachers College Record*, 103, no. 4 (2001): 634–66.

7   THE CONTINUING EXPANSION OF THE FEDERAL ROLE

 1 Maris A. Vinovskis, *From a Nation at Risk to No Child Left Behind: National Education Goals and the Creation of Federal Education Policy* (New York: Teachers College Press, 2008).
 2 Reading Excellence Act, 20 U.S.C. § 6601 et seq. (1997).
 3 Educational Excellence for All Children Act, S. 1180, 106th Congress (1999).
 4 For example, see Academic Achievement for All Act, H.R. 2300, 106th Congress (1999); Educational Opportunities Act, S. 2, 106th Congress (1999); Public Education Reinvestment, Reinvention, and Responsibility Act, H.R. 345, 107th Congress (2000); Student Results Act, H.R. 2, 106th Congress (1999).
 5 Patrick McGuinn, *No Child Left Behind: The Transformation of Federal Education Policy, 1965–2005* (Lawrence: University of Kansas Press, 2006).
 6 Elizabeth DeBray, *Politics, Ideology and Education: Federal Policy during the Clinton and Bush Administrations* (New York: Teachers College Press, 2006).
 7 Giao Phan, "Texas School Reform" (Austin: Houston Schools for a New Society Evaluation, University of Texas at Austin, 2006).
 8 For example, see Walt Haney, "The Myth of the Texas Miracle in Education," *Education Policy Analysis Archives* 8, no. 41 (2000). http://www.epaa.asu.edu (accessed May 15, 2012).
 9 Andrew Rudalevidge, "No Child Left Behind: Forging a Congressional Compromise," in *No Child Left Behind? The Politics and Practice of School Accountability*, ed. Paul E. Peterson and Martin R. West (Washington, DC: Brookings Institutions Press, 2003).
10 George W. Bush, "No Child Left Behind" (Washington, DC: Government Printing Office, 2001).
11 For example, see Congressional Record, 107th Congress, May 17, 2001, H2308; Congressional Record, 107th Congress, May 7, 2001, S4438.
12 Erik W. Robelen, "Key House Democrat Offers $110 Billion Education Plan," *Education Week*, February 7, 2001. http://www.edweek.org (accessed May 15, 2012).

13 DeBray, *Politics, Ideology and Education: Federal Policy during the Clinton and Bush Administrations.*

14 NCLB was passed by a vote of 91–8 in the Senate and 384–45 in the House of Representatives.

15 No Child Left Behind Act of 2001, 20 U.S.C. § 6301 et seq. (2002).

16 20 U.S.C. § 6311(b) (2002).

17 20 U.S.C. § 6311(b)(1) (2002).

18 20 U.S.C. § 6311(b)(3)(C)(vii).

19 20 U.S.C. § 6311(b)(2)(C)(v).

20 20 U.S.C. § 6311(b)(2).

21 20 U.S.C. § 6311(b)(2)(C)(v).

22 20 U.S.C. § 6316(b)(1)(E).

23 20 U.S.C. § 6316(b)(5)(E).

24 20 U.S.C. § 6316(b)(7)(C)(iv).

25 20 U.S.C. § 6316(b)(8)(B).

26 20 U.S.C. § 6319(a)(2).

27 20 U.S.C. § 6303(g)(5)(a).

28 20 U.S.C. § 6317(a)(1); 20 U.S.C. § 6317(a)(5).

29 Frederick M. Hess and Michael J. Petrilli, *No Child Left Behind Primer* (New York: Peter Lang, 2006).

30 Joetta L. Sack, "Federal Spending Burst Nudges Up Uncle Sam's Share," *Education Week*, February 13, 2002. http://www.edweek.org (accessed May 15, 2012).

31 Ibid.

32 20 U.S.C. § 7907(a).

33 In 2003, states faced a combined budget gap of $17.5 billion, and 31 states faced deficits. National Council of State Legislatures, "Fiscal Storm Shows Signs of Subsiding" (Washington, DC: National Council of State Legislatures, 2003).

34 For example, although NCLB was authorized at $26.4 billion for FY 2002, Congress actually appropriated $22.2 billion. Similarly, although NCLB was authorized at $29.2 billion for FY 2003, Congress actually appropriated $23.8 billion. National Education Association, "NCLB Testing Results Offer 'Complex Muddled' Picture: Emerging Trends under the Law's Annual Rating System" (Washington, DC: National Education Association, 2005).

35 General Accounting Office, "Title I: Characteristics of Tests Will Influence Expenses; Information Sharing May Help States Realize Efficiencies" (Washington, DC: General Accounting Office, 2003).

36 Center on Education Policy, "From the Capital to the Classroom: Year 2 of the No Child Left Behind Act" (Center on Education Policy, 2004).

37 William J. Mathis, "The Cost of Implementing the Federal No Child Left Behind Act: Different Assumptions, Different Answers," *Peabody Journal of Education* 8, no. 2 (2005): 90–119.

38 Center on Education Policy, "From the Capital to the Classroom: Year 4 of the No Child Left Behind Act" (Washington, DC: Center on Education Policy, 2006).

39 Ibid.

40 Northwest Evaluation Association, "The State of State Standards: Research Investigating Proficiency Levels in Fourteen States" (Portland, OR: Northwest Evaluation Association, 2004).

41 Robert L. Linn, "Conflicting Demands of No Child Left Behind and State Systems: Mixed Messages about School Performance," *Education Policy Analysis Archives* 13, no. 3 (2005). http://www.epaa.asu.edu (accessed May 15, 2012).

42 General Accounting Office, "Title I: Characteristics of Tests Will Influence Expenses; Information Sharing May Help States Realize Efficiencies."

43 Jamal Abedi, "The No Child Left Behind Act and English Language Learners: Assessment and Accountability Issues," *Educational Researcher* 33, no. 1 (2004): 4–14.

44 Linn, "Conflicting Demands of No Child Left Behind and State Systems: Mixed Messages about School Performance."

45 U.S. Department of Education, "The Secretary's Second Annual Report on Teacher Quality" (Washington, DC: Department of Education, 2003).

46 General Accounting Office, "More Information Would Help States Determine Which Teachers Are Highly Qualified" (Washington DC: General Accounting Office, 2003).

47 Christopher O. Tracy and Kate Walsh, "Necessary and Insufficient: Resisting a Full Measure of Teacher Quality" (Washington DC: National Council on Teacher Quality, 2004).

48 Laura S. Hamilton et al., "Standards-Based Accountability under No Child Left Behind: Experiences of Teachers and Administrators in Three States" (Santa Monica, CA: RAND, 2007).

49 Government Accountability Office, "No Child Left Behind Act: Education Should Clarify Guidance and Address Potential Compliance Issues for Schools in Corrective Action and Restructuring Status" (Washington, DC: Government Accountability Office, 2007).

50 Kristen T. Cowan and Leigh M. Manasevit, *The New Title I: Balancing Accountability with Flexibility* (Washington, DC: Thompson, 2002).

51 Sheila N. Kirby et al., "Schools Identified as in Need of Improvement under Title I" (Santa Monica, CA: RAND Corporation, 2005).

52 Public Agenda, "Rolling up Their Sleeves: Superintendents and Principals Talk about What's Needed to Fix Public Schools" (Washington, DC: Public Agenda, 2003).

53 Center on Education Policy, "From the Capital to the Classroom: Year 4 of the No Child Left Behind Act."

54 Ibid.

55 FairTest, "Cheating Cases Continue to Proliferate" (Jamaica Plain, MA: FairTest, 2011).

56 U.S. Department of Education, "No Child Left Behind Is Working" (Washington, DC: U.S. Department of Education, 2006).

57 John Cronin et al., "The Impact of the No Child Left Behind Act on Student Achievement and Growth: 2005 Edition" (Portland, OR: Northwest Evaluation Association, 2005).

58 Center on Education Policy, "From the Capital to the Classroom: Year 4 of the No Child Left Behind Act."

59 Cronin et al., "The Impact of the No Child Left Behind Act on Student Achievement and Growth: 2005 Edition."

60 Judy Martz and Bill Richardson, Letter to Secretary Roderick Paige, October 6, 2003; James McGreevey, Letter to Secretary Roderick Paige, October 10, 2003.

61 National Education Association, "No Child Left Behind: State Legislative Watch List" (Washington, DC: National Education Association, 2005).

62 U.S. Department of Education, "Peer Review Guidance for the NCLB Growth Model Pilot Applications" (Washington, DC: U.S. Department of Education, 2006).

63 David Hoff, "Education Department Fines Texas for NCLB Violation," *Education Week*, May 4, 2005. http://www.edweek.org (accessed May 15, 2012).

64 *Center for Law and Education, et al. v. United States Department of Education*, 315 F. Supp. 2d 15 (D.D.C. 2004).

65 *Reading School District v. Pennsylvania Department of Education*, 855 A.2d 166 (Pa. 2004).

66 Connecticut State Conference of NAACP Branches, "Press Release: CT NAACP Urges State to Avoid Wasting Additional Funds Pursuing NCLB Suit" (Hartford: Connecticut State Conference of NAACP Branches, 2006).

67 *Association of Community Organizations for Reform Now, et al. v. New York City Department of Education et al.*, 269 F. Supp. 2d 338 (S.D.N.Y. 2003).

68 *School District of Pontiac v. Spellings*, 584 F.3d 253 (6th Cir. 2009).

69 Connecticut brought a similar lawsuit focusing on the funding needed to implement NCLB. In this lawsuit, the court was particularly unwilling to let the lawsuit go forward not just because of the relevant law, but also because of the perception that the courts have limited capacities to engage with complex educational evidence and the lack of precise standards in NCLB to provide guidance. *State of Connecticut v. Spellings*, 453 F. Supp. 2d 459 (D. Conn. 2006).

70 The interaction between law and interests groups over the interaction between NCLB school choice and desegregation is analyzed in Elizabeth DeBray-Pelot, "NCLB's Transfer Policy and Court-Ordered Desegregation: The Conflict between Two Federal Mandates in Richmond County, Georgia, and Pinellas County, Florida," *Educational Policy* 21, no. 5 (2007): 717–46. See also *Californians for Justice Education Fund, et al. v. California State Board of Education*, 2003 Cal. App. Unpub. LEXIS 11713 (2003); *Center for Law and Education, et al. v. United States Department of Education*, 315 F. Supp. 2d 15 (D.D.C. 2004).

71 Standing, the legal ability of a party to demonstrate a sufficient relationship with the harm at issue in a lawsuit, could not be maintained in *Center for Law and Education, et al. v. United States Department of Education*, 209 F. Supp. 102 (D.D.C. 2002). A Section 1983 action which allows private plaintiffs to sue to enforce a federal state was deemed unavailable in *Association of Community Organizations for Reform Now, et al. v. New York City Department of Education et al.*, 269 F. Supp. 2d 338 (S.D.N.Y. 2003). The statutory language of NCLB was at issue in several lawsuits and was the centerpiece of the

unsuccessful claim that Pennsylvania needed to provide assessments in English because NCLB required native language testing to the extent practicable. *Reading School District v. Pennsylvania Department of Education*, 855 A.2d 166 (Pa. 2004).

72 20 U.S.C. § 1412(a)(15)(A).

73 20 U.S.C. § 1412(a)(14)(C).

74 Milbrey McLaughlin, "Evolving Interpretations of Educational Equity and Students with Disabilities," *Exceptional Children* 76, no. 3 (2010): 265–78.

75 20 U.S.C. § 1412(a)(16)(C)(ii)(I).

76 Individuals with Disabilities Education Act, 20 U.S.C. § 1400 et seq. (2004). A statute of limitations is the maximum time after an event happens in which a lawsuit may be brought. Under the 2004 IDEA reauthorization, parents have two years to exercise their due process rights after they knew or should have known that an IDEA violation had occurred.

77 Tiina Itkonen, "Stories of Hope and Decline: Interest Group Effectiveness in National Special Education Policy," *Educational Policy* 23, no. 1 (2009): 43–65.

78 Ibid.

79 20 U.S.C. § 9611 (2002).

80 Maris Vinovskis, "Changing Federal Strategies for Supporting Educational Research, Development, and Statistics" (Ann Arbor: Institute for Social Research, University of Michigan, 1998).

81 Ibid.

82 Maris A. Vinovskis, *Revitalizing Federal Education Research and Development: Improving the R&D Centers, Regional Educational Laboratories, and the "New" OERI* (Ann Arbor: University of Michigan Press, 2001).

83 50 Congressional Record, 107th Congress, H1739–41 (2002); 135 Congressional Record, 107th Congress, S10480 (2002).

84 20 U.S.C. § 9611(b)(1).

85 20 U.S.C. §§ 9612, 9634.

86 20 U.S.C. § 9502(20).

87 20 U.S.C. § 9502(18)(a).

88 20 U.S.C. § 9502(18)(b).

89 20 U.S.C. § 9633(11).

90 70 Federal Register 3586–59 (Feb. 25, 2005); U.S. Department of Education, "Identifying and Implementing Educational Practices Supported by Rigorous Evidence" (Washington, DC: U.S. Department of Education, 2003). To be sure, the Institute of Education Sciences arguably softened its stance on randomized experiments and emphasized the utility of qualitative data. For example, see Institute of Education Sciences, "Education Research Grants: Request for Applications" (Washington, DC: U.S. Department of Education, 2008).

91 U.S. Department of Education, "Identifying and Implementing Educational Practices Supported by Rigorous Evidence."

92 U.S. Department of Education, "Transcript of the Use of Scientifically Based Research in Education Working Group Conference" (Washington, DC: U.S. Department of Education, 2002). Still, only 26 percent of awarded grants fell under research categories that prioritize random trials for FY 2004–2008.

Grover T. Whitehurst, "Rigor and Relevance Redux: Director's Biennial Report to Congress" (Washington, DC: U.S. Department of Education, 2008).

93 Alan H. Schoenfeld, "What Doesn't Work: The Challenge and Failure of the What Works Clearninghouse to Conduct Meaningful Reviews of Studies of Mathematics Curricula," *Educational Researcher* 35, no. 2 (2006): 13–21.

94 U.S. Department of Education, "Transcript of the Use of Scientifically Based Research in Education Working Group Conference."

95 For example, see National Board for Education Sciences, "Annual Report" (Washington, DC: U.S. Department of Education, 2006).

96 Daniel Liston, Jennie Whitcomb, and Hilda Borko, "NCLB and Scientifically-Based Research: Opportunities Lost and Found," *Journal of Teacher Education* 58, no. 2 (2007): 99–107.

97 National Research Council, *Scientific Research in Education* (Washington, DC: National Academy Press, 2002).

98 U.S. Department of Education, "Transcript of the Use of Scientifically Based Research in Education Working Group Conference."

99 Sarah-Kathryn McDonald et al., "Scaling-Up Exemplary Interventions," *Educational Researcher* 35, no. 3 (2006): 15–24.

100 American Recovery and Reinvestment Act of 2009. Public Law 111–5 (2009).

101 U.S. Department of Education, "American Recovery and Reinvestment Act" (Washington, DC: U.S. Department of Education, 2009).

102 U.S. Department of Education, "American Recovery and Reinvestment Act Report: Summary of Programs and State-by-State Data" (Washington, DC: U.S. Department of Education, 2009).

103 American Recovery and Reinvestment Act of 2009. Public Law 111–5 § 801 (2009).

104 U.S. Department of Education, "Guide to U.S. Department of Education Programs" (Washington, DC: U.S. Department of Education, 2009).

105 American Recovery and Reinvestment Act of 2009, Public Law 111–5 §§ 14001–14013 (2009).

106 Public Law 111–5 § 14001.

107 Public Law 111–5 14002(a)(2)(A)(i).

108 Public Law 111–5 14005(d)(2)–(5).

109 Because districts could use SFSF funds for activities authorized by the ESEA, they had almost unlimited discretion over how these funds could be used. Impact Aid, a program authorized by the ESEA that traditionally aimed at helping districts financially burdened by federal activities, allowed districts extreme flexibility in use of educational funds. Public Law 111–5 § 14003(b).

110 Government Accountability Office, "Recovery Act: States' and Localities' Current and Planned Uses of Funds While Facing Fiscal Stresses" (Washington, DC: Government Accountability Office, 2009).

111 Public Law 111–5 § 14006 (2009).

112 Public Law 111–5 § 14006(b).

113 Public Law 111-5 § 14007.

114 U.S. Department of Education, "Guidance: Funds Under Title I, Part A of the Elementary and Secondary Education Act of 1965 Made Available under the American Recovery and Reinvestment Act of 2009" (Washington, DC: U.S. Department of Education, 2009).

115 Ibid.

116 74 Federal Register 59,688, 59,688–59,699 (Nov. 18, 2009).

117 Leslie A. Maxwell, "Obama Team's Advocacy Boosts Charter Momentum," *Education Week*, June 17, 2009. http://www.edweek.org (accessed May 15, 2012).

118 Michele McNeil, "Racing for an Early Edge: States Jockey for Position as the U.S. Education Department Readies Billions of Dollars in 'Race to the Top' Awards – the Stimulus Program's Grand Prize," *Education Week*, July 15, 2009. http://www.edweek.org (accessed May 15, 2012).

119 Michele McNeil "Rich Prize, Restrictive Guidelines: Criteria Would Set High Bar for 'Race to the Top' Eligibility," *Education Week*, August 12, 2009. http://www.edweek.org (accessed May 15, 2012)

120 Michele McNeil, "46 States Agree to Common Academic Standards Effort," *Education Week*, June 10, 2009. http://www.edweek.org (accessed May 15, 2012)

121 Government Accountability Office, "Recovery Act: States' and Localities' Current and Planned Uses of Funds While Facing Fiscal Stresses."

122 Sean Cockerham, "Palin Rejects over 30% of Stimulus Money," *Anchorage Daily News*, March 19, 2009. http://www.lexis.com (accessed May 15, 2012)

123 McNeil, "Rich Prize, Restrictive Guidelines: Criteria Would Set High Bar for 'Race to the Top' Eligibility."

124 Alyson Klein, "'Race to the Top' Standards Link Questioned; Some in Congress Worry Federal Intrusion Ahead Through Money for Testing," *Education Week*, August 12, 2009. http://www.edweek.org (accessed May 15, 2012).

125 Maine, Texas, New Hampshire, and Oregon did not enact new policies favorable to charter schools or enacted policies hostile to charter schools. Erik W. Robelen, "State Picture on Charter Caps Still Mixed, Some Easing Restrictions as Federal Officials Urge, though Others Reluctant," *Education Week*, August 12, 2009. http://www.edweek.org (accessed May 15, 2012).

126 Klein, "'Race to the Top' Standards Link Questioned; Some in Congress Worry Federal Intrusion Ahead Through Money for Testing."

127 McNeil, "46 States Agree to Common Academic Standards Effort."

128 California Education Code §§ 10601, 10601.5, 10802, 10804 (2009).

129 Benjamin M. Superfine, Jessica J. Gottlieb, and Mark A Smylie, "The Expanding Federal Role in Teacher Workforce Policy," *Educational Policy* 20, no. 1 (2012): 58–78.

130 New York State Department of Education, "Race to the Top Application" (Albany: New York State Department of Education, 2010).

131 Rhode Island Department of Education, "Educator Evaluation System Standards" (Providence: Rhode Island Department of Education, 2009).

132 Ibid., A-7.

133 Joseph Murphy, "Turning Around Failing Schools," *Educational Policy* 23, no. 6 (2009): 796–830.

134 Institute of Education Sciences, "Turning Around Chronically Low-Performing Schools" (Washington, DC: Institute of Education Sciences, 2008).

135 Ibid.

136 Ibid.

137 Ibid.

138 Center on Innovation & Improvement, "School Turnarounds" (Lincoln, IL: Center on Innovation & Improvement, 2009).

139 Murphy, "Turning Around Failing Schools," 819.

140 Thomas B. Corcoran, "The Changing and Chaotic World of Teacher Policy," in *The State of Educational Policy Research*, ed. Susan H. Fuhrman, David K. Cohen, and Fritz Mosher (Mahway, NJ: Lawrence Erlbaum, 2007).

141 Ibid.

142 Michael Allen, "Eight Questions on Teacher Preparation: What Does the Research Say? A Summary of the Findings" (Washington, DC: Education Commission of the States, 2003).

143 Corcoran, "The Changing and Chaotic World of Teacher Policy."

144 Ibid.

145 Center for Policy Research on Education, "What Large-Scale, Survey Research Tells Us about Teacher Effects on Student Achievement: Insights from the Prospects Study of Elementary Schools" (Madison, WI: Center for Policy Research on Education, 2000).

146 National Comprehensive Center for Teacher Quality, "The Link between Teacher Quality and Student Outcomes: A Research Synthesis" (Nashville, TN: National Comprehensive Center for Teacher Quality, 2007).

147 Ibid.

148 Public Policy Institute of California, "Determinants of Student Achievement: New Evidence from San Diego" (San Francisco: Public Policy Institute of California, 2005).

149 Corcoran, "The Changing and Chaotic World of Teacher Policy."

150 Alfie Kohn, *The Case against Standardized Testing: Raising the Scores, Ruining the Schools* (Portsmouth, NH: Heinemann, 2000).

151 David K. Cohen, Steven W. Raudenbush, and Deborah Loewenberg Ball, "Resources, Instruction, and Research," *Educational Evaluation and Policy Analysis* 25, no. 2 (2003): 119–42.

152 Michael S. Knapp, Michael A. Copland, and Julie A. Swinnerton, "Understanding the Promise and Dynamics of Data-Informed Leadership," in *Evidence and Decision Making*, ed. Pamela A. Moss (Malden, MA: Blackwell, 2007).

8   CONCLUSION

1 David F. Labaree, "Public Goods, Private Goods: The American Struggle over Educational Goals," *American Educational Research Journal* 34, no. 1 (1997): 39–81

2 Ibid.
3 Benjamin M. Superfine et al., "Promising Strategies for Improving the K-12 Workforce in Illinois: Improving the Educator Workforce" (Urbana-Champaign, IL: Institute of Government and Public Affairs, 2009).
4 Mark A Smylie, Debra Miretzky, and Pamela Konkol, "Rethinking Teacher Work Force Development: A Strategic Human Resource Management Perspective," in *Teacher Work Force Development: The One Hundred and Third Yearbook of the National Society for the Study of Education, Part I*, ed. Mark A Smylie and Debra Miretzky (Chicago: National Society for the Study of Education, 2004).

Index

Made in the USA
Las Vegas, NV
21 August 2021